HITCHHIKING

Vietnam

A woman's solo journey in an elusive land

Karin Muller

The Globe Pequot Press

Old Saybrook, Connecticut

Cover design by Saralyn D'Amato. Front cover photo by Karin Muller.
The following photos were taken by Jay Robinson: Jacket back and jacket flap, hardcover edition; top right and lower left back cover, paperback edition; p. 10, bottom, color insert; p. 13, top left, color insert; p. 16, bottom, color insert. Photo on back cover, lower left, paperback edition by Sheila. Photo on p. 12 of color insert, bottom left, by Manuela. All other photos by Karin Muller.

Library of Congress Cataloging-in-Publication Data
Muller, Karin.
    Hitchhiking Vietnam: a woman's solo journey in an elusive land / Karin Muller.
— 1st ed.
        p. cm.
    ISBN 0-7627-0257-5 (cloth)
            0-7627-0243-5 (paper)
    1. Vietnam—Description and travel.   2. Vietnam—Social life and customs.
    3. Hitchhiking—Vietnam.   4. Muller, Karin—Journeys—Vietnam.   I. Title.
    DS556.39.M85   1998   97-47233
    915.9704'44—dc21   CIP

Manufactured in the United States of America
First Edition/First Printing

Contents

List of Maps

Prologue

I stood on the sidewalk beside a group of shirtless men shoveling gravel in the humid Saigon air. Their bodies were bronze and shiny and speckled with the suction-bruises of the ancient Chinese healing arts.

I was looking for a Mr. Tam, or "Tommy," a private guide recommended by the friend of a friend who had once made a business trip to Vietnam. Overwhelmed by last-minute preparations, I had scribbled Tam's name and a vague set of Saigon directions on the back of an envelope before going back to ordering iodine tablets and wrapping presents for the holidays I'd miss.

Now, standing on the corner beside a cardboard fish stall, watching women snip the heads off frogs, "Tommy" seemed like a long-lost brother. He was the key to unlocking a secret journey, a dream that had carried me halfway around the world: to hike the thousand-mile Ho Chi Minh Trail, all the way from Saigon to Hanoi.

But finding Tam seemed suddenly more daunting than anything I might have to face in the days to come.

"Find Goo Lick," my hasty handwriting said, and "cyclo driver—Norfolk Hotel." He knew Tam, I had been told, and would take me to his house. I summoned my courage and stumbled into the swirling maelstrom.

The white-upholstered cyclos were lined up like a picket fence outside the Norfolk Hotel. Their drivers perked up at an approaching fare with the peculiar sixth sense of hunting dogs on the scent. In seconds they were in full bellow, trumpeting the virtues of a pleasure ride through the old Chinese district, an indispensable visit to the famous downtown theater, and the moral value of lighting an incense stick in a faraway pagoda made entirely of jade. My tattered scrap of paper set them back sharply. They examined it with nicotine-stained fingers, muttering under their breaths until one, more creative than the rest, brightened and said "Gulik!" In seconds the man had produced a ratty cyclo from its hiding place behind a soup stand and, after a sideways glance at the hotel doorman, quickly motioned me into the passenger seat. With a wail of protesting axles and a few lost tufts of horsehair stuffing, we were off.

Every nook and cranny, every inch of sidewalk along Dong Ho Avenue was occupied by budding business men and women, their wares spilling out into the street: fried dog, chickens (live or dead), secondhand plastic pens, single sheets of paper. Here and there a drunk retched into a gutter and a dog sniffed casually at a rotting rat. We turned and shunted into progressively narrower side streets until we entered an alley so twisted that the cyclo squeezed through like toothpaste, scattering old women and knocking over ancient altars smoldering with incense.

Gulik lay stretched across two wooden pallets, snoring off last evening's beer. He staggered to his feet and grinned through a row of decomposing teeth. He flicked the switch on a nearby pump, and stagnant water from the alley's drainage ditch eddied into a plastic tube that led to the parlor sink. Gulik applied a toothbrush to his brown-stained stumps. I stood beside the pump and watched, fascinated, as an algal bloom detached itself from the ditch wall and meandered toward the pump's mouth. A momentary clog, a brief sucking sound, and it was gone. Gulik rinsed his mouth and set the toothbrush back in its Coke-can stand. He motioned me outside and into his rusting cyclo.

I climbed aboard. The patient old women picked up their scattered incense sticks in our wake.

Gulik perched, storklike, above and behind me, his knees pumping and his rubber flip-flops askew on the pedals. "I," he said, inserting the cyclo deftly into the almost seamless flow of traffic, "am the Speeding Bullet. Nobody is faster than Gulik." We hurtled into an intersection, a lawless confluence of three streams of traffic, where life seemed measured in inches, and stunning acts of courage went virtually unnoticed. My feet disappeared momentarily under the fender of an oncoming truck, then reappeared to clip the outermost egg on a moving vendor's cart. Gulik laughed gaily and surged toward the next giddy brush with death while I surreptitiously wiped the yolk off my Reeboks.

We turned onto a side street, where children stopped playing ball to point and shout questions. News of Gulik's unusual cargo—tall, blond, and female—preceded us like a rippling wave. We pedaled through the maze of alleys and culverts into Tam's neighborhood, and he came stumbling out to greet us. His belt was unbuckled, and his face bore the crinkly remnants of an afternoon nap, but he stuck out a brisk hand and smiled without guile. He seemed almost as glad to see me as I was to see him.

"I want to hike to Hanoi," I told him in breathless Vietnamese, as the neighbors gathered. "Through the Central Highlands . . ."

His smile never faltered. "No problem."

"Will you go with me?"

His handshake slowed perceptibly, then sped back up. "Yes."

The journey had begun.

As this map shows, the journey was long and at times rather confusing. It began in Saigon, where I met Tam and asked the Communist Youth League to take me through the Mekong for fifteen days by bicycle. When I returned to Saigon I joined Jay, an Alaskan, on his motorbike heading north. We took Highway 14 to Buon Ma Thout, turned east to the coast and continued up Highway 1 to Hanoi. Once there, we hitchhiked to Sapa, where I trekked among the nearby Zao and Hmong villages. We returned to Hanoi by train and continued to Nha Trang. There I hitched a ride with Jochen to Saigon on his Minsk. Upon being denied a visa extension, we were both forced to go to Cambodia. A week later we reentered Vietnam by taxi and took the train to Cuc Phuong National Park with our animals. From the park it was only a short hop to Hanoi, where I once again teamed up with Jay on the refurbished motorbike and journeyed high into the Tonkinese Alps to live among the tribes-people. Just outside of Phuong Tho, Jay was seriously injured, forcing us to return to Hanoi. Finally I took my pack and hitchhiked alone on a great loop across northwestern Vietnam through Sapa, Son La, Moc Chau, Lai Chau, Lao Cai, and Mai Chau, to return two months later to Hanoi.

Overview of the Trip

The Dream

Long ago, I used to fall asleep to my mother's bedtime stories of Africa. I would climb under the blankets, hold tight to a pillow, and beg her to tell me once again of Fifi, her family dog, who often wandered down to the Mkuzzi River and was one day eaten by crocodiles. Or how she used to march through the coffee fields, beating pots and pans to keep the swarming locusts from landing and eating the crop. Or what the finger-long insects tasted like when they were roasted, crisp and hot, on the coals by her Wakamba neighbors. My mother spent *her* childhood high in the Uzambara Mountains, in present-day Tanzania, where my German grandparents ran a farm and sisal plantation for more than thirty years. She didn't wear shoes until she was twelve. Her stories wove themselves inextricably into my childhood dream-wanderings and lent wings to my daytime fantasies, until the breadfruit trees and bougainvillea of her family farm seemed more real to me than the oaks and potted plants in our New Jersey backyard.

The road from Africa to America had been a long one. Mom was eventually packed off to boarding school in England and continued on to university in Switzerland, then Boston. Along the way she managed to accumulate several new languages, a medical degree, a husband, and two children.

I was too young to remember much of Switzerland. The Swiss dialect we spoke at home merged seamlessly with the English of suburban schooling and childhood friends. I never yearned for Europe, despite the *stollen* breads my mother baked at Christmas or the chiming clocks, the cut-glass goblets, and the hundred other mementos that lay scattered about the house. My fantasies were already taken up in the vivid tales of my mother's childhood farm. But Africa was a far cry from New Jersey, and it was here that I seemed destined to grow up, attend college and get a job, save up for a house, and spend every weekend mowing the lawn.

Then one day when I was eleven, we moved. I didn't have the faintest idea where Puerto Rico was, but as I watched my mother cheerfully stacking boxes and crates, I saw on her face the same expression she always had when she was lost in her African memories. I knew that my other life, the real one, was about to begin.

And begin it did. In the markets of Rio Piedras, where Mum haggled for dirt-encrusted vegetables in a language she had picked up like a penny on the roadside. And on platform ferries crossing brackish rivers, where only a frayed and knotted rope kept our rusty old station wagon from being swept out to sea. We learned to scuba dive and tried to trick each other into touching the anemones that stuck to our fingers and stank for days. At school, a language swirled around me that only gradually made itself understood. I discovered a culture so warm and vibrant that it seemed to gather up newcomers in a passionate embrace. For the first time in my life, reality was as vivid as the fantasies I had created inside my head.

Four years passed. As suddenly as we had come, we left— this time to Australia. I spent my summers working on an outback cattle station or exploring the breathtaking national parks of the continent. I found an array of flora and fauna unlike anything I had ever seen.

But the world kept getting larger. I discovered *National Geographic* and spent entire nights under the covers, silently mouthing the lyrical place-names that sounded like the beating of exotic drums. Bujumbura. There wasn't a photo that didn't seem to be missing that crucial element—me: smoking a pipe with an old man in the Brazilian jungle, roaming the African plains with my hand resting casually on a lion's mane, or high up in the rigging of an Arab dhow. At seventeen, I surreptitiously applied to the Peace Corps. My parents said no, and I went to college.

It was Williams, small and private and nestled in the lovely Berkshires. After a semester of anxiety-ridden phone conversations with my parents, I caved in to the need to be marketable and majored in economics, a subject made only marginally palatable by taking all my elective credits on Africa and Asia. On the side, I took classes in everything else—from philosophy to physics, calculus to Coleridge. That I would someday have to make use of my degree never occurred to me.

Toward the end of my second year, while my brother was busy interviewing for a prestigious corporate internship, I decided to backpack across Europe. To my surprise, my mother, explorer extraordinaire, fearless adventurer, suddenly turned back into a parent. "It's too dangerous," she insisted. After several months of wrangling, we agreed that I should find a traveling companion. I asked my boyfriend. "Well," he said after three microseconds of thought, "it would be nice to have done Europe, but I don't really want to go there." Three microseconds after that, the relationship ended and I left for England, alone.

"I'll get my revenge," my mother told me, "when *your* teenage daughter decides to do something just like this."

It was a minor miracle that carried me from London to Macedonia without tragedy. I floated through Europe with the wide-eyed innocence of a child. In Yugoslavia I stumbled off a twelve-hour bus ride and found myself in the isolated part of Zablak. There was no guest house. Darkness was falling. A young man, a fellow passenger, approached me and used hand signals to invite me to his house. He cut an imposing figure—six feet tall, with broad shoulders and strong arms—but seemed shy and eager to please. He had not harassed me on the bus, as the soldiers often did, and made it clear that his mother and sister awaited him at home. It never occurred to me to say no.

Two hours later I was still following him up a goat path far from any sign of human habitation. I could see nothing but the outline of his burly shoulders in the moonlight. Sanity dawned: I was an idiot. Before I had time to gather my courage and melt into the darkness, we crested a hill and ran smack into a tiny woman with the broad, stocky body of a tree stump. She screamed, threw up her arms, and grabbed all six feet of my young man and swung him in a complete circle before setting him down again. It was his mother. Over the next two weeks, while I learned how to knead ten-pound slabs of dough and gather wild blueberries from the mountainside, his family came to mean more to me than all the half-remembered monuments and tourist traps from Italy to England. A country, I realized, is the sum of its people. To see it I had to learn their language and share their lives. And so, when college was over, I joined the Peace Corps.

This time I was twenty-one and ready, or so I thought. Starry-eyed and brimming over with idealism, I rolled up my sleeves and strode forth to better the world. I tackled Filipino society with explosive energy firmly grounded in the belief that I knew what was best for everyone concerned. *My* village would be a model for the entire Philippine Archipelago, if not for the entire world. I moved into a squatters' village and immediately began to plan. Those areas near the palm trees should be fenced off for gardens, a school could be built near the village square, and for God's sake, would somebody tie up those pigs before they start rooting around in the latrines.

If one learns through failure, then I acquired the wisdom of the ancients during those two long years. Land crabs snipped off the tops of my tomato seedlings. My wells dried up. My rice cooperative grew exponentially, then failed even more spectacularly. My clams drowned. I cultivated all the wrong people and unwittingly ignored the real leaders. I fell into a depression, and recovered only when my mother arrived for a visit.

We traveled to visit another volunteer, a young woman who lived in a tribal minority hamlet high up in the mountains. The night before our departure, we both ate some bad fish, and the next morning Mom seemed hesitant to join me on the roof of the bus.

"What if I need to use the loo?" she asked.

"I'll knock on the roof, and the driver'll stop and wait for you," I assured her.

An hour later we were speeding past miles of newly planted paddy fields, the three-inch shoots poking through beds of brownish mud. My mother pointed out, with remarkable restraint, that there wasn't a tree in sight, nor any other monument to modesty. I offered to ask an old woman to go with her and spread her skirts to ward off voyeuristic roadside eyes. As I watched them troop off, I suddenly realized that Mum was no longer the expert in all things exotic. Somewhere along the way we had become partners in the adventure of life.

Eventually she boarded the plane for home, and I returned to my site, recharged and ready to get back to work, convinced that if only I tried harder, I couldn't help but succeed. My villagers responded with the elasticity of a rubber band, giving way initially but gradually building resistance until my own energy defeated me, and they returned to what they had always been. Along the way they helped start me down the path to a completely different type of learning—about myself—in a new paradigm where nothing is absolute and there are few rights and wrongs, only ways of being.

When it was my turn to board a plane for home, I knew beyond the shadow of a doubt that I no longer wanted to be a part of the civilizing machine. I wanted something . . . else. I donned stockings and became a management consultant.

My salary went up 4,000 percent. I put aside the two obscure Eastern tongues that I had learned to perfection and were now of no earthly use to me. I acquired an expense account and joined a gym, where I paid the equivalent of my entire Peace Corps allowance to be allowed to sit on a bicycle and pedal endlessly, going nowhere. Two years later, I went to the doctor for a mysterious pain in my fingers and was told that if I continued with the long hours and computer-intensive work of my corporate job, I would lose the use of both hands. I had chronic carpal tunnel syndrome and flexor synovitis. The eventual surgery took more than a year and left me questioning the endless treadmill of the Wall Street world, with its inflated salaries, empty lives, and inevitable ulcers.

But if not that, then what? I had tried the corporate route and no longer wanted to pay its price. Moreover, although my salary had skyrocketed these past few years, my standard of living had not, and I now had enough savings to keep me for several years if I stayed true to my old Peace Corps lifestyle.

On the other hand, this was the time when I should've been consolidating my career, padding my 401(k) retirement plan, paying my dues; that was the path I had been raised to follow. But I had also been raised on my mother's stories, and they had cast a spell on me that wouldn't let go. To her tales I had added my own, and it was no longer Africa that haunted my dreams—it was Asia. The land of bright paper dragons and orange-robed monks, of emerald rice fields and mud-brown buffalo. *I could go back . . .*

Most everyone disagreed. My father, who had watched my erratic career moves with a bewilderment firmly rooted in his orderly Swiss upbringing. My friends, all upwardly mobile and increasingly wrapped up in the joys of summer weddings and happy house-hunting. My dog, who wanted nothing more than me, a Frisbee, and a lazy afternoon. And myself. I had tasted the good life. If I threw it all away, I might never get it back.

But I was twenty-nine, and I had neither husband nor children nor mortgage. If not now, then when?

The decision made, the destination was obvious. Deep in the heart of Southeast Asia lay a country as mysterious as it was unforgettable: an enigma only recently opened to Americans. Vietnam.

If the information in my local library was anything to go on, Vietnam's history had started with the 1964 Tonkin Gulf incident and ended in 1975, roughly the period of U.S. military involvement in that country. The Vietnamese language, too, seemed not to exist, a frustratingly empty space between Urdu and Welsh in the foreign-language bookstores. I scoured Vietnamese restaurants in search of a tutor and cold-called anyone with a Vietnamese name in my local phone book. I made language tapes for myself and dragged an unwieldy cassette deck around like a reluctant puppy dog. I tacked vocabulary lists to windows and doors, to the TV screen, and to the wall across from the toilet. At last I stumbled upon a family who agreed to teach me and even produced an obscure, thirty-year-old grammar text filled with words like "tiger-hunt" and "maid-servant."

I read every account of Vietnam I could get my hands on, and I watched *Heaven and Earth* and *Apocalypse Now*. I sat with my gentle Vietnamese family in their tidy living room, mouthing words that seemed more like a song than a sentence, and tried to banish the nightmarish visions of carpet bombings, stuttering machine guns, and villages wreathed in flames. I thought of my own memories of Asia, its graceful people and peaceful cultures. It just didn't make sense.

I wasn't the only one who seemed confused. Every time I said the word *Vietnam*, I heard a different story.

"It's the most beautiful place I've ever seen," one vet told me with tears in his eyes. "The greenest green this side of Creation. And the children have such smiles . . ."

"Thieving, sneaky, dirty little yellow terrors," another growled, his back still rigid with anger twenty years after the war. "They'd as soon kill ya as look at ya."

"We bombed them into the stone age, and communism finished the job," a local journalist informed me. "Their average per capita income is no more than two hundred dollars a year."

"American companies are dying for the chance to invest," I read in a business newsletter. "Cellular phones are the hottest new market."

Everyone agreed, however, on what would happen if I tackled Vietnam on my own.

"You'll be raped," promised a rugged, six-foot-four mechanic, an ex-marine. He jerked at my spare tire with his crowbar, his arm muscles twitching in time with his words. "The place's still littered with bombs. Malaria'll eat your guts." He hoisted the tire free. "Snakes and commies, snakes and commies in the grass. You'll disappear and no one'll ever find you."

"It's a Buddhist country," I said carefully, "a gentle people. The war is over."

He stopped abruptly and leveled his crowbar at me like a machine gun. For the first time, there was real anger in his voice. "How the *fuck* do *you* know?"

He was right. What did I know? I had nothing more tangible than my gut instincts—that war is the real enemy, not communism or Uncle Sam. That a man placed in an impossible situation, whether he be an Ohio farm boy or a Hanoi shoe repairman, will do whatever it takes to survive. I couldn't begin to imagine the horrors the American soldiers had faced in the swampy jungles of a hostile, foreign land—but they had come back and gone on to become loving husbands, caring fathers, and steadfast citizens. The Vietnamese fighters also must have returned home to their plows, their children, and their ancestral shrines. I was ready to stake my health, my virtue, and by my mechanic's accounting, my life on the inherent goodness of human nature. My faith seemed trivial in the face of that accusing crowbar.

"If I came back and wrote a book," I asked timidly, "would you read it?"

"I don't read books."

"What about a documentary? Something you'd see on TV?"

He paused in the act of tossing away the tire and thought about it for a long time. "A movie?" he finally said. "Yeah, maybe."

And so, two short weeks before my departure, between the last of my language lessons and a hundred final errands, I bought a video camera. When the time came, I tucked it into my backpack, waved a cheerful good-bye, and climbed aboard the plane.

In truth I was utterly terrified.

Dear Mom,
I've extended my visa for three months, found a
guide to take me along the Ho Chi Minh Trail, and
bought a bicycle and jungle hammock. Can it
really be this easy?

Escaping Saigon

"When the Americans left I thought I'd never see a foreigner again," Tam shouted over his shoulder as we wove through rush-hour traffic on his tiny motor scooter. We cut sharply behind a cart piled high with charcoal patties and lurched onto the curb next to a street-side soup shop. Tam locked the bike and gestured to the stools with quick, birdlike movements. His eyes were everywhere, weighing the honesty of approaching pedestrians, scanning the tables for chopsticks, and urgently signaling the soup maker for our order. The grisly menu hung in plain view from the awning of the cart: a rubbery yellow chicken with a hook thrust through the gash in its throat, and a nondescript slab of raw meat, indistinguishable but for the bulging white-rimmed eyes that stared through a cloud of flies. The young man behind the wheeled counter worked methodically, handling raw meat and crumpled bills with equal indifference. Steam from the cauldron of bubbling broth caressed his bare chest, and a long finger of ash balanced precariously on the end of the cigarette that hung from his lower lip.

With a barely discernible nod to Tam, he scooped two fistfuls of limp white noodles into a long-handled strainer and sunk them into the broth. Within seconds they emerged, hot and glistening, to tumble into chipped porcelain bowls. Nimble fingers chose several sprigs from a nearby pompom of onion shoots and reduced them to confetti in a blur of fingertips and flashing steel. He hacked narrow strips from the slab of flyblown beef, tossed them in, and followed up with two heaping teaspoons of MSG. A ladleful of rich broth flowed around the buried noodles, melting the salty crystals and turning the dark red beef an earthy shade of brown.

Tam poked at the noodles with one chopstick. His small frame had gained in stature when he sat, his barrel chest and shock of thick black hair belying the short bowlegs under the table. Only his hands gave him away as he nervously shredded fresh basil leaves into his soup. The strong, callused fingers were as tiny as a child's.

"I worked for three years as an interpreter for the U.S. Marines," he told me in his high-pitched, nasal English. "When the Americans withdrew, I was stuck in Danang. We hid in a basement and listened to the radio. The North Vietnamese Army was coming." He and his wife fled south, just ahead of the swelling tide of refugees seeking safe haven in Saigon, the last stronghold of beleaguered South Vietnam. Behind him an endless stream of humanity struggled along the cratered road, pushing wheelbarrows, leading bullock carts, and shepherding their few belongings into an uncertain future. Tam himself carried a heavy burden—his four-month-old son.

His foresight proved in vain. Saigon was terror-stricken, feeding upon itself in a suicidal struggle for individual survival. The Communists advanced in an unstoppable wave. The last hope of rescue that had funneled nearly one million Vietnamese into the city disintegrated into the heaving mobs that swarmed the U.S. Embassy gates. The Americans had left without them. Tam and his family went into hiding to await the inevitable.

An eerie calm descended upon the city as the conquering army approached. "There was no one left on the streets," Tam said, his eyes losing focus. "All you could see were the piles of uniforms where the South Vietnamese soldiers had thrown them down and run off in their underwear." Although almost no bombs had fallen on the city, the southern collaborators suffered no illusions of reprieve. They waited only to see what form the eventual retaliation would take.

The call came quickly. Tam was ordered to report to the Communist command. "They said it would only be for a few days!" he exclaimed. "My wife and child were depending on me." The days turned to weeks and months in a distant re-education camp. "My wife was forced to return to her family," Tam said, his cheeks reddening with remembered shame. "There was nothing I could do." Six days a week he was ordered to the communal fields, where he struggled to tease a meager crop from the arid hills.

Every Sunday he was "re-educated." "We were made to write the names of people we worked with, their units, commanders, and rank. Always the same." He shook his head and poked at a sliver of beef. "I never told them I'd worked with the Americans." Instead, he passed himself off as a radio operator for the South Vietnamese Army. "And," he added, rolling the words around in his mouth, savoring the luxury of using them, "I tried to forget my English. They were shooting American collaborators."

After a year, Tam was released and ordered to a communal village as part of a government project to forcibly relocate four million Vietnamese families into the hinterlands. When the rains fell he worked the paddy, a frayed conical hat on his head, the silt clinging to his bare calves like stockings. Phuong, his wife, arrived and set about coaxing beans, potatoes, and tomatoes from the gray earth and cooking the weedy vegetables over an open fire. During the dry season there was little enough water for drinking and none for crops. In desperation, Tam was prepared to do almost anything to feed his family.

Every morning at four he rose to hike deep into the forest. There he applied his machete, chopping fallen tree trunks into one-meter-long segments. His wife followed to cook his lunch and bring him water from the distant well. Eventually he shouldered the heavy logs for the hike home, where he hacked them into kindling and then carried them four kilometers to the railroad tracks. The train stopped for less than two minutes on its journey south—just time enough for Phuong to clamber aboard while he passed the bundles of kindling to her through an open window. Five hours later the train lurched into Saigon—now renamed Ho Chi Minh City. She sold the wood and then bedded down on the filthy station floor to await the 4:00 A.M. train that would return her to Tam and their son. For three years, and through pregnancy and the birth of their second child, the routine never varied.

Until Phuong fell ill. The sickness—malaria—lingered for months, consuming her body and their scarce financial reserves. The doctor was seventeen kilometers away, and the nearby nurse could offer nothing but sympathy and empty shelves. Without income from the sale of the kindling, starvation loomed. In desperate times they made a desperate decision—to escape to Saigon. Tam peeled a few precious bills off their dwindling resources to bribe a local official to let them go. In the darkest hour of the night, they fled.

They arrived at the crowded station in Saigon with only their two children and a bag of clothes. Tam was an illegal alien in his own country, without the permits necessary to live in the city. He stood only a slim chance of finding work.

For the second time he was forced to send his wife and children back to her family to survive.

(((

By this time Gulik had found us, stashed his cyclo, and taken a seat nearby. He edged closer and closer, increasingly annoyed by an English conversation that was beyond his understanding.

"You take ride, see city," he said suddenly in Vietnamese, pointing at his cyclo. I shook my head, then had a sudden inspiration and turned to reexamine his pedal-powered vehicle. From the midsection back it resembled a regular bicycle. A huge metal chair hung from the handlebars, supported by two wheels on either side of the seat. In poor weather a tattered awning could be raised over the passenger's head. It looked like the perfect chariot to take me into the highlands along the Ho Chi Minh Trail. My pack would be my passenger, protected from the vagaries of weather and thieving hands. Mentally I was already cruising through shimmering green paddy land, scattering flocks of roadside geese to the four winds.

Tam was horrified. "You can't take a cyclo. It's too hard for a woman." Gulik agreed wholeheartedly. He suggested that I be the passenger with a Vietnamese driver. He slapped his bare chest.

The idea of crossing Vietnam in a mobile lawn chair, tossing handfuls of candy to ragged children, made me cringe. I offered to test-drive Gulik's cyclo to see how hard it really was.

"The police would come," Tam said, his eyes flickering up and down the street. "Maybe if you were a man . . ." At any rate, Gulik added, the cyclos were licensed. If I took one out of the city limits, I would be arrested immediately and the owner would be held responsible. It was obviously out of the question. Both men brightened considerably.

Properly chastised, I approached the question of a bicycle with considerably more caution. There were hundreds of thousands of them in Saigon alone. Clearly they couldn't all be registered. I had seen whole flocks of women riding to market, laden with baskets of vegetables and upside-down ducks. How much, I asked, would it cost to rent a bicycle?

"Ten dollars, one day!" Gulik insisted immediately, then tapped himself on the chest again. "I find for you."

I considered his offer. For that price I could rent two motorcycles, complete with drivers. Perhaps, I suggested, I

14

should *buy* a bicycle, seeing as I would be needing it for several months.

Tam and Gulik huddled. A Vietnamese bike was out of the question. Its shoddy construction was sure to be an endless source of misery. A Chinese bike, though heavy, would survive the myriad potholes of Vietnamese backcountry roads. I delicately raised the issue of my oversize backpack and quickly drew a sketch of a two-wheel cart that would solve the problem. Gulik examined it with a jaundiced eye, then nodded reluctantly. It just so happened, he informed me, that he knew a man who was willing to part with his bicycle and a shop that could make my cart. All for the bargain price of fifty dollars. Tam nodded agreement and I handed the money over, the negotiations complete.

My satisfaction was short-lived. "I'm only a private guide," Tam admitted over the inevitable cups of bitter green tea that ended every meal. "I can't get us the government permissions we need to sleep in the villages." Without the proper permits, foreigners were allowed to stay only in officially sanctioned hotels in provincial capitals. Tam saw my crestfallen look and relented. "It might be possible that we relax the local police and militia with money and cigarettes every evening," he told me reluctantly. "I know how to make people happy. You leave it to me."

We parted with Tam's promise to find me a family where I could live for the next few days before embarking on our journey north.

Gulik graciously offered to take me back to my hotel. I quickly lost my bearings in the labyrinth of shortcuts, market squares, and alleyways. With a squeal of brakes we arrived unexpectedly in front of Gulik's now-familiar house. "You may live here," he announced, grandly gesturing at the broken-tile entryway with its half-clogged water pump. "Better than family."

I thought about it while he chained his cyclo to the wall. The narrow alleyway around us teemed with life. A shiny, russet rooster and a naked toddler eyed each other warily. Three basins of moist brown snails and speckled pigeon eggs shared an unoccupied corner. A nearby ice cream vendor was attracting droves of wide-eyed children with his bulbous circus horn. It looked ideal.

I followed Gulik through the parlor, past the family shrine wreathed in incense and offerings of tangerines and instant noodle soup. Up ahead, an old man slowly lowered himself down a ladder and shuffled away. We hauled ourselves up to the second floor.

Gulik led me to a small alcove, separated from the windowless room by a wall of plywood odds and ends. A curtain hung across the door, and a thin ray of sunlight crept in through the only chink in the wall. He stepped inside and presented it to me with a flourish.

Before I had time to respond, the curtain was once again thrust aside, and a young woman stormed in. Without sparing me a glance, she marched straight to Gulik, berating him in staccato Vietnamese and flinging her arms, elbows first, in my direction. The gist of the conversation was clear. This was their bedroom, and she had no plans to vacate it. Gulik responded meekly with muttered dollar signs, to no avail. She marched us both in goose step to a filthy corner at the far side of the room. The walls were dank and runny. Rusty pieces of rebar stuck up at odd angles from the floor. A large, unidentified insect crunched under my foot. It was so dark that I could barely make out a ragged hole in the floor a few feet away. The family toilet.

Gulik recovered quickly and proceeded to point out the glories of my new home. He offered to put up a plastic curtain for privacy and perhaps even whitewash the walls if I stayed long enough. The toilet was nearby, and a loving family environment would envelop me like a long-lost daughter.

"How much?" I asked.

How much, he inquired diplomatically, was I paying at my hotel?

Ten dollars, I said, for hot and cold running water, sheets and a mattress, a private room, and a thermos of piping hot tea every morning.

He nodded happily. "The same."

We shook hands while I promised insincerely to consider his offer. I escaped into the sunlight and fled back to my hotel.

(ℯ (ℯ (ℯ

Kim Cafe was well-known as the local mecca for backpackers and travelers-on-the-cheap. Its tables spilled onto the street, jammed with foreign faces, bushy beards, and incongruously red hair.

I slunk into a Vietnamese soup stall behind the boisterous cafe and eavesdropped on Western voices discussing the best tours, quickest buses, and cheapest restaurants.

"Yeah, Co Giang Street. Floor space for three bucks a night. The coffee's free, but you gotta bring your own milk."

"Just agree to whatever, and give him five thousand once you're there. Happy hour's five to seven."

"They wash and dry jeans for four thousand. If they're real dirty they'll squeeze you for five."

All around us, opportunistic Vietnamese hastened to fill foreign needs. ROOMS FOR RENT signs buzzed and blinked from every window. Shops sold black-market CDs and traded well-thumbed novels, two for one. A message board bristled with necessary knowledge, from "Urta, we gone Mekong, back on 17th" to "Avoid Restaurant 442! Soup tastes like panther piss." On the corner a driver reclined in his own cyclo, thick glasses propped low on his nose, reading *War and Peace* under the light of a magazine stand.

A plump figure clambered out of a nearby cyclo and waved at me. Bill and I had met briefly that afternoon and, in the manner of travelers, struck up an easy and uncommitted acquaintanceship. He looked from my little soup stand to the foreign cafe, clearly torn between a recognizable face in unpalatable surroundings and the more comfortable atmosphere of the backpackers' hangout. He made his decision, paid the driver, and stumbled over. I reluctantly nudged a stool out from under the table with my foot.

He was an accountant by trade, divorced, living in a renovated garage, with few needs and fewer desires. He traveled religiously for one month each year, he told me, in order to experience exotic cultures and people. Thus far, Vietnam had not been a stunning success.

"I mean, it's cheap and all," he said with a shrug, "but there's no culture to speak of. All they wanna do is rip you off." He gestured at the street around us. "Just take a look!"

I suggested there might be life beyond Kim Cafe.

"No," he said firmly. "I've been there. Cu Chi Tunnels, Cao Dai Temple, Mekong Delta, Jade Pagoda . . ." I read the list on the tour board behind him as he reeled off the names. "Nothing worth seeing," he concluded.

The soup arrived. It quickly became clear why my coveted stool under the one fluorescent light had remained empty despite the evening crowd. Dozens of gnat-size flies were throwing themselves in a suicidal stream against the thin bulb above me. Those that escaped the wily geckos fell like rain into my hair, my lap, and my soup. Soon the oily surface was dotted with dazed and drowning insects. I added a spoonful of coarse pepper and stirred. The bugs sank.

Bill continued to slump in a dejected haze. I took pity on his hopeless quest and unthinkingly offered him a place on my journey north.

"By bicycle?" he said in horror, his hands fluttering, searching the air for an excuse. "No no, I don't have time," he said, relaxing back into his chair with obvious relief. "How far could I possibly get in two weeks? What could I see?"

A few hundred miles of the real Vietnam, the land of lazy afternoons on bullock carts, the muted clonk of buffalo bells, and the soft, sensual feel of paddy silt between bare toes.

"I gotta go to Hanoi," he told me firmly. "There's a car heading up the coast tomorrow—two Americans and an Aussie. They're taking a week, stopping in Danang and Hue. It's an *opportunity*."

The gritty remnants of my soup, diluted with sunken gnats, wasn't nearly as sharp as it should have been. Bill handed the stall owner a blue 5,000-dong note and stood, sweating in the sultry evening air, waiting for his change. I pointed out that he was suffering for somewhat less than four cents.

"I don't wanna get them started tipping," he said with barely a glance at the woman who had spent her evening hunched over a steaming cauldron of soup. He snatched the worn bill from her grease-stained hand and stalked off to find Vietnam in a car on Highway 1.

Gulik was waiting for me when I returned to my hotel, his hand draped over a wheeled monstrosity. My bicycle. It was the color of scuffed tar, big-boned and battered. I circled it warily. The seat was torn and lumpy, its springs ready to burst through the paper-thin plastic. I climbed on board. The back end swayed gently from side to side. One pedal performed a decidedly eccentric orbit, and the brakes pulled smoothly but didn't make the slightest impression on my forward momentum. I wheeled it back to Gulik.

Was there, I asked, a cart to accompany this glorious machine?

He pointed silently at a six-inch piece of plywood that, reincarnated from its previous life as a part of his bedroom wall, was now anchored to the frame with bits of rusty wire.

I admired it and once again inquired after the agreed-upon cart. His face crumpled in horror. A cart, he pointed out, would simply be an added set of wheels to go flat at an inconvenient moment. He muttered darkly about wasted axle grease. He wiggled his fingers and plucked at the air to illustrate its susceptibility to theft. And, his features contorted in a rare moment of sincerity, he admitted that certain unsavory countrymen might yield to the temptation to use it as a public spittoon.

I fetched my pack. Even the determined Gulik fell short in his efforts to balance the sizable duffel on such a tiny foundation. After several resounding failures I suggested that he weld a support brace behind the platform, rather like the backrest of a child's seat. He was noticeably unenthusiastic. It would, he insisted, look odd to a Vietnamese.

Not nearly as odd as I would look riding the bike, I pointed out.

But, he countered, the added bar would decrease its resale value.

True, I agreed, but then I wasn't planning on selling it. I wanted to buy it.

He nodded reluctantly. Perhaps for an additional five-dollar bill he could persuade a welder to adulterate its graceful shape for me.

Perhaps, I told him firmly, with the addition of a brace, I could be persuaded to take it. And it wouldn't hurt to have working brakes.

He slouched off like a water buffalo, trailing the unwanted bike behind him.

℘   ℘   ℘

Tam was nobly silent the next morning when I showed him my new acquisition. We parked it in the lobby—to the horror of the staff—and sped away on Tam's moped. I had asked him to help me find a few final bits of gear for our trek: a hammock made of cheap, jungle-green rayon; a lock to discourage those who might be blinded by the beauty of my bicycle; a conical hat; and two pocket dictionaries, one for the villagers and one for me.

"You look, I drive," Tam ordered as we cleared the alley. I

scanned the crowded sidewalk stalls, grateful to have Tam along to lend a hand.

Both the protracted search and the endless bargaining mystified the average foreigner. The Vietnamese, in their turn, could not understand the Western obsession with saving time. In a society with a superabundance of labor and little money, the hours dedicated to preserving that extra dollar were well spent. Despite their bafflement at Western priorities, the Vietnamese were quick to grasp the value of time as a bargaining tool when dealing with foreigners. They delighted in quoting a ridiculously high starting price, then settling back onto their haunches to allow the minutes to wear away their opponent's patience and pry open his wallet. To this end, the vendors had long since perfected the art of dawdling. They picked their teeth with bamboo slivers. They offered their guests endless tea and, under important circumstances, home-brewed rice whiskey. They maintained an unbroken litany of praise for their wares, their silver tongues gathering crowds of onlookers. They bemoaned their shanty homes and dozen children and longingly fingered the unpatched collars of their customer's clothes. I was no exception. Tradesmen took one look at my soft white skin, and even Tam's formidable bargaining skills evaporated under the onslaught of triple prices and firmly shaken heads. He shrugged ruefully and paid.

"It doesn't look like a communist country," I shouted into the wind as we swooped through traffic like teenage skateboarders on a crowded sidewalk.

Tam laughed. "Not anymore! Now just the policies. But it wasn't always so easy. Before, when I didn't have a work card or papers, it was impossible to stay out of trouble." He shook his head. "Very hard."

We stopped for a cup of French drip-coffee, filtered

through battered aluminum sieves into glasses already half-filled with thickened milk and shards of ice. I swirled the mixture into an even chocolate brown and took a welcome sip. I hadn't really come in for the coffee, or even the miraculous stream of cool air that blew out of the noisy air conditioner over our heads. I came to spend more time with Tam.

He was the kind of find-it-or-fix-it handyman every traveler dreams of. He was more, much more, than just a translator and driver; he was a friendly and familiar face in a sea of inscrutable eyes and mahogany skin. Tam had taken me under his wing for no other reason than that I was alone, without family or friends to shield me from harm. He had unhesitatingly assumed the role of older brother and was by now protective to the point of paranoia. He pulled me back if I tried to cross the street alone and worried like a mother hen if I ventured out unchaperoned after dark. In America, such behavior would have annoyed me. Here, I cherished it.

As hard as I tried, I couldn't sit across from him without poking around into his past. I had thought myself so brave before I met him, coming to a foreign land all by myself. Tam's story showed me what a hero really was, and made my journey seem trivial by comparison. I wondered if I would have had the strength to carry on if faced with the despair that had haunted so much of his life.

With minimal prodding he launched back into his tale, by now nearly two decades old but still etched in pain across his face.

"It tore my heart to send my wife and children away," he said. "To take care of them was my only duty in life." He shook his head. "But it wasn't possible under the circumstances."

Relieved of both the burden and joy of his family, he roamed the streets, determined to find work. By day he scoured the marketplace, handing out cigarettes and building relationships that might eventually lead to a coveted place on a labor crew. By night he slept on the sidewalk, renting a straw mat beside the other street people, always on the same corner, ready to flee when the police made one of their periodic raids. He paid an old woman a few cents to allow him to wash at a pump in a back alley.

At last his marketplace tenacity was rewarded by a job as a loader. Every morning at half past three he presented himself at the lot where the trucks rolled in, laden with fruit. For three hours at a time, with two fellow laborers, he shuffled under the weight of bananas and pineapple, coconuts and breadfruit and papaya, to the vendors' indoor stalls. Twenty percent of their pay went to the mobsters who had secured them their jobs. The rest—fifty cents—they split among themselves. On lucky days they had the opportunity to unload three trucks; then Tam had the money to eat at the outdoor cafes and soup stands, perhaps even twice in a day. When sickness loomed or trucks were scarce, he made do with a piece of bread and a cup of green tea. For four years, his life was defined by the antlike lines of fruit, shuffling in long columns along narrow alleys and disappearing into the pitch-black innards of the cavernous marketplace.

Early on, when work was scarce and money scarcer, he was approached by a broken-toothed old man who promised him a day's good wages to lie back and let them take a little of his blood. He followed the stooped, shuffling form into an alley and did as he was told. They took a liter and afterward told him to drink two cups of tea with sugar to make himself strong again. Even so, the next morning he couldn't raise himself off the sidewalk to go to work. Again and again, when times turned grim, he returned to offer his blood for money. On his third visit it took over two hours to fill the bottle to the brim. The blood looked thin, like water, and separated into layers before his eyes. He never went back for fear they would drain every drop of his spirit and strength into the bottle.

With the money from his job as loader, he aspired to a home with four walls and a roof—a shack in the slum. Once again he returned to the marketplace armed with cigarettes and money "to make people happy." The result was a single room, seven feet by five feet, with a ladder up to a tiny loft barely high enough to crawl into. He ran a miniature bulb tapped into a neighboring line, papered the walls with old newspaper, put a lock on the door, and proudly retrieved his wife and children. It became home to their family of six for the next fifteen years.

3

Dear Mom,
OK, so my bicycle developed a few kinks, my guide
can't go with me, and my new visa's only good for
thirty days. The hammock's still working just fine.

Disappointment

I dreamed of grass, deep and dense and soft under my bare feet. I could taste the rich, smooth flavor of German chocolate on the tip of my tongue. I took a breath of crisp alpine air and awoke to the blaring horns and torrid heat of Saigon's dawn traffic. The dream faded with the whine of bloated mosquitoes that had found their way through the tattered sleeping net and clung to its swaying folds. I squished them between my thumb and forefinger until their blood, my blood, ran down my thumb. It did nothing to quell the homesick yearning in my heart.

I had never planned to do this trip alone. I had invited everyone from my mother to the seventy-year-old community librarian. In desperation I had begun accosting the most casual acquaintances—"Would you like to go to Vietnam with me?"—always hoping that some handsome young man would reply, "Vietnam? Why yes, that's just exactly where I've always wanted to go. When do we leave?"

Then one day reality outstripped the fantasy and here I was, alone.

And I couldn't go home again until I made good my foolish boast to hike the Ho Chi Minh Trail. The very words were ominous, filled with the promise of dank green jungles and snakelike, clinging vines. To American soldiers, the trail had been the root of all evil—provider of the bullets that mowed down their comrades and of the snipers who fired them. To the North Vietnamese, it had been the ultimate symbol of courage and sacrifice—young men resolutely heading south, having taken an oath not to return until the war was over and won. I had chosen to hike the trail from south to north, into the heart of enemy territory, so to speak, all the way to the capital city, Hanoi.

But my journey was emphatically not about war, as much as that could be possible in a land that had been fighting off an assortment of invaders for more than a thousand years. I was anything but a war buff. I had no desire to collect fake dog tags or to have myself photographed crawling through the famous Vietnamese underground tunnels or to wear one of those round green hats that looked depressingly like a North Vietnamese Army helmet. And even if I had the interest, I would have no business writing a book about the war. That was the domain of the Vietnam veterans, who spoke with an authority I could never hope to match.

The Ho Chi Minh Trail was for me a means to an end. I had once believed in human nature enough to dedicate two years to the Peace Corps. This belief, somewhat tempered, had come up solidly against American public opinion about Vietnam. I had looked for the truth in American war documentaries, in tourist accounts, and in communist rhetoric. In the end I knew that the answers could be found only in Vietnam, in its rural villages, among the farmers who had once been fighters. And if, after so many years of bombs and bloodshed, the Vietnamese had found a way to forgive the unseen enemy, I wanted to know their secret—and bring it home with me.

My video camera sat on a nearby bureau, its blank eye a baleful reminder of my idiotic pledge to film a documentary of the trip. The sum total of my video expertise was a phone call to a producer friend a few days before my departure, asking for pointers on how to turn the camera on and what to do with it after that. "Hold it steady," he told me without a hint of irony. "Follow the action. Don't try to zoom, and don't pan; you'll give your viewers a headache. Take long shots. And find someone to go with you; you'll need footage of yourself along the way or you'll have no story."

I picked up the camera and held it like an injured robin. I had bought a small consumer model that might escape scrutiny in a country where filming for broadcast still required a host of permits and permissions, each with its accompanying bribes and weeklong delays. Somehow, my footage would have to be so spectacular that it made up for its shortfalls in technical quality. The whole idea was ludicrous and made me want to do nothing more than crawl back under my sweat-soaked sheets and sink back into another dream of home.

One step at a time. Even so, I was overwhelmed.

Discreet knuckles rapped gently at my door. I hurried for clothes. Tam came in, awkward with the unaccustomed familiarity of my bedroom. He had always waited for me in the lobby. Something was wrong.

He sat on the edge of a chair in the far corner of the room, clasping and unclasping his hands. "I have something to tell you," he admitted miserably. "I sat up all night trying to figure out how to say it." His smooth, callus-free palms flashed among coarse knuckles of past labor. He paused, then blurted, "I can't go with you on the bicycle. You see, my family's going to America soon—with the Orderly Departure Program. The paperwork's all ready, and we're just waiting for the tickets. I have to stay in Saigon for my name to be called. Perhaps if you just went on day trips, with the motorcycle . . ." His voice trailed off.

My heart sank. I wanted something more than daylong excursions. I gently explored other explanations. That his wife was having second thoughts entrusting her husband to a foreigner. That, at forty-six, he had rightfully outgrown second-hand bicycles. Or perhaps my initial offer of salary and expenses was a shade too low.

He shook his head indignantly. "I'm not an official guide," he explained. "I was already arrested once for taking a foreigner into the countryside." Another arrest at this stage of his application process could prove disastrous. One phone call from a provincial police chief to the right department and he would lose his place on the list with the stroke of a pen.

"But I gave you my word that I would help you," he added quickly. "I just don't know any other guides that I would trust as I do myself." Nevertheless, he promised to try to find an official guide who could procure the proper papers. An older man, perhaps, with family and integrity. The permits could be readied in a matter of weeks.

He left quickly. I did too, in a dejected haze, to walk aimlessly along the smoggy streets of my reluctant new home. Would I ever manage to escape this grasping city and wander the lush green countryside of my dreams? My feet took me over bridges dense with oxcarts, cyclos, and women shuffling under the double weight of the bamboo baskets they carried like justice scales on one shoulder. Refuse bobbed among the spindly posts of the shanties along the river's edge. A child stared up at me from the safety of her father's arms and waved.

I followed the waterfront to a signboard proclaiming the exotic animal market of Ho Chi Minh City. Behind it a warehouse crouched sullenly among cages teeming with tiny sparrows and snakes as green as new-sown rice. The low-slung building opened like a gaping maw, gloomy and uninviting.

Inside, the corrugated walls reverberated with the din of bird and beast, the joyful song of bulbuls and the searing mew of a newborn kitten being dropped into the cage of a half-grown civet. Dried bear galls hung from suction cups beside bottles of coiled serpents drowned in whiskey. Glass display cases offered flying lizards stiffened like plywood kites and bags of animal parts—teeth, bones, bits of skin and ears and innards, guaranteed to cure every ill from arthritis to impotence. A clouded leopard skin adorned one wall, its lips painted fire-engine red and its eyes huge and glaring.

I tried to shut my ears to the cacophony of yelps and yawls, coos and cackles, and hurried past birds singing out their souls in the suffocating heat. A porcupine rattled its spines against the bars, and the shrill, heartrending cry of an eagle stopped me in my tracks. I crouched beside the cage. A crested serpent eagle stared back at me with unblinking yellow eyes. Its tail feathers had long since worn away from continual contact with the mesh floor, and its wings were torn and tattered. It cried again, a whistle so piercing that I was sure it could be heard across Saigon. I backed away from the impossible sight.

In a corner near a cobra's cage, four men in business suits and shiny black shoes sat around a table, fingering miniature goblets. The stall owner held a pitcher that filled slowly with blood draining from the long, hoselike body of a decapitated snake. He stirred in a measure of rice whiskey and poured. The men drank and smacked their lips.

Excited cries drew my attention to a far corner of the building. A shiny black bird perched precariously under the eaves, inches from freedom. A looped piece of twine at the end of a long pole hovered near its head as its former captor tried to snare it. The bird hesitated for a fraction of a second in the unaccustomed midday glare. It was his undoing. A skinny teenager clambered up the wall like a gecko and reached out to snatch the bird by its tail feathers just as it launched itself into flight. The crowd applauded. The boy climbed down. The bird was stuffed back into a cage barely larger than a teapot.

I heard a mewing sound and turned to see a tiny leopard kitten, a soft bundle of fluffy fur the size of a softball. A baby macaque rode on its back and twisted its ears playfully. I watched the monkey dismount and wrap its wiry arms around the little cub in a huddle of mutual, newborn need. A woman squatted nearby, dabbing tarry paste onto the scabrous leg of an emaciated mongrel.

"How much?" I asked with morbid curiosity and indicated the leopard cub.

She looked at me indifferently. Foreigners made poor customers, neither valuing the animals for their medicinal qualities nor willing to risk customs by transporting them home. She shrugged. "One thousand dollars."

I put a finger through the wire mesh. Both infants ignored me, preferring their own company. It was just as well—I had no way of returning such a small charge to its wild home and I, too, would be leaving one day.

"Five hundred!" she called at my back as I walked away. "I ship for you! Customs no problem!"

I fled.

℮   ℮   ℮

A note was waiting for me in the lobby the next morning, inviting me to lunch with Tam and my "new family." I was out the door at a run and didn't stop until I had lost myself in the maze of alleys leading to his shanty hut. Tam found me swamped by children. The little girls reached out to run gentle fingers over the sun-bleached hair on my arms and laughed behind their palms. Tam pointed here and there among the sea of bodies. "My children," he said, indicating two girls and two boys of assorted teenage years. "Dragon over there, Flower, Forest, and Spirit." The oldest was a stunningly handsome young man of nineteen, standing shyly beside a willowy woman with masses of tumbling black hair.

"My wife!" Tam said with sudden pride. He gestured me forward. "Come, I show you where we live." He led me down a corridor of crumbling cement into an underground burrow of tiny rooms. A continual stream of neighbors trickled out of the gloomy passageways, to use the outhouse or simply to stroll through the tropical twilight of the alley among children playing with chipped marbles, women selling the last of the day's boiled snails, and old men who sat with fading eyes, watching two generations grow up around them.

Tam's wife, Phuong, offered me a limp, long-fingered hand and a rueful smile to indicate that she spoke no English. She had a slender body that swayed with natural elegance and translucent skin that emphasized aristocratic cheekbones. I tried to imagine her hauling wood off a train and sleeping in a filthy station, and couldn't.

Tam ushered me in and gave me a quick tour of his closet-size home. It was bare but for a cabinet in one corner and a pot half-full of old rice. The cracked linoleum floor was spotless.

Two of his children knew no other home. When Tam first found the place fifteen years ago, he immediately called for his wife and two kids. The rent, twenty-five dollars a month, soaked up most of his income from the market. There wasn't enough money to feed four hungry mouths. After some debate, he pawned his beloved watch so that his wife could start a small business selling bananas on the street. Every morning she rose before dawn to shoulder the double baskets and shuffle back and forth from the banana trucks until she had accumulated seventy bunches of the tiny, candy-sweet tropical fruit. She spread her wares out on the sidewalk and learned how to give manicures between sales.

I looked at her with new respect. The years and hardship didn't show on her face as it did Tam's.

"She was eighteen when we were married, and I was twenty-seven," Tam explained in English. He reached out to take her hand for a moment, an uncommon gesture in a reserved Buddhist country. "My family didn't like her when we first met," he said. "She came from a poor background." Everyone, he admitted, was opposed to the marriage. After a period of soul-searching, he approached his parents. "I told them, you will not change my heart," he said, and smiled. "They came to the wedding."

Once married, they moved in with his parents, and the difficulties multiplied. His sister and wife had once been classmates. When Phuong married into the family through an older brother, she acquired the status of senior sister. The demoted sibling rallied the family with gossip and innuendo. Since there were ten children, the noise was substantial. It had taken years for Phuong's natural grace and gentle personality to establish her as a valuable addition to the family tree.

Tam stopped speaking abruptly and pulled out two photo albums.

"Our father died in 1991, one month before we got permission to go to America," he said, flipping open the first album. The fading photos showed an old man lying on a bed, a sheet tucked under his chin. A dozen relatives clustered around him, their heads wrapped in the white scarves of mourning. The smallest children stood in front, their tiny hands resting on the edge of the bed, their eyes wide with fascination and fear.

"He was cremated," Tam said regretfully. "We couldn't bury him." He saw my confusion and explained. "All land belongs to the Communists now. Even if you pay for a plot, they can take it away." He described a huge private cemetery in Saigon that had been turned into a park with the stroke of a pen. "They didn't even move the bones! Just the headstones." Only the official martyr cemeteries were safe, with their look-alike memorials teased into garish, rocket-ship shapes and copycat eulogies in soldierly rows. Even those headstones, it was rumored, often guarded empty graves as officials in charge of reburial pocketed the money and left the bones to rot in the jungle. Tam shook his head. "You never know when they'll come to take away a grave. It made my mother very sad."

He opened the second album, his fingers suddenly fumbling and eager. It held six sheaths of paperwork, all neatly bound, stamped, and stapled. At the front of each was an identification card with a photo of Tam or a member of his family.

They had twice missed their chance at redemption and a new life—once when the chopper lifted off the U.S. Embassy roof for the last time and again when the Americans posted the requirements for postwar immigration status. Applicants had to prove five years in the re-education camps, and Tam had only three. Now, twenty years after the fall of Saigon, a brother who had made it out was sponsoring Tam's family to a new life in the land of hope and dreams.

But Tam was no longer the twenty-three-year-old interpreter, sparkling with energy and ready to bound into the future. Two decades of opportunities had been cut out of his life. Years that should have been spent accumulating retirement funds, fixing up his first house, and taking vacations to Disney World had instead found him looking for a corner of the street to sleep on and scavenging rice for his children. At forty-six, with graying sideburns and creaky knees, he was starting over with few skills other than a basic understanding of English and a pent-up love of freedom that would take him across the oceans to a foreign and frightening land.

I closed the album and sat with Tam and his family, drinking gooey, sweet Vietnamese soda and fielding eager questions. Should he send his children to study computers so that they wouldn't be behind in an American school? His wife was learning how to decorate cakes to earn money; should he buy a blender in Saigon or wait for California? He had always dreamed of driving a car. How might he go about becoming a cabdriver in one of the West Coast cities? I listened and nodded, covertly scanning the tiny hut for a nonexistent phone or flush toilet, and knew the transition would be shattering. I also knew that within a year Tam's children would be at the top of their classes, that Tam would find his taxi and eventually own it, and that he would one day be sponsoring the neighbors' children that clustered at the door, staring wide-eyed at the foreigner. None of these things surprised me.

What really amazed me was his face. Filled with guileless enthusiasm, as eager to take on the world as any young man, I was amazed to see not a trace of bitterness over the hardship and lost years. Tam had long ago learned to forgive. He had learned to carry on without grudge or blame. He had learned to cherish peace and opportunity, wherever it could be found.

It wasn't Tam who was blessed to go to America. We were the lucky ones, to one day have him there.

℮   ℮   ℮

I returned home to discover a new guest sharing our hotel's only bathroom. Steve had been in Saigon for several months and was hard at work on his three goals: learning the language, finding a pretty Vietnamese girl, and starting a nonprofit organization. His Vietnamese, though ill-suited to his booming voice and boisterous manner, was intelligible and endeared him endlessly to the local population. His woman was already picked out and obviously returned his affection. The nonprofit was in serious danger of derailment. He took periodic trips to the Central Highlands, the most difficult area in Vietnam for an American to penetrate, to investigate hospitals that might be amenable to aid. It was tough going.

He was a California boy who had spent twelve years in Alaska before finding his spiritual home in Asia. He still had contacts in Anchorage, where friends were trying to get things started—principally funding—so he could continue his work. "We wanna get a kinda *circulation* going between here and Alaska," he told me confidently, before admitting that little was happening across the waters and that he was pretty much on his own.

He obviously adored his girlfriend. She was, he said, bright and peppy with plenty of ideas and eager to get ahead. He had been dating her for three months and hadn't laid a hand on her. "I know the score," he told me with a firm shake of his head. Instead, he went to dinner with her family three nights a week and took pains to present himself as a serious suitor, not some seedy tourist on the make. I liked him for his earnest naivete and knew that, even if his projects failed, he would have convinced at least one family that not all foreigners scour the streets, looking for a casual screw. I wished there were more like him.

(e   (e   (e

I spent the next week mouthing the lyrical texts of a thirty-year-old Vietnamese grammar book and exploring Saigon's aromatic marketplaces while waiting for word from Tam.

At last he came bounding up the guest-house steps. "I found you a guide," he said by way of greeting and was rewarded with a huge smile and something close to a hug.

"I've only known him for six months," he warned, holding up his hands to ward me off. He elaborated his new find on his fingers. By good luck he was an older man, with two sons my age, and happily married. Despite this he was still fit, having been a soccer champion in his youth. He had played throughout the Mekong Delta and would have many friends in the countryside. Unfortunately, he spoke only Vietnamese and a little French. "In addition," Tam said, pausing to search for just the right words, "you understand that he isn't a friend. I don't trust him as much as I would trust myself with you." But, he concluded, I was welcome to come have a look. We were scheduled to meet him in an hour.

He lived at the end of an alley teeming with cockfights and inhospitable stares. His house was surprisingly substantial—a front cement yard, two bikes, a shrine, and a parlor stuffed with lacquered furniture. He was fifty-five years old, tall, tan, and leathery. The handsome young face in the photos on the wall was still discernible in his features. He offered me a solid American handshake and sat, stiff-backed, on the edge of a chair. He spoke French proudly and unintelligibly. I answered in Vietnamese and cross-checked in English with Tam, whose replies deteriorated into a muddle of strange tongues. We eventually untangled the assorted conversational threads and got down to business.

He was highly skeptical of my plans to hike the Ho Chi Minh Trail and suggested in the strongest terms that he take me south instead, into the Mekong. He knew people throughout the Delta provinces in the timeless way that sharing a playing field under a burning sun cements friendships from all walks of life. Despite his connections, he was a private guide without papers and would have significant problems taking a foreigner into the rural villages. He would therefore accompany me only if I agreed to stay in a provincial capital every night. He spoke with a decisive finality that brooked no argument. I bit my lip in dismay and looked at Tam.

"There is one other possibility," Tam said softly in unadulterated English. "We can go see the Communist Youth League. They take students on tours into the provinces, camping."

I thanked the older man, asked for a day or two to think things over, and stood to leave. He shook my hand again, telling me he wouldn't be available for at least two weeks. His calves were as solid as bowling balls, but traveling with him was certain to include a frustrating litany of noes. We took our leave.

Tam parried my eager questions through rush-hour traffic as we headed back to my hotel on his motorbike. "The Youth League was started a few years ago with the purpose of taking local students into the countryside on bicycle trips," he shouted over his shoulder. "They organize tours to the military bases where parents fought the Americans, and sometimes even go on short visits into rural villages."

The guides were all aspiring Youth League members, working their way toward officialdom. If they studied hard and demonstrated political correctness, they would one day be promoted to Youth League member, then to Communist Party member, and then to bona fide government official. Tam wrinkled his nose at the thought. Apparently not everyone was enamored of the party and its perks anymore. The new emerging class of private businessmen not only had power but money, and didn't have to toe the party line.

"But," Tam added, "the Youth League has much power inside the system. They will be party members one day, so people are afraid of them, especially in the rural areas where they still follow the old ways. The Youth League can get you your permission papers, no problem."

By the time he dropped me off at my hotel, he had agreed to set up a meeting with the Youth League director for the following week. I tried to curb my rising hopes.

℮   ℮   ℮

What a roller coaster Vietnam was turning out to be. The joy of discovering Tam within the lonely wasteland of a foreign city, losing him only hours before our departure, waiting helplessly for a new guide, redesigning my dreams to ride behind those massive calves and learn Vietnamese amid the rubble of my French. The Youth League, with its officially sanctioned bicycle tours and village overnights, seemed almost too good to be true.

I quit my room to wander the streets, my feet taking me unwittingly to the post office, to the torn manila envelopes stuffed with incoming foreign mail. Perhaps if I asked the world-weary woman at counter three, she might let me search through them for a letter from home. The ground beneath me was slipping, and beneath it lay a pool of loneliness and despair.

It was a familiar feeling, the need to talk against a shared background—missing friends and family, the release of uninhibited laughter, my mother's treasured scrawl on a tattered envelope. The boredom that had caused me to discard a pleasant if unfulfilling job in America now seemed foolish. I had exchanged security for risk, friends for strangers, and comfortable confidence for helpless dependency. From this side of the fence, America was looking pretty good.

I tried to push away the deepening depression. Things weren't all that grim. Barely a week had gone by, and already the successes were piling up. I knew my way around the marketplace and had sat for hours with the fruit vendor, sampling her fare; I'd found a pair of shoelaces by myself and bargained them down to something resembling the local price; I had slipped behind a stall to scale a fish amid the laughter of gathering spectators. If I stuck it out, I knew I could tackle the challenges of survival in this strange land until, one day, I would wake up and discover that the frightening had become familiar.

In the meantime life was astonishingly vivid, the details etched in gold against the black and white of my ordinary existence. At home, time flowed seamlessly, April into May and summer, fall foliage and the sudden arrival of snow. Here, unique memories marked the pages of each passing day, every event a paragraph to be reread and relived.

The manila envelope had no letters with my name on them. I stumbled back to my guest house and buried myself in bed.

4

Dear Mom,
I can't get a single, solitary soul to go down to the
marketplace and try the roasted bugs with me. If
only you were here.
*   I miss you terribly.*

The Communist
Party Machine

Tam picked me up several days later in his moped for an
interview with the director of the Communist Youth
League. "Get on," he urged. We were late again.

We sped off through the traffic, clipping bicyclists and
almost getting sucked under the wheels of an overloaded market truck. I remembered Tam's aspirations to become a cabbie
and delicately suggested that he amend his driving style before
reaching America and that he consider losing the habit of paying off the men in blue.

"I am a very careful driver," he insisted, leaving behind a
flurry of feathers as he shot across the path of a bicycle laden
with upside-down ducks. "Especially when I have a passenger!"
He cut around the outside of a truck into a massive surge of
oncoming traffic. "And when that passenger is a foreigner"—
he put down a foot to corner better—"and a woman"—he
waved a languid hand and shot through a stampeding herd of
mopeds—"and like a sister in my own family"—we missed a

turn and inadvertently mounted a sidewalk—"then I make sure nothing happens."

We arrived on time. Perhaps he wouldn't make such a bad cabbie after all.

Youth League headquarters was a blocky monstrosity with a huge cement foyer and hard wooden chairs to accommodate plenty of supplicants. We presented ourselves to the appropriate secretary for our appointment. The director, she told us stiffly, had gone out. Unperturbed, Tam scurried around making friends, passing out cigarettes and skillfully concealing the fact that he no longer smoked. Eventually we were allowed into the director's office and given hibiscus tea in tiny porcelain cups. Tam looked around warily and chose a seat as far as possible from the open window before continuing his story. "I still have no papers to work in Saigon," he told me in a low voice. "If someone should overhear . . ." I cast a suspicious glance around the empty room and pulled my chair up as close as decorum allowed.

Tam's career as a loader in the marketplace ended shortly after the arrival of his wife and two children in Saigon. He had found a cyclo for rent from 4:00 A.M. until noon each day. The price was three dollars and his potential earnings close to ten. There were hidden costs, however. His vehicle was unregistered and therefore illegal to use within city limits. If the police stopped him, it would cost him five dollars on the spot. If he didn't have the money, they would impound the bike for ten days.

"You think driving a cyclo is easy?" he asked with sudden belligerence. "It's not! You have to hold the handlebars very tight"—he gripped the air with both hands—"especially on downhills." The weight of the cyclo rested on the front wheel, under the heavy seat that held the passenger and cargo. The driver steered from behind, maneuvering the bike by hauling on the handlebars to turn the wheel. I could well imagine the uneven pressure those wobbly old bikes would build up on a steep slope.

"The very first time I got in my new cyclo," Tam said, smiling at the memory, "I found a passenger right away. When we reached an intersection, I forgot that the pedals didn't turn backward. I caught my foot, and my passenger spilled over onto the street! I got off to help him up, but he was so scared he jumped to his feet, threw some money at me, and ran off."

Tam quickly learned the idiosyncrasies of his machine and was soon pedaling passengers and cargo all over the city. But no matter how much sweat he left upon the pavement, he still barely managed to pay the rental fee and fines and the expenses for flat tires and axle grease. Eventually, in desperation, he drifted toward the hotel that housed foreign guests. It was a risky venture. The government didn't want outsiders to realize how the city depended on pedal power to move its people and supplies, and had banned cyclos from the area. The police were always on the lookout for stray bikes, and the fine was a whopping thirty dollars. Tam learned to hide his vehicle behind the hotel and lure potential customers away from the alert eyes of loitering informers.

Despite his precautions, the government discovered his whereabouts and, more importantly, his skill in English. "They asked me to become an informer, to report on the number of guests, where they went, and what they said." In return he would get special papers, could sit freely in front of the hotel, and would be allowed to change dollars into Vietnamese dong. At the time, possession of even one illegal U.S. dollar could have dire consequences.

And why not? Every hotel had at least one informant among the cyclo drivers. Not only did they wallow in special privileges, but they also were popular with the other drivers because they could intervene with police to rescue an impounded cyclo or plead a fine.

Tam refused. Even then he dreamed of going to America and was afraid of the consequences should he take a role in the Communist regime. "After that, they were always looking for

41

me and fined me extra when they found my cyclo." He shook his head. "I had to go back to the streets."

A young man poked his head through the director's door, and Tam instantly fell silent. After appraising us carefully, the fellow slipped into the room and sat down without a word. His face was concave like a dinner plate, and obviously only a magic spell was keeping his glasses on his tiny button of a nose. His insubstantial mustache looked like it might disintegrate if he ran his tongue along the corner of his mouth.

The director followed him in through the door, and we shook hands over more hibiscus tea while a dozen cigarettes migrated from Tam's satchel into their pockets. The obligatory exchanges concluded, we sat down to business. I waited through a pregnant pause while everyone stared at me.

"You must tell them why you're here," Tam whispered. I hesitated. The director already knew what I wanted. Moreover, no one at the Youth League spoke English.

"Go ahead, I translate," he urged. I took a deep breath and sketched out my hopes in one sentence before Tam was off and running. Twenty minutes later he was still hard at work, and everyone was nodding agreement. My attention wandered. A movement caught my eye, and I craned my head to see through the louvered window behind the director's desk. It faced into another room, where a limp form collapsed to the floor among a litter of bodies. It was midafternoon, and after a strenuous morning of shuffling papers, the Youth League was taking a well-earned communal nap. I longed to join them.

Tam pulled gently on my sleeve. "The director says they've never taken a foreigner out before," he said. "They're not sure they can fill all your needs."

I assured him that my needs were tiny, trivial, mouselike. The director interrupted with a question.

"What is your purpose in undertaking this journey?"

I waxed loquacious about envoys and ambassadors, about peace and friendship and bringing the world closer together, straight out of my old Peace Corps handbook. Tam translated in less than a sentence. I was glad he was there to save me from myself.

"You wish to see battlegrounds?"

"No." On that point I was quite sure.

"There are a few problems," Tam admitted, then hurried on as he saw my face crumple, "but nothing that cannot be resolved—if we can make the right people happy."

The cigarettes obviously hadn't done the trick. "What kind of problems?"

"They must apply for official permission to allow you to stay in the villages. It will be very hard for them to find a member of the Youth League who is willing to go with you. They must extend your visa beyond the allotted time. And they say you should go first into the Mekong for a practice trip before they will take you north." He paused for breath. It sounded daunting.

Things were not as grim as they seemed, though. Money, apparently, was the universal palliative for a whole host of problems. I promised to grant happiness in every way I could to a wide variety of people. Everyone relaxed.

Once we were outside I caught up with Tam. "What do you think?" I asked breathlessly.

"It's good that you go with them," he replied thoughtfully. "They have strong power in the provinces. Much better than a private guide."

"But the Mekong wasn't exactly what I had in mind."

He lowered his voice and looked over his shoulder. "I heard that the director just returned from a party trip—two months along the Ho Chi Minh Trail from Hanoi. They say the government wants to turn it into a tourist attraction. Perhaps if this trip goes well, they will let you be the first to undertake the journey north."

I couldn't believe my luck.

    (&   (&   (&

A week later we were back for a follow-up meeting. The director met us at the door to his office—a good sign, but his brow was furrowed, and he sat down immediately with Tam without the pretense that I was anything more than an accoutrement. After several weighty moments Tam turned to me. "He say lots of students want to go with you, but not alone."

I had never really seen myself as a particularly intimidating example of Western womanhood, but it was a rather intriguing idea. I waited for the solution.

"Two should go," Tam said firmly. "One that speaks English and another who knows the Mekong well."

It sounded like a fine idea to me, at the bargain price of five extra dollars a day, a few tire repairs, and happy-money in the end. Everyone relaxed and we got down to the real business. The bill.

The director pulled out a crumpled sheet of paper and began a long itemized list. One hundred dollars for the flimsy permission that had my name at the top and a stamp at the bottom. Forty dollars to encourage happiness among the officials along the way. Fifty dollars to the Youth League headquarters for having shared tea with me. Thirty dollars for medical insurance that I didn't need. Twenty dollars for a secondhand bicycle pump—enough to buy a whole new bicycle out in the provinces. One hundred dollars in salary for the two fine young men that were to accompany me. Ten dollars per day for food, gifts to the villagers, and miscellaneous needs, principally cigarettes and beer for my guides. And, of course, the tip.

I haggled over the medical insurance, knowing that all the fees were manufactured and not wanting to capitulate too completely. They eventually deleted it, provided I agree to carry enough Western medicine for all of us.

I sat back with a sigh of relief. I was satisfied. They were not. More tea was poured.

An older man took the floor, pacing back and forth with his hands clasped firmly behind his back. He had close-cropped hair and the intense, forward inclination of a drill sergeant. They were all very concerned, he announced, that I be comfortable on the journey. Could I sleep in a hammock? Did I know how to ride a bike? Would my skin shrivel under the intense sun of the Mekong? Everyone knew Americans drove their cars everywhere. Could my legs manage more than a few hundred meters without turning to jelly? Would I eat the food, even low-class, local food, rather than shame my guides? My head bobbed up and down while Tam kept up a running supportive commentary. And the final and preeminent question, did I know how to make my guides happy? Yes, I had that figured out by now as well.

They introduced my future companions, who it turned out had been sitting with us the entire time. Both were twenty-five and looked eighteen. Fung showed one purple inch of gum in a pumpkin smile and flashed a gold-capped tooth that stuck out at such an angle that it hung over his lower lip even when his mouth was closed. He made a short speech in Vietnamese, slashing the air with long painted fingernails as he spoke. Chau had the dinner-plate face and button nose, and a curious laugh that sounded like a skin-diver who had inadvertently taken water through his snorkel. We agreed to meet at the office at five the following morning. I was to bring the money, and they would provide a send-off committee. At last, everyone was happy.

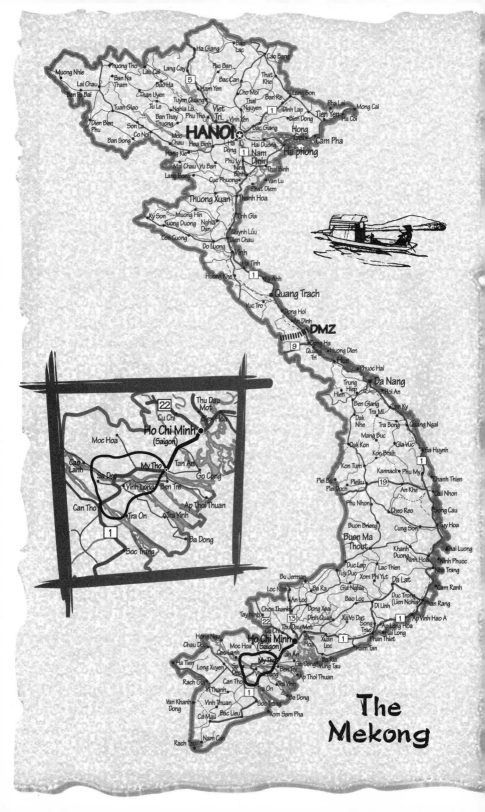

The
Mekong

5

Dear Mom,
I've discovered the essential cure for traveler's
diarrhea:
   2 Immodium
   2 Pepto-Bismol
   2 Ciproflaxin
   The Immodium acts like a cork to stop up the
works. The Pepto-Bismol is the protective padding
and the Cipro the depth charge that blows the
little suckers out of your system.
   Unless it happens to be a parasite.

The Mekong

The air was dark and heavy with coal-fire soot. The streets were deserted but for a few old vendors crouched next to their braziers, tickling the embers into a warm red glow before laying on crisp corn to roast. Every doorstep and alleyway sheltered a body or two, sometimes an entire family nestled together like spoons to ward off the predawn chill. I rode past old men squatting along the sidewalk, hurrying to complete their toilet before the rush-hour hordes took over the roads.

The Youth League offices were shuttered and empty. Gradually the shadowy figures of more than a dozen young men took shape, and finally the director himself. Money was exchanged, quickly and furtively, and counted several times by assorted hands. As a tentative sun sent pale fingers across the sky, we moved off in formation—eleven young men surrounding me in a cocoon of bicycles and mopeds.

My bicycle developed a personality almost immediately. The seat spring burst through its plastic cover and drilled into my buttock like a corkscrew. Even with my pared-down kit lashed low on the rack, the rear end wobbled like a well-endowed matron. Gulik's brake job evaporated halfway down the first gentle incline. I struggled to keep the bike in a straight line and to avoid the solicitous young men who pedaled alongside. My entourage showed no signs of fading away. We maneuvered as a unit, the size of a Mack truck, through the developing traffic.

The bristling rebar of city construction gradually melted into closely spaced houses of cement or thatch, then ended abruptly as the Mekong began. The Mekong! Pearly white gravestones protruding through the dense green rice like teeth, multicolored pagodas with rooftop dragons clawing at a cloudless blue sky, and flocks of motley ducks flowing like quicksilver from one paddy to the next. It was the perfect prelude to the Ho Chi Minh Trail—three weeks of cycling from village to village, learning the language and getting to know the people.

Fung pulled up beside me, his protruding gold tooth flashing in the morning sun. "Euhafy?" he asked.

I thought about it for a moment, hoping in vain that Chau might turn out to be the English speaker. "I beg your pardon?"

He licked his tooth. "Eurhafy? Eu hafy?" he repeated, getting louder. He flashed a stunning two inches of gum in an explanatory smile. I grinned back. I was indeed happy, deliriously so, to be riding among endless fields of emerald green in the Mekong Delta. It was a dream come true.

Two hours later I was dreaming about smooth roads, cold drinks, and shade. We pulled into a roadside eatery with a tiny soup cart near the entrance. The proprietor hurriedly pushed tables together to accommodate our continually multiplying crowd of fourteen.

The meal, with early morning beer and assorted desserts, came to an astonishing fifty dollars. Fung looked pointedly at my money pouch. I had already given him ten, the agreed-upon expenses for the day. I silently dug into my reserve brick of Vietnamese dong and watched with relief as the mob climbed onto their bicycles, without bothering to say good-bye, for the return trip to the city.

"How much further?" I asked, flexing sore muscles and stiffly mounting my forty-pound clunker.

"Twelve kilometers," Fung said, then reconsidered. "Forty-seven."

"Seventy-two," Chau mumbled in Vietnamese.

Twelve would be easy, forty-seven feasible. Seventy-two would be a nightmare, but Chau had surely misinterpreted my question. We wobbled off.

Then, with a six-inch drop onto boulder-strewn rubble, the road turned to rot.

It didn't get narrower or lose the appearance of a road. It simply sprouted ruts and protrusions in such profusion that the rideable path became a single-lane bike trail that wove in and out among the rocks. Occasionally it left the road altogether to dip down into a sunburned garden or gutter. To Fung and Chau's wide-eyed surprise, I had little trouble maneuvering the bike between obstacles, but soon a more pressing problem emerged. The track had become a funnel for all two-wheel vehicles, and I was quickly introduced to the only steadfast rule of Vietnamese country driving—the Law of Tonnage. Smaller vehicles were expected to give way to larger ones, no exceptions. Given the rather unintimidating dimensions of my chariot, I wasn't much of a threat to anything larger than a chicken or an exceptionally cowardly pig. I quickly learned to distinguish among the squeaky horn of the moped (barely worth edging to one side for), the rusty honk of the ubiquitous Minsk 125 cc, the rare and endangered Honda bike bleat, and the deep, reverberating blast of a bus, demanding instant compliance. I resolved to buy a bus horn.

And to find courage somewhere in a corner of my soul. It was self-defeating to give way every time I heard a honk behind me, to nudge my bike onto the jarring cobblestone rocks, only to discover that I had been displaced by a smirking six-year-old who was years from growing onto the seat of his oversize bike.

If I didn't have courage, at least I had spite. I watched the young male motorcyclists, frustrated in their attempts to force me off the path, take matters into their own hands. They gunned their engines and assaulted the road, using their bikes as weapons to jackhammer the recalcitrant stones into submission. I felt the morbid satisfaction of seeing two enemies beat each other to pieces.

I pedaled along, watching schoolgirls in spotless *ao dais* weaving gracefully along the road, young men revving their fickle engines to slew around sandy turns, and gnarled old-timers in cranky three-wheelers, their skin turned to leather under the relentless sun. The country road was an obstacle course of sleeping mongrels, antique trucks, weary bicycles with quarter-ton loads, and the mercurial ebb and flow of geese. Graduates of this rural training ground eventually migrated toward the bright city lights—armed with maniacal courage, lightning reflexes, and an utter contempt for such infantile restrictions as traffic signals, stop signs, and one-way streets. Saigon city driving was starting to make a lot more sense.

(℮)   (℮)   (℮)

I had long since ceased sightseeing and limited my rather blurry horizon to the immediate implications of the next rock or rut. My bowels rumbled with the acidic warning of incipient diarrhea. From deep in the nether regions of stiff-backed, prickly-skinned, head-pounding hell, I saw Fung take an abrupt turn onto a brambly footpath and disappear.

We pulled up at a run-down shack with a stereotypical third-world mutt—an object the size of a toaster oven with short, dun-colored hair, pointy ears, and a moth-eaten, curlicue tail. Like its brethren, it emitted an endless series of shrill yaps and slunk around behind us to feint at our bare ankles. It looked ripe for the cooking pot and I said as much, sending foolish little kicks in its direction and making myself look ridiculous. Chau's great-uncle-in-law came out to greet us. He was an old man with sad eyes that pulled his face downward and a smile that tugged it back up. He kindly took me around back to where a cement vat held blessed rainwater high above the thirsty ground. He touched the bottom of a hollow gourd to the surface of the water and swirled it around, creating ripples that eddied away floating insects and debris. He dipped out a jugful and poured it, glittering like liquid diamonds, over my waiting hands. I tossed it gleefully onto my throbbing face and neck. He smiled and dipped again, then pointed at a green coconut propped against the back doorstep. I nodded eagerly. Nothing would quench my thirst better than the smooth, milky fluid that came in nature's own antiseptic container.

Fung materialized behind me, standing stiff and straight. "No," he barked. It was rapidly becoming his favorite word, the one he used by default whenever he didn't like my questions or couldn't be bothered to answer. This time he made me to understand that drinking coconut milk when I was hot would cause me to sicken with fever.

I made him to understand that after my dousing, I was no longer hot.

He touched a fingertip distastefully to my burning cheek and sauntered away without a word, leaving behind the light impression of his long, curved nail, like a cat's claw.

The old man and his wife were making lunch, cheating nature of her quota of sweat by moving with economy and a complete lack of haste. He squatted against the back door, eviscerating several fish and laying the bones out in the sun to dry. She stoked the brazier with explosively dry kindling and laid on an immense black wok puddled with congealed cooking oil. He brought the fish to the fire and they changed places as smoothly as in a ballet, in a ritual perfected over forty years of marriage and unchanging daily chores.

She showed me how to peel the skin off a celerylike vegetable, its flesh spongy with moisture. We plucked apart ivory-white flowers, pulling off the stamens until our fingers were sticky with bright orange sperm.

When we sat down to eat, the old man spoke to me for the first time, offering to adopt me as his daughter since I clearly had no parents of my own. His wife smiled and nodded agreement, and I felt privileged at the thought of becoming a part of their gentle home.

After lunch I sagged and looked longingly at the heavy bench that filled one corner of the sitting area. It was the only solid piece of furniture in the rickety hut—flat, hard, and cool to the touch, a perfect place to lay out a bedroll and take an afternoon nap.

I marshaled my meager Vietnamese. "More bicycling today?" I asked Fung with some trepidation. We had ridden at least two hundred miles since breakfast. My legs told me so.

"No." The word seeped out in a cloud of smoke. He was lying in a hammock in the desiccated front yard. The cigarette haze hung, unmoving, in the still air. Several chickens had dug themselves down into the cool dirt in the shade, and even the dog was too busy panting to chase me around. I sagged gratefully onto the bed.

A hand disengaged itself from the folds of the hammock and waved lazily down the path. "You go out," Fung ordered. "Learn rice-drying."

An old woman, blood kin to my scarf-bedecked hostess, stepped forward with a luminescent smile and beckoned me with a callused palm. She had obviously been waiting patiently in the background since we arrived. I hesitated, then crumpled under her eager smile and followed her out into the blistering bush. "Be back two-thirty!" Fung called after me.

The house next door was built around a central cement courtyard for drying the one essential element of Mekong life—rice. It lay in foot-high pyramids on plastic sacking. An old woman with crusty bare feet smoothed it back and forth like icing with a bristleless broom. Mottled geese darted in and out, their beaks chattering as they scooped up the dusty grains.

Together we gathered the corners of the sacking and poured the golden, unhusked rice into woven baskets. We carried them on our heads, like Egyptian offerings, to a cement platform beside the pond. The nearby ducklings went manic, wagging their tails and arrowing toward us in bomber squadron formation. They quacked incessantly, an endless background murmur like conversation in another room.

The old woman arranged me like a store-front mannequin, tilting the basket forward on my head, forming my right hand into a cup, fingers spread, to scatter the grains as they fell. She gave the basket a little push to start the flow and stood before me, strenuously flapping a large woven fan to manufacture a breeze in the torpid air. The heavier rice kernels fell straight down onto a piece of sacking while the chaff wafted away. Fine white rice powder sifted through the basket bottom and settled on my head and arms like baker's flour. A pile of white gold gradually grew at my feet. The life-giving grain. This was only one of the many steps that began with the seedbeds, carefully prepared nurseries of newborn rice that grew thick and impossibly green in the soupy mud. After several weeks the seedlings were transplanted, stalk by stalk, to the larger paddy—tedious work that took days of stoop-backed toil. The paddy was weeded and fertilized with manure or night waste, guarded from birds and other vandals. The seedlings took nourishment from the rich mud, growing dark and tall and, eventually, heavy with dusky yellow seed heads. Then the harvest, the threshing and drying and husking; months of work before a single bowl could reach the hand of hungry man, woman, or child. Long before the next seeding, the paddy had to be flooded and weeded, plowed, and smoothed until it again took on the texture of chocolate pudding. No wonder the villagers held rice sacred. Just watching the mesmerizing fall of grains, I wanted to drop to my knees and run my fingers through the rising pile.

Fung came to get me, to pry me away from the ducks and blowing chaff and the old woman's lovely smile. On the way home he pointed at my white hair and face, my arms sticky with sweat and coated with rice paste, and said "*Su ngua.*" I assumed he meant "dirty" and bent down to scoop up some paddy water to wash it off.

"No." He waved for my dictionary, leafed through it, and showed me a word, underlined with one long thumbnail. *Itch.*

There was no time to wash up. We strapped my unused bedroll back on the bike and pedaled off, governed by a distant ferry schedule demanding that we ride another forty kilometers by five o'clock.

At four o'clock we wheeled, panting, into a sizable town. We turned down a side street and took a sharp right hook into a private courtyard. Chau dismounted, hugged the stocky, middle-aged woman who stood by the door, and began unloading his bike. It was his mother's sister-in-law, and we were spending the night. The ferry, the schedule, and the urgency had mysteriously disappeared.

She was friendly and eager to please, bringing me tangy star fruit and slapping me on the back until I began to spit out smiles despite my overwhelming fatigue. She disappeared into the kitchen and I into the shower, and when I came out, a veritable feast was set on the table—leaves and noodles and fish and a mountain of hard-boiled eggs. I snagged two eggs and tucked one into Chau's hand to play a childhood game—cracking the ends together, the loser has to eat the broken egg. Mine cracked, my stomach rumbled, and I looked inside. A milky, sightless eye stared back; beneath it, a sodden wing. It was a fertilized embryo that had been allowed to incubate until the day before hatching and then hard-boiled. It lay on my plate, mustard yellow and looking like a fledgling about to fly from its nest. An image of the militant old man from the youth offices appeared in my mind's eye: *Will she eat local food rather than shame her guides?* Everyone was watching. I scooped out a spoonful. It crunched between my teeth.

Our hostess brought out a sheath of pliable, cardboardlike disks, and everyone fell silent to do justice to the meal. The rice paper was dipped into a mixture of fish sauce and chili, filled with noodles and leafy greens, rolled like a cigarette, and sealed with a generous dollop of saliva. Chau demonstrated and handed me the result. I could smell a trail of cigarette smoke along the sealed edge as I took a bite.

After dinner I slunk off to the much-needed privacy of my mosquito net and a few quiet moments with my grammar books. Within minutes my bedroom window was packed with giggling kids. Eventually three teenagers burst into the room and huddled in one corner, talking in whispers and pushing each other forward to speak with me. A young man finally squared his shoulders and sidled up toward me.

"Hello. Where you from?" he asked in English, to the instant applause of his female entourage.

Fung had ordered me to say I was from Switzerland and speak only French. A small devil took hold of me.

"America."

His grin widened. "America number one!" he said, and raised his hand in a thumbs-up sign. My mouth fell open.

"Please be happy come back," he added. My jaw dropped a fraction wider.

His two friends surged forward and began offering carefully rehearsed questions and phrases: "Would you like to dance?" "Does your family eat rice?" "My cat is name Harry," and "Do you drink a lot?" I detected the emerging outlines of an English exercise book, and they produced it upon request. It was almost illegibly tattered and dirty, produced on cheap newsprint and bound with glue, and fingered by generations of eager young hands. The modules were riddled with typos and stilted 1950s' dialogue. They had been studying the book diligently for four years. I was the first native English speaker they had ever met.

We worked through their entire lesson plan twice, while I gradually wilted and they blossomed into happy-go-lucky teenagers having the time of their lives. At last, torn between the desire to encourage these dedicated young students and my desperate need to be with my own thoughts for a while, I pleaded illness and prayed that they would take the hint and leave.

"You sick?" the young man said, leaning forward in sudden, wrinkle-browed concern. His girlfriend took my hand and slipped into bed beside me. A rapid-fire conversation ensued over my head, with the obvious conclusion that they must keep me company until the illness passed, throughout the night if need be.

I sank back onto my bedroll and tried in vain to summon the Vietnamese vocabulary to explain my desire for privacy. The concept had no meaning in a culture where "alone" was synonymous with "lonely," where everyone ate, slept, worked, and sometimes defecated together. Only in times of extreme anger were people asked to leave, and even then the Asian face-saving solution was to grit one's teeth in silence and avoid the offender in the future.

But I hadn't grown up sharing a room with eighteen people. My head throbbed, my eyeballs ached, and a small ball of nausea was growing in the pit of my stomach. How could I explain the importance of being able to scratch my ear and wiggle my toes without having it commented on by a cheering crowd of onlookers?

I stood and herded them gently away from the bed and tried not to cringe as I shut the door on their bewildered faces. I crawled back into bed and fell instantly into exhausted sleep.

℮   ℮   ℮

The next afternoon Chau and Fung roused themselves from their drunken sleep only long enough to stagger out to the veranda chairs. Fung noticed me and issued strict instructions not to leave the house, or risk being assaulted by angry mobs of anti-American activists. He sank into a stupor and I left.

I hadn't gotten very far along the road before they found me, hordes of them—three-foot-high munchkins in shiny white shirts and flip-flops, energetically swinging their plastic satchels on the way to school. They surrounded me in ever-deepening layers, shouting *"Lyn So"* with cheerful glee. They thought I was Russian. I set them straight, and they brightened considerably. When I walked off, they followed, showing no intention of making their way back to school.

I crossed a small bridge spanning one of the myriad canals that make up the flat and soupy Mekong and waved to a young man poling a wobbly boat beneath my feet.

"Where are you going?" he asked in Vietnamese.

"For a walk."

He pointed at the bottom of his boat. "Come for a ride."

I agreed, as much to escape my meteor trail of children as to experience life in a flat-bottom canoe barely larger than a coffin.

He was returning from his fishing nets, and several six-inch fish flapped and twitched around his legs. But from 9:00 P.M. until 6:00 A.M. every night, he made French baguettes, he told me. He offered to take me to the bakery where he worked. I hesitated for a moment, but he had flour in the crook of his arm and along his hairline, and seemed harmless.

The canal, barely twenty feet wide, was strewn with gossamer gill nets dangling from wooden posts. Bottles, with a stub of candle in each one, hung here and there to warn off nighttime traffic in a land that traveled by water. I imagined returning home in the evening to the song of crickets and the rhythmic whisper of the pole, guided by flickering candlelight in thick green bottles, and it seemed the most poetic place in the world.

Then we turned the corner and maneuvered around a row of outhouses the size of packing crates, each with a narrow walkway connecting it to shore. One was occupied, its owner plainly visible from the hips up. A scant few feet away, a clutch of women stooped over the river's edge, washing cabbage for their evening meal. We paddled on.

The bakery was in full swing when we arrived. The owner sat in the front room before an enormous accounts book filled with columns of tiny, penciled numbers. "Come in," he said in greeting, his face wreathed in a genuine smile. He seemed not the least put out by an uninvited stranger in the middle of his morning shift. He insisted on leaving his books to give me a personal tour, and his joy at discovering my stumbling Vietnamese was without bounds. He seemed more proud of me than of his hard-won bakery and plied me with a steady stream of soft drinks and buttery candy while escorting me through his cottage factory.

We followed the beehive activity into the oven room, where two shirtless young men seized unbaked sausages of dough, sliced their tops, and loaded them into ovens that lined one wall. Beams of sunlight filtered through air so dusty with flour that it seemed to hang in translucent curtains that danced and swirled.

The bread that emerged was golden brown, and steamy soft inside. It tasted like the perfect Parisian baguette, one of the few positive remnants of the French occupation. I obviously wasn't the only one who thought so. "The ovens run for eighteen hours at a time and make ten thousand loaves a day," the owner told me proudly.

"Where do they all go?" I asked, for I had seen neither trucks nor loading docks.

In response he took me to yet another room, where the loaves were disappearing through a side door into the waiting baskets of an army of bicyclists and market walkers. I watched as a dozen young women covered their wares against the roadside dirt and pedaled away, taking turns to sing out the lyrical

"Ban meeeeiiii" ("bread") as they carried them to every house and shanty for miles.

I ducked back inside and found my way past vats of dough and an assembly line of tousled black hair and shiny shoulders. In the darkest, deepest corner of this human-powered bakery, I caught a brief glimpse of a lone man standing silently. He was covered with flour, like an old wraith with a halo of gray, powdery hair. He spent his days pouring sacks of flour onto scales whose weights he could hardly lift, then smoothing out the lumpy mixture with fingers gnarled with age. The air was so thick that it tickled my nose.

The men worked nine hours a day, six days a week, and earned twenty dollars a month. I had rarely seen such attention to detail and efficient use of human energy anywhere in the world. It belied my earlier impression of Vietnamese productivity—an old woman sitting long hours beside a few scattered bananas, waiting for a sale. I was impressed.

The bakery owner begged me to come back and meet his wife, and sent the boatman to return me to the bridge where we had met. I snuck home before Chau and Fung stirred from their afternoon nap.

59

6

Dear Mom,
Fang is a discourteous, drunken, light-fingered,
lazy warthog. I have nightmares about those
chilling nails and dangling gold tooth.

Greed

We were under way at the first light of dawn, before the sun melted the small stretch of tarmac in the center of town. My body creaked more than my bicycle, and my sunburned skin felt like that of an overripe melon about to explode. My guides solicited an extra wad of money for a gift they had supposedly purchased for our hostess, despite having spent the entire evening in the lawn chairs on the veranda. I asked to see it, only to be told that it was bad luck to open a package meant for someone else. When we took our leave, she pounded me companionably on the back and told me to come back, and I wished she really did have a memento of our visit beyond old fish bones and eggshells.

We cycled back the way we had come. I no longer had any idea of our route and no longer cared. I had impressed upon Fung my desire to settle into a rural village for a few days, and they had promised me that nightfall would find us in just such a place. In the meantime, I was learning to enjoy the simple act of pedaling through the lush countryside and scattered roadside hamlets. I treasured the freedom from being told to hold my chopsticks just so, from the struggle to apply the proper salutations to everyone I met, from being pinned under the critical eyes of my watchdog guides. It was a peaceful time, the road so flat that the endless pumping on the pedals became as automatic as the sway of a train along its tracks. The landscape slid by, slowly enough to savor, quickly enough to keep my interest. Because the dreamy green fields left me feeling peaceful and content, I called out greetings to candy sellers and paddy diggers, toddlers and tired old men.

They responded with a smile and a wave. Behind me I heard a rippling wake of wondering comments: "on a bicycle," "she spoke Vietnamese," or "white lady."

Fung pedaled up beside me to practice his newest phrases. His pronunciation had improved dramatically, though he seemed far more interested in adding to his vocabulary than in meaningful conversation. I kept a small dictionary in my back pocket, and we rode side-by-side, exchanging snippets of information and non sequiturs.

"When you weah twawsahs, I t'ink you old woman. When you weah"—he searched for the word, then slashed his leg just above the knee with one hand—"I t'ink you yhoung woman."

"Thanks." He was stork skinny, with droopy lips and that double set of chilling, polished nails. With his protruding gold tooth, my rebellious mind had long ago relabeled him "Fang." Despite his compliment, I resolved to wear twawsahs, even in the sweltering midday heat.

I was slowly relearning the thousand words I had crammed into my head while still in America. In my haste to make progress, I had paid scant attention to the squiggly, slanted lines and dots above each new bit of vocabulary. They were, I eventually discovered, critically important pronunciation guides for a language that was more sung than spoken. Without them I was unintelligible. A common word like *ma* could have half a dozen meanings, from rice seedling to horse. Since every word had several tonal variations, the potential for misunderstanding in even the simplest sentence was astronomical.

I studied my latest vocabulary list for a moment, my eyes darting back and forth to check the potholes and traffic. Fung reached over and took it from me, gave it a perfunctory glance, and tucked it into his shirt pocket. Similar slips of paper had been disappearing from my belongings since the trip began. I suspected they would eventually find their way into some government anti-espionage file. I wondered what insights they would provide the powers-that-be and resisted the temptation to scribble a list of CIA instructions addressed to Fung in college-level English and wait for him to take it off my hands.

He grabbed suddenly for my dictionary and searched through it for a new word. "No lay-ziness!" he barked at me before riding on ahead, my dictionary still tightly clamped in his fist.

We pedaled steadily throughout the afternoon and into the tropical twilight. Traffic thickened and the scenery turned from waving paddy to squalid urban congestion. Darkness fell. We had neither lights nor reflectors, and neither did the trucks that came barreling down the road at us.

"How much further?" I asked peevishly. My backside hurt, and the ghostlike traffic made me nervous. Surely we wouldn't have stopped for a three-hour lunch if it meant we would be pedaling into the night.

"Twenty minutes," Fung said.

An hour later we were in bumper-to-bumper bicycle traffic on the outskirts of a large city. The homebound urban dwellers carried every imaginable form of cargo on their rusty bikes, from full-size pigs to thirty-foot lengths of bamboo that trailed along behind them like dinosaur tails. They were unabashedly friendly and took the opportunity to ride with me whenever possible, smiling broadly and trying out bits of unusual English gleaned from contraband recordings by Bruce Springsteen and Madonna.

A young man swerved into the momentarily empty space beside me, his cargo a grinning friend who sat sidesaddle on the back rack. They were students, one studying French in the local university, the other English. On the unlit road I could make out nothing more than the moonlit glow of their smiles. I was captivated. The miles slipped by beneath us.

Why, I asked, English and French? The language of the invaders.

"Business!" they chorused, and laughed happily. Western languages, particularly English, were the key to a coveted job in a foreign firm. Everyone aspired to American dollars, American contacts, and eventually a chance to emigrate to America. Besides, if no job opportunities presented themselves among the multinationals, it was always possible to get by teaching English to future wannabes. The university course was immensely popular, and only the best and brightest were accepted. Russian was no longer even offered, due to a complete lack of interest.

Fung pushed his front wheel between us and pried my young friends away. He spoke to them roughly in Vietnamese, then turned on me.

"Bad men, no good. No talk."

Our rapid-fire, unintelligible English had made him uncomfortable. I weighed my new friendships against the thought of having to spend the next twelve days in Fung's company, and sadly waved them good-bye.

"How much further?"

"Twenty minutes."

Another hour went by.

After crossing the same intersection so many times that even I recognized it, I knew we were lost. Chau's relief when we arrived at the steps of a run-down hotel was palpable. So was mine. We pulled into the lobby, and I wearily unloaded my packs. Chau padded away with my permission papers, padded back, and shook his head. We got back on our bicycles. The next lodging house was sure to take us, Fung assured me, and it was no more than twenty minutes away.

This hotel was huge, run-down, and expensive. Chau booked three rooms for three days. I was too tired to argue. We agreed to meet at nine for dinner, and I climbed the seven flights of stairs beside the long-expired elevator.

The restaurant they chose was shabby, the menu hugely overpriced. We sat down with five young men, friends of Chau, who had been waiting for us in the company of a dozen bottles of beer. They ate and drank with gusto, and soon the table legs were surrounded by empty flasks and the floor was littered with fish bones. I waited wearily for our guests to leave. When they finally did, Fung beat me to the punch. He demanded two hundred dollars for the hotel rooms, gifts, and miscellaneous expenses.

I had brought a sizable emergency fund with me, over and above the agreed-upon expenses for the entire trip. The daily budget, which I handed over to Chau each morning, disappeared without a trace, and I had been asked repeatedly to dig into my reserves. By now there was very little left.

I took it out and counted it—$176—and asked them if that amount, in addition to our budget, would cover the remainder of the three-week trip. Fung pulled out his pocket notebook, scribbled through a page of careful calculations, then slapped the result down on the table. By his account our entire twenty-one-day budget, plus several hundred dollars in emergency reserves, were scheduled to run out two days hence. I realized to my horror that the trip was costing not twenty dollars per day, but well over two hundred.

I took up the pencil and reminded them of our original deal—to stay, if not within the budget, then at least close to it, to sleep in villages and enjoy the local cuisine. My guides became hostile and silent. Fung pointed out, stiff-lipped, that hotels could not be accounted for in the negotiated package. I heartily agreed. I had brought a hammock. Why didn't we use it? Surely their student trips didn't cost two million dong per person per day. That was a year's income for the average Vietnamese.

"Election time," Chau explained, while Fung took short, irritated puffs on his cigarette. The city government was cracking down on foreigners, and they hadn't been able to get me into a village, despite the permission papers. It would clear itself up in a few days.

I made an effort to accept this conciliatory note and turned back to Fung. "Twelve more days," I said. "How much money?" Fung went back to work, tapping his nails on the table and thinking hard. Nine hundred dollars.

I had nowhere near that much money with me, and no plans to spend it if I did. We bargained. They refused to consider a penny less than five hundred. I told them I would have to return to Saigon by bus to replenish my reserves. Fung agreed with a wave of his hand and tossed me his scribbled notes as a reminder. Dinner was silent.

I excused myself to go for a stroll. Fung barked an angry order, then recovered enough to inform me that I was not allowed to go out at night alone, and they were far too tired to accompany me. I was, however, allowed to pay the bill, a hefty one that included dinner and drinks for all his friends. They escorted me back to the lobby. The last I saw of them was their sweat-stained backs as they headed for the nearest bar.

℮   ℮   ℮

The next morning was a local election day. The red Vietnamese flag brightened the gray streets with random splashes of color. Processions crept by like millipedes: men in masks and banners, dancing and twirling to the riveting beat of drums and cymbals. Ubiquitous posters proclaimed the joys of the coming elections—"Voting is our greatest freedom!" and "Preserve your right to vote!" with life-size paintings of white-clothed schoolgirls freeing flocks of doves.

It was all a sham. Party membership was a prerequisite for candidacy, and political platforms were dictated from the central organizations in Saigon and Hanoi. The flags were required by law on posted "red flag days." Although the government brought the vote to the old and sick, everyone else was subject to a fine—money or labor—if they didn't present themselves at the appointed hour. Those who were out of town had to petition the police for special dispensation. Ninety-nine percent voter attendance and the veneer of democracy hid nothing of substance or meaning.

Chau, the lower-ranking Communist, was ordered to accompany me back to Saigon. We arrived at the station in early afternoon and just barely managed to squeeze on board the last bus, filled to bursting. Traditional gender constraints disappeared once the wheels began to roll. I had yet to see a Vietnamese couple kissing or even walking hand in hand, but within the confines of public transport, moral restraints gave way to practical necessity. People nestled together, and sleepy heads dropped onto unknown shoulders. Even Chau, freed of Fung's intimidating presence, scrutinized my dictionary for the first time and helped me through some of the more convoluted Vietnamese pronunciations.

Grammar soon fell by the wayside in favor of dedicated conductor-watching. The man was as quick and agile as a cricket, leaping down and jogging alongside, scooping up babies and manhandling women up the steps. When we pulled over to pick up larger groups with bicycles and cargo, he clambered up on the roof like a gecko. A helper slung the bikes up, and he snatched them out of the air and lashed them on board in record time. I pulled out my watch and clocked his best efforts. A woman with children cost us three seconds; two bicycles and a fifty-kilo sack of rice set us back less than twelve; and for the single young men, the bus barely slowed.

I was just drifting off when the rattan bag hanging from the seat in front of me took a deep breath and began to crow. It was answered by a series of identical bags scattered throughout the bus. I drifted off to the volleys of rough-throated roosters, with a cauldron of twitching shrimp between my feet and my head resting on a strange man's shoulder.

℮   ℮   ℮

I left a message for Tam and retired to my guest-house room. Twenty minutes later he burst through the door. He was concerned that I hadn't yet seen the inside of a village, shocked that my guides had managed to spend so much of my money, and appalled that they had once casually asked me whether I had stored any of my belongings with Tam. "You must see the director," he insisted, muttering, "Why should they want to know where your things are? It's none of their business. How often did they ask you?" To my surprise he refused to accompany me to the director's home. Instead, he made elaborate plans to "drop by" at the critical moment and offer to "lend a hand." I began to realize how fragile his position in society was and what a risk he was taking in helping me.

We ate at a street vendor's rice stall, run by his wife and sister-in-law. They sold omelets and fried fish by the plate and cut up their offerings with a large pair of shears. The tables and tiny stools, the rice cauldron and the food, were portable to avoid frequent police raids. If they were caught and didn't pay an immediate bribe, their day's worth of food would be overturned into the street.

Dinner with Tam was like eating with an old friend, and in the end he called for dessert and wouldn't allow me to pay the bill.

℮   ℮   ℮

The director's front parlor was a hairdresser's salon where he kept his young wife and several relatives gainfully employed. The hair on the floor was uniformly black, and the mirror warped like a carnival booth. A young girl brought us tiny cups of tea, and the snipping fell silent as employee and client alike strained to hear our conversation. My English was straight and to the point, Tam's translations long and friendly. Chau sat in sullen silence, periodically shooting to his feet to vehemently argue a point. In the end Tam turned to me with a compromise. "They promise no more hotels, you must double the budget to forty dollars each day, and they will give you an accounting of their expenditures." We shook hands all around, agreed that we now understood each other perfectly, and left.

The Saigon bus station was an island unto itself, with high walls to keep the untidy vendors with their carts and merchandise outside. We entered and were immediately bustled on board a half-filled bus. The engine was already running, the driver sitting behind the wheel. I blessed my luck that we had arrived in the nick of time and sank into a nearby seat. The driver honked twice, surged six inches forward, rolled back, and disengaged the clutch.

Bodies filled the bus, their heat adding to the palpable waves coming off the engine. The driver put the bus in gear. I silently urged him forward. We rocked forward, settled back, and sat.

An hour later I was preparing to bludgeon the driver, toss him out the door, and pilot the bus myself. He nudged the clutch into gear for the umpteenth time and urged the bus forward. I refused to be taken in by this sadistic trick. We kept moving.

We eased into rush-hour traffic and immediately slowed to a crawl. An unruly herd of bicyclists wove back and forth across our front bumper. Now, instead of cringing at the indifferent behemoth that was bearing down on me with blaring horn, I was inside the monster's mouth, staring out. I rained curses on the heads of the unresponsive bikes that blocked our way and lengthened for one millisecond my confinement in this smelly oven. The driver did his best to humor my unspoken wish. He nosed the bumper to within inches of the wobbly bikes. He punched his horn and roared across intersections, secure in the belief that pesky bicyclists would get out of his way. So they did, though the occasional laggard disappeared from view under the front windshield for a heart-stopping moment before emerging to pedal off to one side.

By the time we arrived, the air was so sodden with fumes that I could feel a veneer of oil clinging to my face. I wiped a sleeve across my cheek and left three fingerprints of black dirt on my gray-tinted shirt.

Fung was waiting for us in the hotel lobby, his nails newly polished and his ever-present beer and cigarettes close at hand. He looked at my disheveled hair and sweat-soaked clothes with poorly disguised disgust. "Did you bring the money?" he asked.

7

Dear Mom,
My best friend appears to be a scrawny white
chicken. I wonder if he has a hidden agenda too.

The Village Life

W e were on our way again. This time, they promised me, we were going to a village. Unfortunately, our path to rural serenity took us not down quiet country lanes past lowing cattle, but along a major Mekong artery where trucks and buses roared by endlessly. I discovered an entirely new sound: not the single, heart-stopping blast of a bus bearing down from behind, but the mingled cry of two road monsters, the second intent on overtaking the first. They appropriated the entire road, scattering drying coconut husks and bicycles and leaving pandemonium in their wake.

The gravel shoulder sloping down into the paddy provided a measure of safety, but it was littered with broken-down bicycles and stalls selling grapefruit. Neat rectangles of drying rice appeared at intervals, their corners anchored with football-size rocks or broken chairs to discourage encroaching drivers.

With the added traffic Fung had taken it upon himself to ride beside me, to play David against the oncoming Goliaths. I was grateful for his concern but much more comfortable pedaling single file. Disaster struck almost immediately. A bus in a hell-bent hurry bore down on us from the front while a truck being chased by demon furies raced toward us from behind. Fung pedaled on, unconcerned. The road clearly wasn't going to be wide enough to accommodate all four of us. At the moment of truth I lost my nerve and plowed through a thicket of red and yellow incense sticks drying on the shoulder. Chau tittered behind me. Fung shook his head knowingly and clicked his tongue. I wished him dead.

I wheeled my bike back onto the road, leaped on board, and sprinted to the front, forcing us to ride single file. Neither Fung nor Chau were happy, and they made frequent attempts to overtake me and ride at my side. I increased my pace. So did they.

We pedaled past intermittent paddy and an occasional roadside eatery. Fung was inching up on me again. I could see him out of the corner of my eye. He motioned that he had something important to tell me. I reluctantly allowed him to close the gap.

"Are you tired?" he asked, planting himself firmly at my shoulder. I shook my head and tried in vain to shake him loose. He rode in a straight line, just on the edge of the shoulder, and gave me no room to squeeze past the broken-down vehicles and tossing buffalo horns. I asked him to ride behind me. He shrugged and shook his head. "You no know how drive bike," he said.

This time it was a bus. It chose the narrow strip in front of us to pull over and let off a passenger. Fung recognized the conductor's shrill whistle seconds before I did and sprinted for the narrowing gap. He plugged it completely. I swung off the road, rolled heavily down an embankment that was far too steep for my fickle brakes, and buried my front wheel in the paddy mud.

Fung pulled over above me and lit a cigarette.

My bike came free of the ooze with a loud slurping sound, and I hauled it with difficulty up to the road. I contained my rage and pushed off, ignoring the splatters of mud that flew off the wheel and speckled my clothes and legs. Fung was sneaking up on me again. This time I was ready for him, cutting him off sharply when he tried to pass me on the inside. He slalomed across my back wheel like a water-skier and inched up on me from the other side. I sped up, all thoughts of lovely scenery forgotten, my mind filled instead with fantasies of scattered thumb tacks, poisoned oil slicks, and rear-mounted tommy guns. Perhaps the war wasn't such a bad idea after all.

The roadside houses multiplied, and I knew a bridge was close at hand. I tired of the race and pulled over to film the river with its bright blue boats with proud, fine lines. Their graceful bows were painted with two glowing red eyes to ward off evil spirits and find the way through dangerous shoals.

Chau tapped me lightly on the shoulder, then pointed at a thick wire strung along the bridge inches from my forehead. He pretended to touch it, made a hissing sound, and indicated the smoldering tip of his cigarette. A live wire carrying live current. I remembered seeing the government placards describing the perils of electrocution. At first I had thought the warnings, showing men tumbling headlong from poles and rooftops with Xs in the place of eyes, were public service bulletins. Later on I heard that electrocution was a leading cause of death in a country so poor that stealing power was a necessary national pastime.

At last we pulled over at a large house with a stone floor and two fishponds in the front yard. Chau embraced the old man sitting on the steps with understandable familiarity—it was his father. He shared Chau's flat, almost concave face and wide forehead. His teeth were unnaturally even and in far better shape than Chau's. He motioned us inside while he gathered the last of the stove kindling that had been put out to dry in the afternoon sun.

Chau had six brothers and three sisters, including the lovely young girl who was padding flat-footed through the parlor, herding a gaggle of ducklings that flowed past us like the incoming tide. His mother's picture stood on one of the altars, behind a much larger plastic bust of Chairman Ho. "She dead ten months before now," Chau said, in the simplified Vietnamese he always used with me. "She die of"—he thought for a moment—"stomach." He lit a cigarette from one of the incense sticks. A plastic Coke bottle of hard liquor appeared, and his father took out his teeth. I left them both to a long, smoky reunion.

The young girl silently pointed out the toilet. It was one of those packing-crate affairs that stood on stilts over a fishpond. When I clambered up the wobbly plank, the mirror-smooth water beneath me suddenly began to churn and boil with expectant fish. They had felt my footsteps and were gathering under the hole. Bits of paper, handwritten receipts, and used shopping lists floated on the surface. I took a deep breath, dropped my pants, and tried to distract myself from the painfully public setting by closing my eyes and assuming that if I couldn't see anyone, no one could see me.

The shower was a cement cubicle with a small hole in the corner that served as a drain. I bathed with a bucket and scoop, and watched long, snakelike strings of frothy gray suds slither through the wall and disappear.

When I returned, the reunion was over and the old man sat alone in front of an ancient TV. Chau had taken Fung out to track down a case of beer. I pulled up a chair and sat with a white chicken that had kept vigil under my chair all through teatime and thus become my friend.

The show was a Chinese import, its half-dozen characters dressed like Hindu deities with flowing robes and powdered white faces with bright red lips. They popped in and out of the story with loud boinging noises and never failed to wreak havoc on anyone in peasant's garb. The Vietnamese voice-over was done by one translator, so even the bearlike warrior spoke in a shrill, high-pitched squeak.

It looked like a comedy, but the old man sat grimly silent and played with his teeth.

The next morning Chau's father was up bright and early, laying wood out to dry in the courtyard and calling the goslings together with singsong chirps. He walked once to Chau's bed and stood for a moment, watching with sad eyes as his son snored off a night's merrymaking. I felt sorry for him until he caught my gaze and smiled, gently shrugged away the generation gap between young and old, city and country, and cheerfully returned to his chores.

I was not as forgiving. I shook them both awake at noon. "Good afternoon," I said in carefully rehearsed Vietnamese. "We are going to our village now?" Fung sat up and rubbed one hand across his mouth. "This is a village," he told me.

I tried to curb my frustration. "This," I said, "is a house near a road. No fields. No livestock." The only wildlife I could hear was the bleating of impatient Minsk motorbikes and the throaty roar of trucks. "Just traffic."

Chau rolled his eyes. Fung heaved a prolonged sigh and collapsed back onto the bed. I went to pack my bags. My plan was simple. I would ride away, take the first likely feeder road I came across, and follow it to its end. I was tired of brother Chau's genealogical tour of South Vietnam. I was in an agrarian country; villages couldn't possibly be that hard to find.

Faced with the inevitable, Fung took over and sent Chau to buy flashlights, mosquito coils, and whiskey for the trip. He waited until I had finished packing, then ordered me sharply to unload my bicycle; we were going by boat.

The engine shaft was almost as long as the boat itself, with a tiny prop buzzing at its tip like a tethered dragonfly. We clambered on board beside a grizzled old driver whose right hand seemed permanently twisted into the shape of his engine's starter cord.

Soon we were under way, peacefully puttering through the calm water, turning unexpectedly into side canals, ducking under monkey bridges just high enough to clear the bow. The narrow channel was sluggish and full of vegetation, and the engine clogged often. The enforced interludes allowed us to drift silently down waterways fringed with waving grass, where white-feathered egrets and brown-skinned farmers waded calmly side by side. We passed several moored fishing boats, their long, sinister poles extended from their prows like rigid antennae, the scoop net drooping between them. I imagined the net being lowered into the water and churning implacably through the muddy canals like the maw of a great white shark. Despite the rich, soupy breeding grounds among the growing rice seedlings, the Mekong was clearly not a healthy place to be a fish.

It was a land that existed somewhere on the interface between earth and water, and people seemed to move about more comfortably in the three-plank paddleboats than on the uncertain mud. It was also the season to prepare the paddy for planting. Farmers speckled the landscape—men, women, and children—wading through waist-deep water and scooping up armfuls of the weeds that choked the flooded fields. They carried them, dripping and rotten, to the edge of the dikes and dumped them to die and dry in the sun.

We steamed past a large cement compound, incongruously solid amid the battered shanty huts with grass thatch roofing. A wood-and-wire fence isolated it from its neighbors, a Vietnamese flag flew proudly from every building, and a single pole rose from its central courtyard, topped by a loud-speaker nestled in a tangle of barbed wire.

"A school?" I asked.

Fung shook his head. "Police station," he said. "No photographs."

Several huts dotted the final stretch of canal. A narrow-gauge electrical line ran down one side of the waterway, sprouting even thinner metal threads that disappeared through bamboo walls. One side had light, the other darkness. I wondered if illicit romances ever sprang up across the murky channel. We docked on the side of the have-nots.

The hut was tiny and shabby, its owners young and beautiful. She had a smile of such friendly innocence that I couldn't believe she lived in such abject poverty. He had high, finely chiseled cheekbones and an earnest, helpful face. Toddling between their legs, their daughter was, quite simply, captivating.

Their home was too small to have separate rooms; a well-mended pink mosquito net curtained off the sleeping area. The extended roof behind the house served as an outdoor kitchen. I saw no sign of chickens, pigs, geese, or any other form of accumulated savings, not even a mangy dog.

The house next door, however, fairly buzzed with wealth. It had real wood siding, a shower cubicle built next to the canal, a half-dozen pigs just limbering their vocal chords for the evening feed, and a raised cement porch that ran the length of the front yard. Freshly cut wood lay in stacks beside a foraging flock of ducklings. Why, I asked Fung carefully, did the neighbors seem so much . . . luckier than our hosts?

"Policies changed in 1986," he translated from Thuy, the earnest young man whose hut we were in. Some farmers had been given back their land, and the old-man patriarch next door had amassed quite a bit of paddy. "You cannot make something from nothing," he said. I watched a stout old woman, filthy to the waist, cross the neighbor's bridge with a large basin of snails resting on one hip. "And," Fung added with a smile, "there was a flood." For three months the Mekong lay under a blanket of water, and the rain poured ceaselessly from the heavens. The young man pulled me eagerly inside to make his point. A coat of gray mud ringed the legs of the plywood bureau and left a corrugated washboard along the walls. There had not been one foot of solid land, he breathed, and everyone traveled in boats. They had raised their sleeping platform and watched the dead rats floating by in the night. Their crops had been destroyed, as well as many dikes and houses. They were only now beginning to recover.

"Did anyone die?" I asked morbidly, thinking of the malignant spread of cholera and parasites once the open sewers were set free. Thuy shook his head. One old woman had gone out, but at the age of sixty-nine she was living on borrowed time and perhaps it was right that she should die.

They had had more than their share of such sadness. A five-year-old boy had graced their hut not half a year ago—their firstborn child. Thuy's wife—her name was Flower—stumbled through the details in halting, half-whispered sentences, with gruesome gestures that could only have been possible after many repetitions of the tragic tale. The little one had been playing on the dirt path that fronted the house and hadn't seen the three-wheel truck, barreling down the road too fast to stop or swerve aside. My first thought was, how could that unpaved lane, barely wide enough for two bicyclists to ride side by side, have hosted such a deed? And then I wondered how they could have allowed a small child to play in so dangerous a place. And then I looked up and saw the pain fresh in her face, and was ashamed.

After dinner we set up our hammocks, and Fung settled down to tell tales in a cloud of store-bought smoke. He seemed under no obligation to share his expensive cigarettes with his hosts, though we had bought four cartons for just such a purpose and for their part they readily plied him with homemade whiskey. The evening's entertainment seemed payment enough, and soon he had them holding their stomachs and rocking back and forth with unsuppressed hilarity. From the way the old women held their hands over their toothless gums and looked me up and down, I knew the jokes were largely at my expense. Still, there seemed nothing harsh about their laughter, and a small boy swung with great energy from the ropes of my hammock. How great could the damage be? Suddenly a stout old woman was towering over me, her hands on her hips and her wrinkled thighs inches from my face. She glared at me and demanded loudly in Vietnamese, "Do you ever even *think* about your mother?" and I knew that all was lost.

℮   ℮   ℮

It was 5:00 A.M. and black as pitch outside. I saw neither the light of a candle nor the shadow of an early riser and heard

77

only the predawn sounds of roosters and a groggy cricket or two. All was quiet—until someone flicked a switch and the sudden blaring of Michael Jackson, hideously loud, erupted from the big house next door. The neighbors were getting up.

By five-twenty they were hard at work on their house, hammering and sawing in the pale light of dawn. At least half a dozen young men were cutting yet more tree trunks into neat planking. The patriarch was up on a ladder with his back to me, hammering a new awning into place. I had expected a portly fellow with a voice rough from too many cigars, and diamond rings recessed into the fat of each finger. This old man was wiry and strong, with a mouthful of nails and plier-like toes. He whipped his body back and forth like a garden hose, throwing his weight behind each stroke of the hammer. I watched the busy household for the next hour as an additional wall gradually took shape and the womenfolk came out with teetering loads of laundry to dip into the canal and pound against the rocks. The music shifted at random from the deep thump of American disco to Eastern instrumental, full of flats and warbling keys, and back again.

At last, when the rising sun had turned our little hut into a toaster oven, there was a stirring behind the mosquito net, the mewing of a small child, and the sound of someone rising. They opened the back door and arranged themselves along the edge of the pond, to do their toilette beside the dirty dishes and the drying laundry. I thought nostalgically of knee-high boxes and expectant fish and went next door to beg the use of the neighbors' shower stall and fishpond.

Later, I warily followed Thuy's toothless old father into an unstable three-plank boat and sat as low as possible, cradling my cameras and watching a ten-year-old squish mud into the many wormholes that were welling water around our ankles. We poled down a canal barely wide enough for the boat, stopping at intervals to lift narrow walkways aside. The soupy trenches I had taken for drainage ditches were in reality waterways for these tiny, canoelike craft. No wonder the Vietnamese had left no footprints during the war and passed like silent wraiths under the very noses of the American sentries.

We broke free and cut across a flooded paddy. Along one edge two men bent over homemade shovels, digging new farmland. It was backbreaking labor, the herculean task of moving eight vertical feet of clay for every hard-won foot of new paddy.

Not many young men would have the opportunity to carve a place for themselves among the few remaining islands that peppered the endless fields. Firstborn sons inherited their elders' fields, I was told, as well as the task of caring for their parents in their declining years. "Other sons go out and find work"—as laborers—"one dollar, one day." Thuy's father paused briefly and fluttered his hands at the horizon. "Or go My Tho city, or Saigon. Never come back." He murmured the names of the two sons he had lost this way.

Of the ones that stayed, not many escaped the spiraling descent into poverty and multiplying children. Those that struggled upward were often struck down by drought, flood, sickness, or the pleas of their less-fortunate relations. The few that made it followed the painstaking road to Delta wealth, which Thuy's father summed up on arthritic fingers. "First land," he said, his face lighting up at the thought, "then an engine!" His lips split in a huge grin, and he fell silent for a moment to contemplate such a wondrous thing. "And then a boat—*big* boat." He slapped the gunwale to show me what he thought of our paltry craft. I prodded him for the next step, but he couldn't seem to imagine luxuries beyond these three. But no—he held up a fourth finger. "An altar." One grand enough to give proper thanks to the ancestors who had heard his pleas.

Or, if they were truly graced, they might accumulate enough cash to buy a pair of water buffalo to till their fields, or even one of the mechanical plows that could be rented out to others for the princely sum of three dollars a day. We pulled up alongside a field where just such a contraption was churning up the mud in preparation for planting.

It bucked and kicked in the grip of the young man who walked behind it, and left a trail of well-chewed mud in its wake. Several other men were plodding through the ooze, bending down occasionally to pick up small, wriggling objects and drop them into rattan baskets slung over their shoulders. I watched, fascinated. After years of shell collecting and berry picking, the temptation to discover what buried treasure they were grubbing out of the knee-deep paddy was irresistible. I gingerly lowered myself into the muck.

Their catch seemed to include every living thing that squirmed, crawled, wriggled, or crept through the mud. Or, as they told me, everything that showed its back to the sun. They emptied their baskets into the bottom of the boat until it became a specimen collector's delight: a seething, slithering mass of fish, shrimp, snails, tadpoles, snakes, crabs, eels, and assorted larvae.

When the bulk of the paddy's inhabitants had been accounted for, we gathered up Fung and Chau from their resting spot under a tree and paddled home for lunch. There, Flower took the wriggling delicacies and, with a minimum of gutting and rinsing, dropped them into a wok. I was just framing a polite refusal to lunch when I saw Flower's hopeful smile and, behind her, Fung's smug smirk. I took a hearty helping, speared a sluglike lump, and banished the sudden memory of my brother, sitting at the dinner table, describing the "mouth feel" of a good red wine.

Afterward Fung and Chau sank into their hammocks and prepared for a few hours in well-deserved slumber. I minced over on feet that were already heating up with infection from my barefoot foray into the morning's mud. I wanted to go out again, to see the rice being planted and, if possible, to lend a hand. Fung gave me a look of irritation and informed me through tight lips that no one worked through the heat of the day.

I cocked my ear to the incessant hammering of the old patriarch next door, putting the finishing touches on his awning.

Fung's long, bony finger rose trembling skyward. The sun would wither my skin and loosen my teeth, he said, and turn me into an even greater hag than I already was.

I flourished a tube of sunscreen and my wide, conical hat and cackled like the Wicked Witch of the West.

His hand sank back into the hammock. The heat, he croaked. It drove men wild and made them do unsightly things, such as he would not even speak of with me.

I promised to protect him with my life from the trespasses of murderers and rapists, if he would just get out of bed.

Without further ado he rolled over and went to sleep, and when I tried to leave without him I found that he had locked my shoes and cameras in the bureau and hidden the key.

The earth steamed with the first heavy drops of afternoon rain, like an overheated skillet doused in cold water. An old woman walked back and forth along the covered porch next door, calling "chi-chi-chi-chiiiie" to urge the ducklings to safety from the coming storm. As the heavens burst open, the earth separated itself into layers—a thin sheet of rising dust from the pounding of the rain on parched ground, then the mist ascending slowly in thin tendrils, to be beaten down by the approaching downpour that swept across the paddy like a great, gray curtain.

Its steady drumbeat drowned out the thump of passing engines in the canal and the shrill laughter of children splashing through puddles. It ran down the brittle thatch, dropped into bamboo gutters, and cascaded with the sound of harps into the earthenware urns that squatted along one wall. It fell solidly into the pond, sending fish and struggling bugs together to the murky bottom.

The land turned to glutinous mud. Ragged cracks in the earth filled with water, softened and melted together, then disappeared under a gurgling layer of soupy runoff. The children stampeded through the door, stained to their armpits with diluted earth. I stood just inside the fringe of thatch and watched the water run in beaded threads from the roof to the ground and eyed the vague, gray land beyond. When I turned back inside, the insistent sounds of moving water settled over nearby conversations like a blanket, until it seemed I was sitting in silence for the first time since I'd arrived in this boisterous land.

Flower squatted by the back door, watching the rain fall with the same patient resignation I had seen on the faces of the old men crouched beside their fields of growing seedlings. I handed her some photos I had brought with me from America and sat down to help her through them. I had, with what I thought was considerable foresight, chosen only pictures that I knew would be of ready interest—a family Christmas shot and some close-ups of my favorite pastime, hang gliding.

The women gathered around. They surveyed my parents' living room, discussing every detail. What a lovely place, they breathed. No, far too grand to be a house, a temple perhaps. "And this"—someone pointed to the Christmas tree that stood off to one side—"so strange . . ." I tried to explain its shape and the blue-green needles that had no counterpart in the lush, big-leafed tropical Delta. They waved me away. They were captivated by the ornaments—the shiny red balls and airy straw stars—that hung from every branch. They must be the fruit of the tree, they decided after a prolonged argument. They were quite sure the balls would be sweet and soft inside, the stars brittle and bitter. They offered to give me a basketful of ripened guava if I would send them some Christmas fruit from America.

I tried the hang-gliding photos. This, at least, they could have no preconceptions about. I struggled to hold their attention while I leaped and gyrated through a long, tortured explanation: carrying this strange, triangular device up a steep mountain, hooking myself onto its underbelly, running like a headless chicken, launching and soaring like an eagle. They waited, listening and watching and nodding their heads wisely. "What," one asked at last, "is a mountain?"

The clouds drew back to uncover the piercing blue of newly washed skies. The saturated ground carried the scent of fresh, moist earth. The cacophony of crickets ebbed and flowed, like an orchestra tuning its instruments. Soon they launched into full symphony, louder than the rain had been, loud enough to drown out the sound of motorcycles puttering along the path outside, loud enough that I had to raise my voice to be heard across the tiny room. I again stood under the eaves and strained my ears, trying to hear beyond the crickets, to other emerging wildlife. There was nothing. No warbling birds, neither bullfrog nor scurrying rodent. Everything had been eaten in this overused land until the only sound left was the trill of uncooked insects.

The kindling for the cooking fire had been left out in the rain and was unusable until the sun found it and dried it out again. Dinner was a plate of gray, precooked plantains, dense and tasteless. Fung roused himself, and Chau put on a clean new shirt. Flower laughed behind one hand and whispered that he'd surely pass by the house of the young girl who had caught his eye earlier in the day. Fung informed me curtly that there were problems with the local police and I was not to leave the hut. Now that it was getting dark, they had returned my shoes and cameras but pocketed all three of our flashlights. Chau gave his hair a final swipe, and they marched off in good humor. Flower raised her thumb to her mouth behind their backs and made a drinking motion, then shrugged her shoulders to say with patient resignation, "This is what men do." Her husband had gone with them.

I gathered together a bar of soap and fresh clothes and wandered next door for a shower. Despite my firm resolution to live like those around me, I couldn't bring myself to drop my pants and crouch by the fishpond in full view of a score of admiring spectators. Like a thief in the night I waited until darkness, used the shower as an excuse and my clothes as a prop, and crept up the ramp to the knee-high box over the neighbor's fishpond. The fish gathered in joyful welcome.

I emerged from the shower well-scrubbed and clean and tried not to dwell on the muddy ditch that supplied the shower urn and had its source in the very same fishpond that serviced the toilet. I slipped past the neighbor's porch where a dozen young men were rounding off a day's work in the fields with the carcasses of several fish and a bleach bottle filled with homemade whiskey. One of them spotted me, and the old patriarch waved me over. He called for a chair and gently welcomed me into the rowdy circle, pouring me a cup of tea when the young men became too persistent with their whiskey bottle and waving them away like pesky flies when their glances lingered. He spoke not a word of English and seemed indifferent to my labored Vietnamese, content to pluck pieces of candied ginger from a nearby dish and present them to me on the end of a homemade toothpick. He was thin-chested and stringy, but his carriage was ramrod straight, and the look of calm confidence on his grizzled face commanded more respect than all the bulging biceps I had seen in crowded Western gyms.

A loud young man, the self-appointed spokesman of the rowdy crowd, plucked insistently on my sleeve. His village Vietnamese, liberally diluted with whiskey, was unintelligible. He shouted repetitiously into my ear in the hope that sheer volume would overcome my ignorance. I pulled out two pocket dictionaries and offered one to my host. He gave a tiny sideways jerk of his head, barely noticeable, that told me he had no use for the written word. I looked around the table, making eye contact with each man, hoping for some receptive glimmer. There was none.

I had seen this happen again and again in a country that boasted ninety-five percent literacy, among the highest in the world. Even those who could sound out a few syllables had never seen a dictionary, and leafed through it like a paperback novel.

Their conflict with the written word ran deeper than poor schooling or lack of books, libraries, newspapers, and even comics outside of the larger cities. Written Vietnamese, in its current form, was barely two hundred years old. It was created by a French Jesuit missionary, Alexander de Rhodes, who romanized the ancient Chinese script in order to make the Bible more accessible to an almost illiterate population. The various tones were depicted through hats and accents, squiggles and dots above and below the vowels. His scheme was wildly successful, and his new text became standard usage after World War I.

But no language matures in two short centuries, and the dialectical differences between north and south compounded the difficulties of hammering down the spelling and pronunciation of a fluid and developing tongue. The most common signboard word in Vietnam was "to fix"—fix bicycles, Bic pens, disposable lighters, shoes, motorcycles, flat tires, furniture, watches. The word had nearly a dozen written incarnations: *sua, chua, rua, xua,* and so on. To find such a word in the dictionary was an impossible task. And, I had heard, each province was aggressively proud of its pronunciation, refusing to accept a national spelling that did not adhere to its own local dialect.

Despite the hurdles, even the most remote Vietnamese were eager to learn and endlessly curious. I rarely sat in a group for more than a few minutes before a pencil and paper appeared in someone's hands and they implored me to impart the English half of the Vietnamese greeting catechism. This consisted of eight questions following the discretionary introduction "Hello": "Where are you from?" "How old are you?" "Are you a tourist?" "Married?" "Why not married?" "You have children?" "How long you stay already in Vietnam?" "How much you earn in America?" Once this information had been extracted, you were an acquaintance and were invited to sit in companionable silence while they passed the particulars on to new arrivals and the nearby hearing-impaired elderly.

Or the whiskey-impaired. My companions were getting rowdier and apparently stuck on the question of my earning power, which I had avoided answering. I gathered my shampoo and soggy clothes, accepted a final piece of sugary ginger from the twinkly-eyed old man, and disappeared.

8

The final Confrontation

I was back on the paddy dikes again, carefully placing my bare feet to keep from toppling into the thick black ooze. I looked up to see my patriarch in a splattered shirt and rolled-up pajama pants, his skinny legs coated in stockings of mud. He seemed to be everywhere at once, and always working. If this old man had acquired a measure of wealth, it was by dint of sweat and daily discipline, and not by a simple policy change on the part of the government, as my guides would have me believe.

He came over and sat beside me on the dike, pulling out a plastic bag of homegrown tobacco and rolling himself a thin cigarette. A paddleboat arrived on cue with several baskets of pre-germinated seed stock, protected by moistened rice sacks and looking exactly like a million tiny sperm. We watched the young men shoulder the baskets and step carefully down into the knee-deep mud. Each gathered a handful of rice and flung it with a flick of his wrist in a wide arc across the mud. With every other step the seed arced across the sky to fall like gentle rain onto the soft, accepting earth. One. Two. Flick. The rice would be left to grow until it was several inches high and then the women's work began—pulling out each seedling and replanting it in endless, orderly rows to make the maximum use of every inch of available paddy. It was a painful lesson in superabundant labor and insufficient land.

The patriarch carefully unrolled the butt of his cigarette, emptied the shreds of tobacco back into his plastic bag, and returned to his work.

I had left Fung and Chau alone for the morning, thinking they might be more malleable after a good night's sleep. I returned just as they were rousing themselves for a midday brunch.

I had chased this conversation around in my head for days. By now I detested everything about my guides, from their city shoes to their droopy-lidded lies. They no longer made any effort to hide their disdain for me, nor their intention of acquiring maximum amounts of my money with minimum effort. There was nothing I wanted more than to quietly pack my bags and disappear, and spend the next few blissful days riding the Mekong while relishing the image of their panic when they awoke to find their meal ticket gone.

But Tam's words came back to haunt me. The Youth League had power, both in the provinces and with the central government. One word from them and my visa would be revoked, my dream to hike the Central Highlands abruptly ended. On the other hand, what did I have to lose? If there was nothing more to Vietnam than a set of flashing, painted nails and a hundred iterations of the word "no," then I'd best redesign my dream to trek the steaming jungle lowlands of Papua New Guinea or the frozen tundra of the trans-Siberian railway.

So be it. I resolved to tackle Fung and Chau head-on, no matter what the consequences.

I found them lounged around the hut's only table, waiting for Flower to serve them lunch. I gathered my courage and the bits and pieces of my carefully rehearsed Vietnamese.

"When we leave this village," I told them firmly, "I want to go out in a fishing boat on the coast for a few days—and nights."

Chau rolled his eyes and looked longingly at his hammock. Fung lit a cigarette and lodged it under his gold tooth. They huddled briefly together, then retaliated with an arsenal of excuses. "The boats," Fung said, "they go out for two weeks at a time." The crews disliked strangers, particularly foreigners and most particularly women. It wouldn't be possible to get permission. Customs. Storms. Seasickness. "I don't get seasick," I said. Fung looked at Chau, who looked at me. "We do," they said in unison. I invited them to stay on shore. They argued for a few more minutes, then gave up and agreed. The following morning we would take the boat back to our bikes, then pedal down to the shore and arrange for a boat out to sea. I felt foolish. Why hadn't I stood up to them long ago? They accepted my surprised thanks with dismissive nods and disappeared to check on the midday meal.

Lunch turned out to be oily green beans and snails in their shiny black shells. I ate two helpings of the vegetables and then pushed my bowl away with what I hoped was a satisfied smile. Fung watched me over the edge of his bowl, then deliberately picked up a snail with his chopsticks and dropped it into my bowl. I protested silently with my hands. Fung stirred it around with his chopsticks, his eyes brittle and hard. I had thus far eaten every bit of food that found its way into my bowl, received countless corrections of my eating habits, and gone without meals when my guides had already satisfied their appetites with beer. But this was different—I knew what the snails lived on, where they flourished, and what parasites dwelled inside their guts. I shook my head. Fung picked up my chopsticks and pushed them into my hand. I put them down, feeling like a rebellious two-year-old refusing to eat mashed peas. Two adults drawing battle lines over a plate of food. My mother would have been appalled.

Both Fung and Chau rose at dusk to wash themselves and disappear without a word down the road. When it came time for dinner, Flower faced me with tearful defiance and insisted there was no food in the house because we had eaten it all and offered no payment to buy more. My face burned with shame, for I had been told that my hosts were being paid a princely sum, enough to feed us all and leave plenty to ease their lives for many days after our departure. I didn't have the words to explain this in the face of her distress, so I rummaged through my pack and brought out the sum of money that she should have received. But the tiny village stall had long since closed, so the cash had little use until morning. Instead, we wandered across the road to pick worm-ridden guava fruit off an abandoned tree. We bought several bottles of creamy, sweetened soy milk from the nearby whiskey stand and sat on the edge of the canal to drink and eat and have boat races with the empty rinds in the receding tide.

I sat with my bags packed, waiting for Chau and the boat that would take us back to our bicycles. He was making a final visit to the "police station," well armed with a bottle of whiskey and carefully oiled hair. I wondered if the girl would be coming back with us.

By ten o'clock even the grizzled old boatman was getting impatient, and I was frantic to film life on the river before the golden light turned to midday glare. I prodded Fung until he decided that Chau could follow when his important business was concluded. We clambered on board, took the new growth off several nearby bushes with our thrashing propeller, and were off.

The children were out in full force, swimming alongside their gill nets like shiny brown tadpoles or crouched like tree stumps on the water's edge, intently watching a bit of line with a tiny hook at its end. Little girls peeped over the prows of three-plank boats while their mothers paddled, tall and stately, in the stern. The boys waded the shallows beside their fathers, throwing miniature nets and proudly reeling them in.

They were all skin and stringy muscle, these kids. They catapulted into the water like sinewy cannonballs and emerged to climb geckolike up the banks and hurl themselves back into the air. Not a single boy was fat, and the girls, far from mincing around in frilly frocks, joined in the muddy games with enthusiasm.

They were certainly wanting in many of the staples of Western childhood—they had neither jelly beans nor ice cream, and television had yet to become a part of their vocabulary—but for this they were eternally barefoot and never lacking for playmates, could make as much noise as they pleased, and when they were dirty, drop their clothes in the river and leave them to dry on a rock in the sun.

Moreover, they had a connection to their parents that Westerners had lost deep in the coal mines of the Industrial Revolution. Latchkey children were unknown here. Parents and relatives were always within reach. The bond ran deeper than mere availability. A father's occupation was accessible to his child in a way a Western desk job simply couldn't be. The rural children were first carried, then supervised, and finally allowed to take part in the activities that brought food into the house and filled the family's needs. For their contribution the children earned respect and trust. Four-year-olds were given matches to start the cooking fire. A half-ton water buffalo was left in the care of a child barely three feet tall. No family possession was off-limits to them, and they responded with maturity beyond their years.

Their social position was reflected in their childhood games. Where I used to make mud patties and chase fireflies, these children sieved the canals for fish. When they caught one, no matter how small, they rushed it home to watch it added to the midday meal. They carved miniature boats, alike in every way to the larger models their fathers built.

The girls could plant rice almost from the moment they began to walk and were carrying infant siblings on their backs by their fourth year. What need had they of plastic fire trucks and Barbie dolls? They were kings and queens of all they surveyed—the canals and paddies, the bridges, trees, and shrubs; there wasn't a house they couldn't run through with impunity. They made kites out of bits of paper and flexible twigs and flew them with the total concentration of fighter pilots. They crafted flutes from bamboo twigs and ocarinas from clay and marched down the paths like soldiers off to war.

I thought of my mother's bedtime tales of Africa. Her stories were all around me, come to life at last.

(℮   (℮   (℮

We arrived at the thundering highway and disembarked to wait for Chau at a roadside eatery. Fung tracked down a hammock with bloodhound accuracy and ordered an iced coffee from its comfortable folds. Chau showed up several hours later, reeking of whiskey and wearing the dejected look of unsuccessful love. He had just enough energy to call for lunch, string up a hammock, and topple into it. Fung looked at his watch and spread his hands helplessly. It was six hours of hard riding back up the road to our seaside village, and there was only five hours of daylight left.

"Tomorrow," he said.

"I'm going," I said, "by bus if necessary."

"No bus," they informed me happily.

I got on my bike. Their faces fell. Fung slapped his forehead and muttered that he'd be an old man by the time we got back to Saigon. Chau closed his eyes and blew smoke out of flared nostrils. They talked briefly, came to an agreement between themselves, turned to me and said, "No."

I rode away.

It took them an hour to catch up. I saw them a mile back

along the flat plain, Fung's shirttails flapping in the breeze, both of them pumping hard. I'd had a lovely ride, my body relaxing into the steady rhythm of the rotating pedals, savoring the freedom of the road. They arrived, puffing and furious and thin-lipped, accusing me of riding fast to keep them behind. They were right. They forced me off the highway at the first roadside eatery and ordered plate after plate of food and drink in retaliation. I had my first good meal in days and saved the leftovers in plastic bags against future guava nights.

We had barely gotten back on our bikes when it began to pour. The road turned iridescent with oily puddles, and Fung waved us under a nearby eaves to wait. We were soon joined by an unusually hefty, dour-looking man with a horseshoe of hair around his graying head. His face broke into a smile when he heard where I was from, and he welcomed me back from a war I never fought. His name was Vu Dat. He was forty-six and the father of six sturdy sons. The sons had followed each other into soldierhood and were now scattered throughout the Mekong in run-down wooden barracks, drilling for a war he hoped they would never see. They must have been in their twenties, too young for the war against Cambodia and too distant to have fired a shot when the Chinese came tumbling over the border north of Hanoi in 1985. They were the first generation of children who had had time to drill before they died, and he was the first generation of fathers who could speak of them without sorrow in his eyes.

But without war there were few promotions, paltry salaries, and no perks. Their father was clearly well off in his dapper plastic rain suit and shiny motorbike, but even his burgeoning construction business couldn't support six new families and a score of offspring. By mutual consent none of the young men had yet married, agreeing instead to save themselves for whatever wealthy allegiances their father could arrange. He invited me to visit them.

I pointed dismally to my guides. Vu Dat snorted with contempt at their long nails and slicked-back hair, clapped my free hand firmly onto his shoulder, revved his engine, and we were off.

I caught a brief glimpse of the astonished Chau and furious Fung, and then all my attention was needed to control my bicycle, one-handed, through the road's potholes and oil slicks at motorbike speed. I didn't dare look back. I would certainly pay for this, but by God it was fun.

My conscience eventually got the better of me and I reluctantly let go. Vu Dat waved a cheery good-bye and sped off in search of other marital material for his gaggle of ambitious progeny.

We were once again in the suburbs, and this time I immediately recognized the run-down huts on the outskirts of My Tho. Twilight was falling, and the road would only take us deeper into the congested heart of the city. Fung had lied. There was no village. I stopped and straddled my bike in the middle of the street, filthy with oil and splattered dirt. The traffic rumbled by, and my anger slowly boiled over. I imagined eviscerating Fung with his own fingernails. I dreamed of Chau drowning in a huge vat of hair tonic. I pondered the conductivity of dangling gold teeth. My visa be damned, and the whole stinking Youth League and Communist Party power structure be damned, I had had it with my greedy guides and their schoolboy tricks. The guided tour was over.

Now that I had faced the inevitable, my rage evaporated. When Fung and Chau finally arrived, I let them lead me to a converted sugar mill at the end of a dark, dirt alley. It was the home of one of Chau's friends, a young woman by the name of Lang Ly.

She was twenty-two and whiling away her days in the cavernous old mill, waiting for her father to import her to America. Every evening and morning, after lighting incense sticks on the altars of her Buddhist ancestors, she tuned her shortwave to the Voice of America and scribbled their lectures into cheap notepads, to study until the next scheduled broadcast. After eight years of religious discipline, she spoke almost flawless English, hardening her consonants and carefully conjugating her verbs. In her spare time she studied the photos her father sent her of her sophisticated siblings, standing in front of the mirror experimenting with an eyebrow plucker and shades of rouge. She had two housemates: a younger cousin who did the cleaning, cooking, and laundry, and a pregnant mongrel with an attentive face and teats covered with mosquito bites.

She made us welcome and ordered up dinner, and spent the meal torn between the unexpected attentions of the two urbane young city dwellers and the opportunity to practice her English. Afterward I slipped under my mosquito net, and Fung and Chau made haste to hit the streets. Once they were gone Lang Ly appeared in her pajamas, clutching a huge white teddy bear. She crept onto the mat, her face fresh and clean without its layer of makeup, and told me of her childhood.

Her father had worked as a menial at the airport during the war, and in consequence spent five years in a re-education camp after the fall of South Vietnam. His wife and child were sent into the barren hinterlands, to farm rice and vegetables during the rainy season and starve in the dry. For four years they sold their jewelry, bit by bit, and when it was gone her grandparents paid off the police to secure them permission to live in My Tho. Armed with a prewar business education, Lang Ly's mother found a job as secretary in a sugar plant and eventually started her own factory.

In the meantime, Ly's father had been released from the camps and reunited with his family. His wartime collaboration was a brand that would forever mar his prospects under the new regime. He tried again and again to secure a job despite the generous income from his wife's mill. At last, convinced that there was no future for him in Communist Vietnam, he determined to escape his past, brave the high seas, and make a new beginning in a land where others before him had found unfettered wealth and happiness.

His wife refused, utterly. When he persisted she fought back with bloody visions of cutthroat pirates, rape, and murder, of bloated blue corpses and starving, sticklike children. Lang Ly, just fifteen, lay on her mat and covered her head with a pillow to shut out the images that had taken shape in her imagination, to haunt her dreams and unguarded thoughts.

The arguments continued, spoken in low, harsh whispers that wouldn't carry beyond the woven bamboo walls to the neighbors and, through them, the police. The one had a dream, the other a hard-won life and a child to raise.

And because there could be no compromise, they separated.

One morning Lang Ly awoke with the sun streaming onto her pillow, where a note from her father lay beside a blood-red hibiscus bloom.

In utmost secrecy he had gathered a thousand dollars and sought out those who took a pot of gold in return for the dream at the end of the rainbow. Even as she read, he was on his way to the Delta, to slip like a wraith through the spearlike mangroves, find a candlelit paddleboat, and make his way to the waiting ship with dozens of other tiny craft, their lights like fireflies converging on a sacred banyan tree.

But the note spoke of none of these things. It told her only that he loved her and that she must think of him as dead and try not to grieve. He admonished her to take care of her mother and be a dutiful daughter, always.

Two years went by without a word. Lang Ly placed her father's photo beside the tangerines and teacups on the ancestral altar and lit incense for his departed soul. Then one day a letter came. He was in a crowded refugee camp in the Philippines, waiting to be processed for transshipment to America. He wrote over and over how much he loved her and missed her and wanted her by his side. He made no mention of his wife, her mother.

Lang Ly kept the letter secret from her family for an entire year, not daring to share the news of her father's survival and thus be forced to share the letter itself. How could she? It said not a word about her mother, not even a polite inquiry after her health.

In time, her father reached his promised land. The ambition that drove him from his home and family held him in good stead, and he soon built two furniture factories and employed a dozen men.

Lang Ly paused and pulled out a plastic photo album. It was filled with a hundred snapshots of her father, standing rigid and unsmiling in front of several dozen monuments. He had a horizontal face with narrow eyes and thin lips squished between a pointy chin and receding hairline. His expression was as stiff and unapproachable as the statues he had chosen to pose beside.

"Why," I asked, "didn't he sponsor you to go to America long ago?"

Lang Ly blushed and faltered for a moment, then flipped over the album to several photos tucked into the last page. "My father had nine children by another wife," she explained, and pointed at an older woman with a bitter face, surrounded by a crowd of polished young men and women staring smugly into the camera. "He left them all to come live with my mother. When he went to America he could only sponsor one wife, and she was his first."

Divorce was illegal in Vietnam and overt polygamy almost unheard of. Lang Ly must have had a rough time growing up. She nodded. "I couldn't cry at home, so I went to school and cried with my girlfriends and teachers," she told me. She gradually withdrew from her schoolmates because their parents disdained her as the secondary offspring of a man with two wives.

University was unavailable to a daughter of the South Vietnamese Army. All of Lang Ly's hopes centered on

America. Her aunt had migrated to California nearly a decade ago and soon afterward sponsored her mother. Lang Ly was meant to go with her as a dependent, but a few weeks before the tickets arrived she turned twenty-one and so had to begin the process all over again. In the meantime, her father sent her one hundred dollars a month to live on, which she meted out to her cousin for household expenses and squirreled away for minor luxuries. She had bought a video player and expensive electric organ, but her toilet had no toilet paper and her mosquito net was old and torn. She never rode her moped without first donning purple, elbow-length gloves and a snappy hat festooned with ribbons. She had lived in My Tho all of her adult life but refused to visit its attractions without a proper chaperone and so rarely ventured beyond the local baker and the marketplace. She had her heart set on going to Berkeley. I thought of rollerblades, hashish, and hip music and wondered if her purple gloves would protect her.

When it became clear that Fung and Chau were out for the night, Lang Ly bolted the door and popped in a English teaching video called "A Weekend Away." She sat transfixed, watching the British countryside glide by while I stole her teddy bear and drifted off to sleep to the sound of British voices saying, "Look there, my dear, it's Westminster Abbey!"

The next morning, fearful of my increasingly irritated pacing as I waited for my missing guides, Lang Ly offered a pacifying diversion. Due to her mother's association with the sugar industry, she announced, she was willing to accompany me to a nearby mill, unchaperoned. She pulled out her moped, gloves, and festive hat, and we were on our way.

The mill was in the center of a vast yard of kindling needed for the eternal fires that smoldered under the vats of agitating molasses. A river meandered behind the cords of wood, and a ship lay tethered to its bank, lazily regurgitating tarry black sludge.

The raw molasses had come all the way from Can Tho province at the southernmost tip of Vietnam. Rather than waste the space between barrels, the entire hold had been gutted and molasses dumped into the bilge. It was now being sucked out by a vacuum cleaner, looking like the world's ugliest bilge water. Bits of debris floated among the dirty brown bubbles, and the pump made convulsive sucking sounds. When the hose ate a brick and ceased to function, a young boy was sent down with a plastic pitcher and a bucket. He dipped the molasses to the last half inch and then used a dirty rag to sponge up the rest. Two crusty men waited on the deck for the last sticky tinful, then shouldered the immense vat hung on a bamboo pole and trotted down the narrow walkway with extraordinary nonchalance. I followed warily, my sneakers sticking to their footprints.

The molasses made its way through the back door, where it was poured into one of several kiddie-pool vats built atop a glowing fire and continually agitated by several rotating paddles. It would churn for seven days, gradually changing hues from black to mahogany to beige, until it was lumpy with sugar granules and the paddles slowed to a standstill.

The breadlike mass was then culled out of the vat by shirtless young men, their skin the color of half-cooked molasses and glistening with a sugar glaze. From there it went into a centrifuge, where it was washed until it turned the color of bleached sand. This time it crumbled when they tossed it onto a knee-high pile on the floor, burying dozens of greedy bees and flies. I had the tremendous urge to kneel and carve a sand castle out of that glistening white mountain. It looked so dense and shapeable, just asking for tunnels and turrets and tiny sculpted stairways.

Lang Ly was moved to action as well. She picked up a scoop and began shoveling it into the ten-kilo paper sacks that lay scattered on the floor.

"This is what I used to do," she said as she heaved the sack onto a scale, then expertly added another quarter pound, "after school each day until dark. To help my mother out." She whipped several strands of packing string around the bag and tied it off, enthusiasm obliterating all trace of her earlier sophistication. I suddenly liked her very much.

She was an enigma—a young woman who refused to see her own neighborhood without a chaperone but aspired to Berkeley; who had spent four years content to watch videos and experiment with makeup but had at the same time disciplined herself to learn a foreign language with little more than a radio and a pencil stub. She was twenty-two and had never been on a date. That seemed unusual, even by Tam's rigid standards.

"I don't want to marry a Vietnamese man," she told me bluntly. She wanted to go to school, to have a career and be able to support herself. She loved children and had taught them briefly in grammar school but wasn't sure they fit into her scheme for the future. "Being a wife here is like being a maid and cook," she said with a bitter laugh. It was a comment I had heard from nearly every ambitious unmarried woman since I'd arrived in Vietnam. The men of Fung and Chau's generation were in for a shock.

And yet she refused to change the light bulb that hung on a naked wire over the sleeping mats and deferred to my guides on almost every subject, from how to cook rice to the proper pronunciation of *Coca Cola*. An enigma.

We arrived home to the angry tapping of Fung's nails on the cracked linoleum table. "Where were you?" he snapped.

Bored, I told him. My Tho was supposed to be nothing more than a brief stopover.

He dismissed my comment with a flick of his wrist. They were waiting, he informed me, for directions to a friend's house in the countryside where we could stay. They had arranged to meet the fellow at three o'clock and he had graciously agreed to lead us there on his motorbike.

"How far to this rural village?" I inquired suspiciously.

"One kilometer," Chau replied. That placed it squarely in My Tho's suburbs, and dozens of miles from the sea. I wanted to range further afield. We had permission to go anywhere.

"Impossible," Fung said, and sallied forth with his latest vocabulary. "We are in a military area. All foreign travel is severely restricted."

"Then we can bicycle until we are out of the military area so that we may be unrestricted."

"Impossible," he told me. Permission had to be authorized three days in advance by the provincial and local authorities.

"Well," I said, "get to it."

"Impossible," they said, and pointed smugly at the calendar. "It is Sunday. Police stations are closed."

Lunch was black. Chau chatted animatedly with Lang Ly while I picked at my rice. I had hoped to wait just one more day before aborting the trip, to shield the gentle Lang Ly from our final confrontation. Even that now seemed impossible, and I was faced with yet another long afternoon with nothing to do but watch the roof rot.

I couldn't do it. Once we had cleared the table, I bounced to my feet and was out the door before a meal-heavy Fung could register a squawk of protest.

Lang Ly caught up with me before I had turned three corners, having followed the meteor-tail of gossip that trailed every white-skinned foreigner through the streets. "Get on," she said gaily, and patted the seat of her bike. "Fung and Chau say you'll be leaving soon for the village."

She was fairly bubbling over with news. "Cousin Emma says Chau was asking many questions about me while we were gone," she shouted over her shoulder while we slalomed through midafternoon traffic on our way home.

I asked why, hoping that her association with a foreigner wouldn't lead to future interrogations, or worse. I'd heard stories.

"I don't know," she yelled, then grinned. "Maybe he likes me." She seemed delighted by the idea. "He's had such a difficult childhood, you know. Just like me."

"Really?" I said. I had no idea.

"He was the youngest in a family of twelve and his parents couldn't feed him, so they gave him to his grandmother, just like that." The old woman had apparently put him out on the street at the age of six to sell fried dough to the early morning market vendors. For years he wandered the streets barefoot, calling out *"Ban Meeei"* until his throat burned and his head ached from the terrible weight of the rattan basket. Lang Ly shook her head in disbelief at such cruelty. "And so when he turned twelve he had no choice but to run away and become a street orphan in Saigon." After eight years of cold and hungry nights, he had finally cajoled his way into evening school. The Communist Party quickly noticed his outstanding talent and hastened to recruit him. He regularly sent money to his ungrateful family and held no grudge against his tyrannous grandmother. "He even attended her funeral in his best suit with a pair of wreaths to lay on her grave." Lang Ly sighed and fell silent.

I wondered if this was the communist version of a romance novel and squashed the urge to mention the old man with a white chicken between his feet or the pretty young thing in the Mekong. We hurried home to see the silver-tongued Casanova again.

Chau was taking a disciplined nap beside his equally talented soul mate. I packed my bags and shook them awake. Fung told me, never shifting from his prone position, that we couldn't leave until noon the next day since their friend had failed to show up at the rendezvous. They were resting before pursuing him through his favorite haunts and brew dens. "And," he added casually, "we have no money." An itemized bill lay on the table for my convenience. It had already been paid from the hidden reserves they had looted from my backpack while I was out. Fung instructed me to wake them at sundown, then rolled over to go back to sleep.

"No," I said. No more fictitious villages and morning lie-ins. "We're going back to Saigon. Today."

Fung and Chau sat bolt-upright. They called Lang Ly over to translate. They got furious. They threatened me with breach of contract. I responded in kind. Excuses rained down upon my head, and accusations. I cycled too far, or not far enough. I ignored their explicit instructions. I talked to strangers, and spoke too much Vietnamese.

I sat, unperturbed. We both knew what the central issue was. They were scared of losing their tip.

"Why," Lang Ly finally asked in bewilderment, "do you want to go back to Saigon?"

"Why," I countered, "are we carrying hammocks and mosquito nets, flashlights and bug spray, if we never use them? And why pay for permission papers and bribes we don't need?"

Lang Ly seemed certain that Chau, at least, hadn't known about the bribe money, despite my itemized receipt written in his hand. Chau, by this time, was up and pacing, puffing irritated clouds of smoke, raising his eyebrows and rolling his eyes. Fung was practicing to be a government official, his long nails slicing the air, eyelids drooping, his head jerking sideways in an involuntary "no." He drew up a second bill, much larger than the first. I looked it over and began to cross things off. The price of Fung's camera, which had followed him into the canal as he staggered drunkenly back to our hut. Payments for meals to my village hosts. Mysterious gifts to obvious recipients.

"Lang Ly, did they pay you for food?" I asked.

She was clearly torn. "No," she finally said, and added quickly, "it doesn't matter."

"Yes it does." I counted out the equivalent and handed it to her. She wouldn't take it. I looked over to see Fung's eyes boring into us both, and put it away. I suddenly realized the position I was putting her in and why she had to side with them.

In the end we all took pity on Lang Ly, doing her best to soften harsh words and to moderate accusations, and simply agreed to go home. Chau walked by me, stiff-backed, and refused to share the dinner table. Fung pulled out his filthy shirts when he saw me scrubbing laundry and threw them in among the suds.

On the bus ride home they jumped down to buy themselves drinks and breakfast with the remaining money, leaving me to sit with the gear. I didn't mind. Despite all the heartache, the Mekong trip had been a remarkable success. I was convinced that the average citizen was friendly, warm, and receptive. My Vietnamese had progressed in leaps and bounds and I'd ridden all the kinks out of my lovable old clunker. I was ready to hit the Ho Chi Minh Trail—alone, if necessary.

9

Dear Mom,
Saigon, the second time around . . . My bike and I
have ironed out our differences, I've put in for
another visa extension, and I don't need a guide.
And my faithful hammock still works just fine.

The Ho Chi Minh Trail

Tam and I circulated through all the universities, posting "Guide wanted" notices that were torn down immediately by grim-faced administrators. We interviewed eager young applicants who evaporated like morning mist upon hearing that their leg muscles would be put to good use. I sat back wearily after yet another downy-cheeked young man turned to me and said, "You use moto-car, vroom vroom! Ha!"—then climbed onto his ratty school bike without another word to pedal away.

"They don't want to go so far from home," Tam explained charitably. The truth was far more depressing. Anyone with English skills had had good schooling, which meant family wealth, and wealthy kids didn't sleep in hammocks and carry backpacks.

"Tam, I want to go alone."

He argued. In the few weeks that I had known him, Tam had grown into more than just a friend. He had taken me into his family, become a protective older brother, looked after me, and developed a personal interest in my hopes and dreams. He wanted me in the protective custody of another trustworthy man. I was touched by his concern. I promised to look for another Westerner and secretly made plans to pedal north as soon as my next month's visa extension was processed.

℮   ℮   ℮

A new face had joined our small group at the guest house. I came home to find him sitting on the peeling plastic sofa, holding court. He wore a three-day beard liberally grouted with grime and a stained shirt, torn in several places. A filthy backpack nestled against his calves like an adoring stray. A half-dozen tourist-travelers sat in a semicircle around him, absorbing his stories in awed silence. I slid in among them.

He had come down from China, across the impossible border north of Hanoi, and journeyed high into the Tonkinese Alps to live among the tribespeople. He spoke fluent Hmong and Vietnamese, he told us, though the few words he sprinkled among his anecdotes were garbled and nonsensical.

He had hitchhiked, mostly in military vehicles or on trucks, following the border south through some of the most rugged mountains in Southeast Asia. At night the drivers invited him to share lodgings at the cheap flophouses and feted him with orgies of homemade whiskey and roast dog. I asked him about police and permission papers. He gave a great, snorting laugh. "The police won't go near the tribal areas," he said. "They're afraid of the minorities—think they're savages." My heart leaped.

The South had been less to his taste. He was now on his way overland into Cambodia and eventually to Laos, where he planned to spend six months living with a Hmong family in a remote village. Unwilling to pay the five-dollar taxi fare for the trip to the Cambodian border, he was looking for someone to take him by motorbike for free.

I approached him once the others had dispersed. He listened to my sales pitch about the Ho Chi Minh Trail. "Sounds interesting," he said noncommittally. "I'll be back in about three weeks—if you wanna wait." He had already picked out a travel companion, a helpful young Chinese man who carried a bulging notebook stuffed with hundreds of Vietnamese business cards, every unlettered inch covered in lacy Oriental script. The Chinese man was sitting cross-legged on the floor with three Hanoi-bound tourists, earnestly explaining without the use of the letter *r* how to get around the foreign prices and gouging conductors on the buses between Nha Trang and Danang.

"You must wait until one houa befo bus leave. Then find local Veennamese man and ask him buy ticket fo you. You jump on bus two minute befo go. When conducto ask fo ticket, you tell him you no pay foleign plices. You fight, it cost only twelve t'ousand dong, not eighteen." A difference of about sixty cents.

"But," he added with a sad shake of his head. "You take expless bus, they t'low you off. Must take local bus." A difference of about four and a half hours.

I was trying to decide if I could stand Saigon for another three weeks when a doughy young man reached over from his spot on the sofa and tugged at my video bag. "You taping?" he asked. I nodded, a little ashamed. Between my guides and the sweaty bike rides, my filming efforts had been feeble, at best.

"Let's see." I took out my camera and handed it to him. He turned it over, examining it critically. "You're not gonna broadcast with this, are you?" he demanded.

"Sure," I said stupidly. "Why not?"

"It's a piece-o'-shit camera. Home video use only. Let's see your tape. Sony. That's what I thought." He dropped the cartridge as though it had just burned him. "The dropout on this stuff's terrible. You should've taken Fuji. That's what I've got."

He systematically inspected my equipment, denigrating filters and wrinkling his nose at my battery packs and their connecting cables. "I," he finally said, "charge my camera with the engine of my motorbike." It sounded like a good idea.

He was a Canadian producer, filming a documentary about the ancient Mandarin Way. He had planned to buy a bike in Thailand and follow the route through Cambodia, up Vietnam's coastal highway, and into China. As luck would have it, recent tourist deaths in Cambodia had temporarily closed the overland border, and immigration officials had turned him away. He had been forced to sell his bike at a loss in Thailand and take a plane to Saigon. Now he was short on cash and seeking a companion to share a motorcycle for the journey north.

A cameraman! I took a second look at him. We could film for each other. I could pick up some pointers to augment my shaky skills. I momentarily ignored his shape, which resembled an overfed Syrian golden hamster, and invited him north with me. By bike.

He was not overwhelmed by my generosity. "Is it a good bike?" he asked suspiciously. "Not a piece of Vietnamese-Russian shit?"

I thought of my old Chinese clunker. Not Vietnamese, I said. And almost as good as my camera.

"Speaking of cameras," he said, "you got any desiccant? It rained on my bag. Camera's on the blink. Just needs to dry out."

My camera, I noted, was waterproof. And working.

"Yeah, right," he said, and scratched his belly.

I was relaxing in my closet-size room, with its freestanding toilet bowl in one corner and oversize calendars of naked Vietnamese women with impossible breasts, when I heard a knock on the door. I hoped it wasn't the hamster. I hadn't taken long to regret my impulsive offer to drag him, panting and sweating, into the Highlands.

It was a stranger, a tall man with sun-bleached hair, a thick brown mustache, and incongruously blue eyes in a tan face.

He fingered the doorknob. "I hear you have two motorbikes for sale," he said.

Bike had become motorbike, one had become two, and "seeking travel companion" had become "for sale" in the lightning-fast grapevine of the travel community. I set him straight. And, what the hell, invited him along.

There was clearly something about bicycles that repulsed these Indiana Jones-type travelers more than a goiter or a dose of gonorrhea. He helped himself to recover by tapping a cigarette out of a crumpled pack of Marlboros.

"I've got my eye on a big Honda 450 cc. Classic bike, old enough to've been around during the war. Real pretty." He paused and surveyed me through a swirl of cigarette smoke. "It could take two."

He planned to buy the bike in Saigon, spend a couple of months riding it to Hanoi, then sell it at a profit and fly to Laos. He was an Alaskan who had been coming to Asia every winter for eight years to escape the arctic cold. During the summers he worked as a carpenter, a builder, an expediter during the *Exxon Valdez* oil spill, and a general handyman. Mostly he liked to fish—especially for those king salmon that evidently grew larger than his arms were wide. "My friends always check the tide tables before bothering to call me," he said with pride.

He was forty-one, with a boyish smile that spread the hairs on his mustache and leathery skin that was gradually submitting to the relentless tropical sun and endless, gritty cigarettes. He wanted me to split the price of the pretty motorbike. I wanted him to buy a bicycle and quit smoking. He lit another cigarette.

I thought about his offer. It wouldn't hurt to scout the Highlands before committing to them heart and soul for the next six months. In truth I knew very little about the Ho Chi Minh Trail beyond a few secondhand tales of humorless police and impassable roads. I could spend a few weeks on the motorbike, then hop a local bus back to Saigon and do it for real.

We agreed to share the cost of fuel and repairs as far as the now-defunct demilitarized zone. I offered five dollars a day rental toward the bike and pulled out a topographical map to show him Highway 14, a thin line that snaked through the forbidding central mountains instead of following the more hospitable coast. Less than a year ago it had been off-limits to Americans. The infrequent travelers' tales were not encouraging. He agreed to try it.

After he left, I realized I didn't know his name.

ɵ   ɵ   ɵ

Tam was thrilled. He bustled around, humming like the father of the bride-to-be, pleased to be tying up a few loose ends before handing me off to another capable man.

Our first stop was the infamous Communist Youth League headquarters. Tam had visited the director after my return—to apologize for my behavior, I suspected, even though he agreed that my guides had not fulfilled their roles. In return the director had offered to get me a coveted three-month visa extension, which would eventually save me a visit to Bangkok in search of a whole new set of papers. By Tam's frequent references to my guides' tips, I knew he was uncomfortable with my refusal to pay them a voluntary bonus for their services. In his world of street survival, the money would be well spent to secure a relationship that might prove useful in the future, regardless of their behavior in the past. Images of Chau entertaining eight friends to a lavish dinner at my expense and Fung sleeping off an all-night spree while the sun crawled into the afternoon stiffened my spine. Justice was a luxury I was willing to pay for.

And pay I did. The director informed us politely that visa extensions were unavailable to Americans in the foreseeable future. In a few months I would be forced to make the costly journey overland to Phnom Penh or Bangkok to apply for a new visa when my allotted time ran out. Pride in Asia was more expensive than I had bargained for.

℮   ℮   ℮

Our next stop was the home of Gulik, the Speeding Bullet, the man who had sold me my overpriced bicycle. If I was going to tackle the forbidding Highlands in less than two weeks, it made sense to do it on something better than a forty-pound, one-speed school bike. I carefully instructed Tam to tell Gulik that he had cheated me, that we both knew it, and that I wanted him to take the bike back at its purchase price.

It took Tam twenty minutes of solemn conversation to translate my single, pointed sentence. Gulik listened carefully, sent me an appraising glance, and then scratched his chin.

"What did you tell him?" I asked.

"I said you had to leave the country immediately with visa problems and asked him if he would pity you and help you to sell the bike," Tam replied without blinking.

Gulik tugged on Tam's sleeve. "Fifteen dollars," he said in Vietnamese. Four weeks earlier it had been worth fifty-five.

I shrugged and gritted my teeth and watched Tam hand over the bike with many protestations of gratitude. The system clearly worked. It was up to me to become a part of it, or drown.

℮   ℮   ℮

A shiny chrome-and-black Honda motorbike sat outside the guest house. My mysterious stranger stood proudly beside it. His name, the proprietress had told me, was Jay. He showed off his newest purchase with the enthusiasm of a car salesman, unscrewing the gasoline cap to let me peer into the tank, nudging the soft vinyl seats, and eventually sliding on to assume the exaggerated hunch of a motocross driver.

"Wanna go for a ride?" he asked.

I had just the place in mind. Ten miles north stood a smoldering mountain of garbage, the dumping ground of Saigon's two million inhabitants. For weeks I had been pestering Tam

111

to take me there, to talk to the ragpickers and see their trade. He had been extremely reluctant, having heard that foreigners were forbidden and that a Danish camera crew trying to film there had been arrested.

"Let's go," I told Jay, and slid on behind him. "I'll navigate."

The football field of garbage crawled with roaches, rats, and ragpickers. They swarmed over the bulldozers that pushed the trash back and forth, ready to snatch anything of value that might surface among the rotting grapefruit rinds and wispy plastic bags. At least half the pickers were children, some as young as six years old, expertly sifting through the refuse with curved metal hooks and nimble fingers.

A small area near the road had been piled high with mounds of gathered garbage—eight vertical feet of black galoshes, six feet of women's blouses, a smaller heap of gray bones, black with flies.

The mountains of accumulated wealth were deceptive. Pickings were surprisingly slim. The garbage that made it to the final dumping grounds had already been sifted a dozen times by the Saigon pickers. Little of value escaped their eagle eyes. Even a discarded wok, dented and worn through in several places, would attract the attention of a steady stream of city homeless who, mounted on bicycles or carrying double baskets of rusty cans, spent their days plodding from one potential find to the next, racking aside dead rats and rotting cabbage in search of something to eat or sell. At five in the morning the street sweepers made their rounds—delicate young women with elbow-length gloves and white surgical masks, using homemade brooms that had been worn down to stubs. Once again the city pickers flitted by like silent wraiths, to stoop briefly over the mounded garbage and be gone. Eventually the piles were shoveled into a truck which labored slowly to the dump, leaking a trail of rubbish and clouds of bitter black exhaust. There the process began all over again.

But there was something odd about the ragpickers that scurried over the rotting field, competing with roaches and mangy dogs for society's scraps. They moved, not with the mind-numbing rhythm of farmers planting rice, but with quick, birdlike gestures, their eyes alert and their hands ready to snatch a valuable find from the refuse. The children laughed often and gave each other brief glimpses of their discoveries, like kids on the beach looking for colored sea glass.

It made sense, somehow. A farmer surveying his paddy knew just how much harvest he could hope for, even under the most benevolent conditions. In this field of filth, the possibilities were endless and a lotterylike mentality prevailed. The very next pass of the rake could uncover a gold ring, a bracelet, a working carburetor. Anyone, young or old, male or female, could strike it rich—if their luck prevailed.

Alongside the highway a group of ragpickers squatted among the trash, their rice sacks disgorging armfuls of junk to be sorted. A young boy sat under a wide-brimmed conical hat, his fingers slipping like snakes through the tangle of wires, bottle caps, washers, broken pens and cutlery, old bones, forks, and bits of copper. Everything had a market. An entire basin was reserved for toothbrushes, their bristles bent almost horizontal, their handles cracked and jagged. The boy held each new item just long enough to assign it a value and then tossed it into the appropriate pile. He tested pens across the back of his hand and slipped a crooked pair of sunglass frames over his nose before dropping them into a heap with a dozen similar sets.

An old man approached, offered me a Vietnamese cola, and waved me onto a salvaged chair with one missing leg propped up on bricks. He surveyed the field. "You don't see much of this in America, do you?" he asked in perfect English. I sank into the seat. He laughed at my surprise.

"I spent years in Minnesota, working as a mechanic," he explained, and inclined a languid hand toward the West, disturbing a host of flies. "You have better garbage, but terrible winters." He pretended to shiver and chuckled. In a curious reversal of the trend, he had chosen to return to his family in Saigon rather than import them to America. He now spent his time foraging for the parts to build himself a car. He pointed at a rusty hulk listing heavily against the edge of a tar-paper shack. "When she is done, then I'll become a cabdriver," he announced and looked at me with sudden hope. "You have nine-sixteenths socket wrench?" I shook my head. He nodded serenely and settled back into his chair, waiting for one of the scurrying forms to approach him with yet another piece of his dream machine, in what was probably the most environmentally sound car manufacturing facility in the world.

℮   ℮   ℮

Although he hadn't actually set foot on among the ragpickers, Jay had impressed me to no end by his willingness to accompany me to a garbage dump. Now that we had hammered out the details of our route up Highway 14, it seemed time to tackle a more delicate issue—my documentary. *Find someone to go with you; you'll need footage of yourself along the way or you'll have no story.* I needed Jay to film me from time to time—at those critical moments when I had to show that I was part of the scene.

"No problem," Jay said, looking pleased with the idea. "I've always wanted to make films. Let's see your camera." He fingered the buttons and pointed it at the table. The record light went on a couple of times. "Sure, I can handle this baby. I've used plenty of equipment like this." I hastened to point out that there was little chance that anything would ever come of the footage and offered to compensate him for his efforts by taking over the day-to-day details of our travels. He wasn't listening. The record light was on again, a swath of blue sky was being captured for posterity, and a broad grin lit up his face as he played with his new toy.

114

℮   ℮   ℮

Our bags were packed, a few minor luxuries sadly stored away as the limits of the bike's ability to carry two Americans and gear became apparent. All that was left was to secure a Honda rack and we'd be off.

Motorbike shops were as common as soup stands in a city where rush hour was a congested knot of two-wheeled traffic. The first shop owner circled the bike twice, beeped its horn, and sadly shook his head. Private citizens were forbidden to own a bike larger than 150 cc, he told us. Jay's 450 would need a custom rack, several sizes larger than the Russian 125s or German 100s that clogged the streets. He directed us to his brother in old Chinatown.

The second shop had no rack, nor did the third, fourth, or fifteenth. I no longer needed to apply my sagging mental resources to translate for Jay. I simply watched the mechanic's hand creep out, almost of its own accord, and answer on his behalf. If he held it palm to the ground and wiggled it, then the outlook was grim, no matter how long he told us to wait or who had the keys to the storage shack. But the potential information went well beyond a simple no. Did the callused fingers flutter like a butterfly's wings or roll gently like a wallowing buffalo? Did they hover below the shoulder or, heaven forbid, career about at ear level? One hand held at medium height, twitching like a heartbeat, meant Honda racks were unavailable in the immediate vicinity or perhaps anywhere in the city. Both hands held away from the body and jerking spasmodically were clearly pointing at Thailand and the United States.

By midafternoon even Jay was willing to adulterate his classic machine with a simple welded rack and had gone so far as to procure a couple of curved bars. The first shop owner turned them over mournfully and shook his head. They were the wrong shape. There was no place to weld them. He gripped one bar and tried, unsuccessfully, to bend the sturdy metal. They weren't nearly strong enough, he said. And his men were busy; it would take at least three days.

We made the rounds, again. By now even the unflappable Marlboro man was beginning to flap. At last we returned in defeat to the first shop. Five days, he told us. We argued.

One week later, we were ready to go.

Dear Mom,
The Ho Chi Minh Trail is by turns mud, craters, deep sand, unfriendly police, and nonexistent. It rains every day, the mosquitoes are the size of grapefruit, and the only thing we can count on is at least one motorbike breakdown before lunch.

Highway 14 and the Beast

The packs were on, strapped firmly in place by strips of inner tube. Jay wheeled the heavy bike through the alleyway to the street, crushed out his cigarette, and hit the starter button. Nothing happened.

He tried again. And again. The admiring crowd of Vietnamese started to snicker. Jay straddled the seat and threw his weight down on the kick starter. Nothing.

An hour later the locals had lost interest, Jay had lost his cool, and the bike had backfired twice. We wheeled it into a shop. They tinkered with it until late morning, kick-starting it several hundred times until it finally roared to life in a cloud of blue smoke. The shop owner held out one hand for payment while keeping a careful grip on the accelerator with the other, gunning the engine to make sure it didn't quit. We scrambled on board, shouted our thanks, and were off.

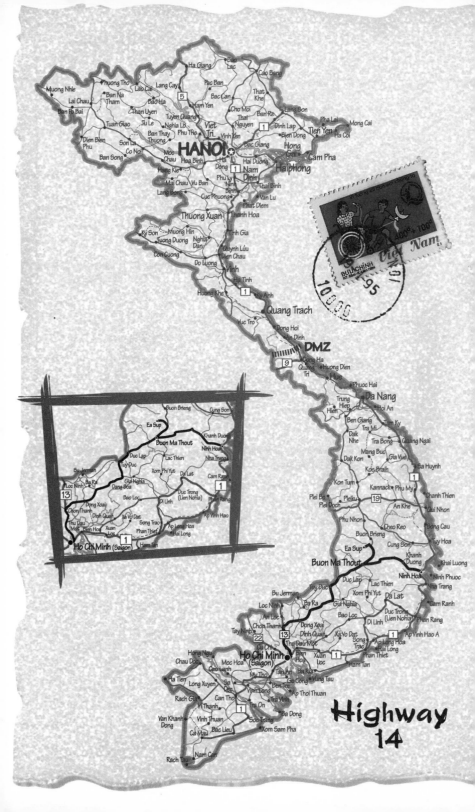

Highway 14

❧   ❧   ❧

Highway 14 was an unusual name for a road that quickly petered out into a one-lane dirt trail. The cement houses gradually turned to bamboo, then to palm leaf shacks, and finally disappeared altogether in a sea of thin brown trees and graying, sharp-edged grass. The vinyl seat that had once felt so soft developed sudden lumps and protrusions. I had long since stopped holding my breath at the variety of rattles that accompanied every impact with a pothole and begun cursing the twenty-two-year-old shocks.

Just as I was preparing to throw pride to the winds and beg for a break, the engine obliged by coughing twice and quitting. We coasted to a stop. Jay stared balefully at the dusty chrome.

"What's wrong?" I asked.

"How should I know?" he snapped, fiddling with the accelerator.

He had regaled me with stories of his motorbike treks through Thailand, month after month of rugged roads and unexplored trails. I had assumed some measure of troubleshooting skills from all that reckless adventure.

"I never broke down," he mumbled.

Eventually he jiggled the gas tank and was greeted with a hollow echo. Suddenly he was the Marlboro Man again, reaching over to switch on the reserve and ordering me to get on as he revved the engine and lowered his visor.

A hundred meters later the reserve ran out and we again coasted to a stop. We resolved our differences with a flip of a coin and Jay hiked off down the road in search of a liter of gasoline while I sat in the baking heat and watched over the beast.

He returned almost immediately, having hitched a ride on the back of a cheap Russian Minsk that purred with annoying reliability. Apparently every hut along the road kept a few liters of gasoline stored in the outhouse or under the roof of the pigpen, ready for quick sale to foolish strangers.

An hour later we hit a particularly deceptive pothole, and one of the mufflers dropped off. I walked back in silence to wrap it in a towel and rode the rest of the way into the next small town with the sleek, crowning glory of our classic machine cradled in my lap.

The Vietnamese seemed determined to make up for the bike's shortcomings. They hummed admiringly over its impressive size, wheeled it into a used-tire shack, lit an arc welder, and cheerfully stuck the muffler back on. They pointed out that we were running on half our horsepower, since the other exhaust was not passing the thick clouds of blue smoke they deemed necessary to a healthy engine. They handed us each a glass of sugarcane juice, shooed us out of the way, and set to work taking the bike apart.

Two days later the beast bucked to life with a reassuring roar, and we unhooked our hammocks from among the old tires hanging in the back of the shop. It was a joy to be back on the road. A late evening thunderstorm had beaten down the dust and insects, and the early morning air was crisp and clean. The rubber trees gleamed in the golden light, their coconut-shell bowls filled with fresh rainwater and drowning bugs. The entire countryside seemed newly scrubbed.

Except the road. Water and dirt had conspired to create truck-size mud wallows that swallowed up every dip and depression. The Honda, a hefty road bike meant for smooth tarmac and banked curves, shimmied mercilessly in the slippery muck. It took all of Jay's muscle to keep the beast upright while I walked ahead, plunging a frayed stick into the puddles and heaving rocks to bridge the gaps.

And then, halfway through a hair-raising slalom across a pond-size puddle, the gearshift worked itself loose and fell into the mud with a soft plop.

Jay skidded to a stop and stared wordlessly at the glutinous mud. He pulled out a squashed pack of cigarettes and dug one out. For the first time in my life I considered taking up smoking.

We didn't reach the next town, Bu Dang, until late afternoon, a total of nineteen miles in eight hours. The scattered settlement boasted a hundred feet of pavement, three open-air pubs, and a flophouse. We pulled up next to one of the pubs, sank gratefully onto seats that didn't move, bump, or grind, and ordered lemonades. Jay was exhausted, his normally tan face gray, his eyes and mouth offset by a darker layer of dirt and grime. I had spent hours enveloped in smoke as I pushed the bike from one bog to the next, and my arms and legs were lacquered with a mixture of oil and spattered mud.

The bike, despite looking like a buffalo after a long wallow, was apparently more attractive than the nearby kung-fu video, and a steady stream of young men trickled out of the pub to surround it, squeeze the clutch, and twist the accelerator. Crowds attract crowds, and soon even schoolgirls were worming their way forward to see what was going on. Jay's face lit in a glow of pride.

I finished my drink and wandered across the street to the flophouse. The proprietor, an ancient woman wearing one shoe and smoking a soggy cigarette, demanded our papers before divulging the availability of rooms. She snatched my passport out of my hand and stuffed it into her pocket, then peered over my shoulder and unaccountably offered it back. Her lips retracted into a smile, but the cigarette didn't move, lodged firmly in the hole where a front tooth should have been.

I followed the direction of her gaze. Jay stood next to the bike, surrounded by a hundred jostling spectators. Several stony-faced policemen were examining his papers and shaking their heads. I waded in and summoned up my meager Vietnamese, handing over a blizzard of smudged photocopies: our passports, international driver's licenses, motorbike registration, and visas. The head policeman shook the sheath of papers in frustration. What he needed, he insisted, was a local driver's license. We had tried to secure one in Saigon, but the list of prerequisites was daunting: a year's residency, work permit, embassy approval, vehicle ownership papers, and fluency in Vietnamese. Since Americans weren't allowed to own motor-bikes, we had given up the quest.

I whipped out Jay's international license and turned to the page of participating countries. By some miracle of oversight, Vietnam was among those listed. The policeman nodded uncertainly. We took advantage of his confusion, thanked him profusely, and hopped on the bike. Another small miracle: It started at once.

But we hadn't reckoned with the crowd. The spectators hemmed us in, eagerly eavesdropping on our predicament, shouting advice at us and the cops in equal measure. Impatient for a confrontation, they would not let us pass, pulling at our elbows and forming a solid wall of curiosity, bolstered from behind by those who were pressing forward to see. In the few minutes we lost trying to force our way clear, the military arrived. I heard a shrill whistle blast and the befuddled police-men sprang into action. We were under arrest.

Several men sat in the dirty police station, fingering our papers and smoking fiercely. I had been negotiating with them for the better part of two hours, responding politely to their demands for cigarettes and citizenship, local licenses and last names, and trying not to panic while the sun crawled across the afternoon sky. Buon Ma Thout, the nearest provincial capital, was seventy miles away. Navigating those muddy roads after dark would be a nightmare. Besides, I had more pressing concerns. My period had started.

"Pardon me, do you have a bathroom?" I asked politely. The man lifted his hand three inches off the desktop and wig-gled it, not bothering to glance in my direction.

"A bathroom," I repeated, annoyed.

This time he pointed at the front door, layered with curious locals and leading to nothing but the street. They wouldn't let me into the courtyard behind the station and turned deaf ears to my repeated pleas. I sat.

At last, the voice in the back room ceased shouting into a moldy phone and the superintendent appeared in the doorway to bark orders, confiscate a pack of Jay's cigarettes, and disappear. An underling assessed each of us a twenty-dollar fine for driving a motorbike without registration.

"How," I asked, "can we both have been driving when we only have one bike?"

He shrugged.

"But," I needled, "you have the registration in your hand." I was annoyed about the bathroom.

He scribbled a few words across a sheet of paper. I looked them up. "No pay," they said, "stay put."

We paid.

Along with the nonnegotiable fine came the order to return to Ho Chi Minh City. Buon Ma Thout and all points north, we were told, were off-limits.

Thoroughly cowed, we puttered out of town heading south and didn't stop until we were well beyond the long arm of the law. Ho Chi Minh City was a depressing 200 miles away, and the short tropical twilight was fading fast. There was only one thing less appetizing than sitting in that smoke-filled room with its peeling walls and patronizing police, and we were staring right at it.

The mud.

We turned around. It was well after dark when we crept up to the town limits, put down our visors, gunned the engine, and raced through the market square, heading north.

Nothing happened. No sirens, no barricades, just a drowsy village with one sleepy soup shop and a couple of mangy dogs on the street. I felt silly.

Then the tarmac ended with a six-inch drop onto uneven dirt. We were back on our old nemesis, Highway 14.

Two miles later the front wheel hit its first fist-size rock and the headlight blinked out. The road faded into inky blackness.

"This is as good a place as any," Jay said. We wheeled the bike into the undergrowth and covered its few remaining reflective surfaces with greenery. I wandered among the trees,

.ce to string my hammock, until I heard Jay's
ـer. "You know what Buon Ma Thout was famous
 ه pattle. Americans dropped lots of bombs. So did the
ـmies. Don't step on any mines."

၆   ၆   ၆

We approached the border of Cambodia, and the weather
turned to match my mood—gray, dark, and rainy, the wind
blasting across the sandy road to scour our faces raw. Even the
countryside was desolate, bereft of bird and beast and home to
little more than the military bases and installations that dotted
the landscape with increasing regularity.

We had become more cautious of the police as time went
on. They were a well-oiled mafia that made a business of
shaking down travelers. The sight of two foreigners on an
overdeveloped bike invariably set the money machine in
motion. Jay had become a master of skirting roadblocks on
the lee side of unwitting trucks, and we were both prepared
to plunge the beast into the undergrowth and lie low if a
passing uniform took any interest in our affairs. Despite our
precautions we were occasionally stopped, and I kept a five-
dollar bill tucked into my passport to make everyone happy. I
felt foolish for our behavior that first day—allowing ourselves
to be hauled into the police station and intimidated into a
double fine. We had learned since then. Always bribe the first
man who asks for your papers; the more officials involved,
the higher the eventual price tag. Never hand over original
papers you aren't prepared to buy back. Accept the negotiations for what they are; you are purchasing your freedom and
your possessions. How much you pay is a function of how
long you are willing to sit, how desperate you look, and
whether you can make them laugh. That first time we had
failed on all three criteria and had gotten off easy with
twenty-dollar fines.

But I was still annoyed about the bathroom.

(e   (e   (e

Buon Ma Thout, the forbidden city, was communism at its worst: squat gray buildings that hadn't seen a new coat of paint in decades and bits of war paraphernalia strewn about to remind its inhabitants of their glorious past. The weather didn't improve the city's appeal. Blustery rain had turned the roads to mush, and the ubiquitous mud had even managed to creep into the cauldrons of broth and flavor the soup with the taste of river residue.

Nursing a broken clutch cable and a fiendishly fickle gearshift, we limped past a full-size memorial tank perched on a pedestal in the central square. I consulted an older man who sat on a corner stool, using a syringe full of ink to resuscitate a handful of Bic pens. He told us of a mechanic, a man famous throughout the province for his skill with all things metal and who by good luck happened to live just around the corner. We pressed on.

The famous mechanic had set up shop on the sidewalk in front of a convenient parts stall. He was small and lanky, with sharply pointed elbows and a ferret face that became increasingly somber as I listed the beast's many ailments. He turned and ran supple fingers over the mud-clogged engine casing, oblivious to my continued litany of complaints and advice.

Someone else told us to come back early the next morning. Repairs had already begun.

Buon Ma Thout was Saigon's poor country cousin, the dark side of communism that foreigners weren't supposed to see. But even here capitalism was making a comeback. The sidewalks were crowded with novice entrepreneurs, and every nook and cranny was filled with oven-size stalls, open for business. A secondhand bicycle pump, set out on the edge of the street, advertised tire repair. A mirror tacked to a tree and a three-legged stool made a fine barber shop. Almost every corner sported a man with a magnifying monocle and a set of tiny screwdrivers, ready to fix watches and eyeglass frames. Three-wheel carts sold one-menu meals: thin onion pancakes, fresh pork omelets, or a queer but tasty concoction of coconut milk, sugar, and a gelatinous thickener made from the hooves of cows.

Vietnam had found a way to participate in twentieth-century luxuries despite its crippling poverty. Photocopying was done by the half page, and tea sold by the quarter cup; batteries were recharged or socks darned while you wait. Few Vietnamese could afford a camera but why bother? Roving photographers offered their services one picture at a time. Broken eggs went at half price. Even day-old bread, stale and chewy, could be found reincarnated in the marketplace, fried as an accompaniment to soup and rice. Both the microsale and resale had been developed to a fine art.

The beast was fixed, its gearshift solid as a rock and the headlight reliable at last. The little mechanic seemed immune to our praise, insisting on a few final adjustments long after he had been paid and standing anxiously on the sidewalk as Jay took it for a test run. The bill was astonishing—an entire day's labor cost less than the price of a new spark plug, and the replacement clutch cable, fully installed, came to about thirty-five cents. We promised to seek his services should anything else go wrong and drove off, fully expecting to be clear of Buon Ma Thout within the hour, never to return.

Dear Mom,
I've developed a great, lopsided bulge in my
Vietnamese vocabulary. I can say just about
anything having to do with motorcycle innards.
"Excuse me, do you have a Honda clutch cable?
No? How about a socket wrench?" What I haven't
learned are words like "wine" or "steak" or "ice" or
"fork."

Into a Village . . .

Arrests, breakdowns, mud, and rain. I had found the Ho Chi
Minh Trail, but events seemed to be conspiring to keep
me out of the villages along its route. The small-town flophouses we frequented were a far cry from what I was looking
for. My dream had always been to find a rural family who would
take me in and let me share their lives. So when a soup-stall
proprietor told me about a village forty miles north of Buon Ma
Thout, I was determined to find it, stay a few day or weeks, and
begin my real journey into the heart and soul of Vietnam.

The next morning found us speeding along the dirt road,
watching the cement houses turn to huts, then suddenly rise
above us on stilts. Old men in loincloths plodded along the
shoulder, trailing gaunt buffalo with clonking bells. The
women all wore homespun black skirts and shuffled under the
weight of smoke-stained rattan baskets filled with roots and
weeds. The faces became darker, rounder, and flatter. We
were getting close.

Then, abruptly, the road narrowed. We passed two soldiers on a tiny moped and redoubled our speed, hoping they wouldn't follow. We were so preoccupied with the rear-view mirrors that we blundered into a military installation before we registered the distinct white C painted on the rattan fence on one side of the road. A restricted area. Without a word we turned and fled, dashing down the first side trail that presented itself.

It was barely as wide as a set of train tracks and fraught with sand traps and rocky riverbed. We lurched and bumped over it for nearly an hour until my body felt like a giant accordion, my ribs slamming against my hips with every sickening drop. At last Jay rolled to a stop and lit a cigarette. The trail in front of us looked exactly like the one behind. Even I no longer believed my confident assertion that every road had a reason and an endpoint. I just couldn't bear the thought of the long drive back to the city for nothing.

Jay's head snapped around in a listening stance, and I too heard the distant buzz of an approaching motorbike. If the soldiers had bothered to follow us this far off the road, then we were in serious trouble. There was no place to hide the beast among the slender saplings. Jay puffed furiously on his cigarette, and I squatted down to wait.

A rusty moped puttered into view, heavily burdened with an older man, his wife and child, three chickens, and a sack of rice. He stopped in the friendly manner of country folk to ask us our business and offer a hand.

Yes, the path had an end, three or four kilometers further along. It led to a Hmong village, some two hundred people living in raised huts along the river's edge. We were quite welcome to follow him; he would be glad to show us the way.

We accepted with enthusiasm, and the ungainly beast was soon shuddering up the trail after its more fleet-footed cousin. My hoped-for village solidified into lovely raised longhouses with tidy, ten-step ladders and polished bamboo floors. Swayback pigs staggered along the footpath leading to the river, its gentle current eddying around rubber-tree roots in lazy brown whorls. Perfect.

The Hmong man motioned us to carry our packs inside against the gathering storm. His wife served us bitter green tea while I made careful inquiries for directions to the headman's hut, to pay our respects and ask permission to look around. The old man grinned toothlessly and pointed at the floor. He was the village elder and we were welcome to stay, he told us, but first he would take us to his friend who spoke both French and English and would make everything clear.

We obligingly climbed back onto our motorcycle and followed him along the grass-lined lane, where dusky girls in plastic sarongs beat sheaths of rice against the ground and pushed frantic chickens aside with their toes. A leathery old man stared down at me from his perch atop a hand-carved elephant saddle. Bent old women flashed blackened teeth and spat streams of blood-red saliva laced with betel.

We passed through a gate strung with the rusty remains of American razor wire and were suddenly staring at a cement building and a drooping Vietnamese flag. Communist headquarters. The gate had already swung shut behind us.

The man in charge was incongruously young, with none of the wrinkles and puckered scars of the village elder who deferred to him. We had disturbed his afternoon nap, and he stumbled around with puffy eyes, pushing aside the mosquito net strung over an army cot to make room for us to sit. We stared at each other in silence. He was clearly as unhappy to see us as we were him. The old man whispered into his ear, elaborating on the circumstances of our arrival in unintelligible dialect. The young official nodded unsmiling and turned back to us. "Your papers," he said, and held out a hand.

I took a chance. He spoke neither English nor French, there was no phone in the room, and the capital was several hours away. I played dumb.

For the next hour we stumbled through a series of deliberate misunderstandings. He inquired our nationality, and I mumbled a few phrases in French. He demanded our passports, and I handed him a pack of Jay's cigarettes. He obviously wanted to escort us back to the station in Buon Ma Thout but was afraid of the beast's horsepower compared to his little Minsk. I agreed wholeheartedly. "Good bike, vroom vroom!" At the prompting of the old man, he asked for my dictionary. I reluctantly pulled it out and he pounced on it, leafing back and forth in search of the word "documents" on a page I had long since torn out. By now he was chain-smoking and looking to the elder more and more frequently, his imperious demands long since replaced by what sounded like plaintive requests for advice.

I played my hand. "We could," I said carefully, "just leave."

His face lit up in a boyish smile, and their heads bobbed in unison. They whisked us out the door, offered us cigarettes, a tour of the village, anything short of an invitation to return. In record time we were deposited back on the beast, our belongings carefully strapped to the rack by a dozen helpful hands. They stood in a long line and waved us off.

We puttered along the trail, our relief gradually draining away. It was raining. The riverbed was no longer dry, and neither were we. We faced four hard hours of driving with less than an hour of daylight left. The narrow track in the dark would be close to impossible.

We were a hundred meters short of the main road when the bike slalomed into a rock and hammered the back brake into the "on" position. The gearshift had long ago worked its way loose and migrated into my pocket. We crested the road, and the headlight blinked off. I pulled out my flashlight, but its beam was too dim to pick out the potholes in time, and soon other odds and ends began to jar loose. We crawled past a herd of knobby-kneed cows with their young keeper strolling along behind them. Half the engine quit, and the merest hint of an incline forced me to get off and walk beside the laboring bike. I heard clonking wooden bells, and the cows overtook us. Jay started to smoke.

Then we ran out of gas.

Jay was looking quite evil, so I slid off and wandered over to an open shack where several young men were playing pool. They called to an old woman, who took one look at my empty plastic bottle, grabbed my wrist, and tore off down the road. We went from one boarded-up hut to the next, the woman hammering on the walls and loudly explaining my plight until a slender hand passed out a liter of gasoline in exchange for a crisp new ten-thousand-dong note. The old woman marched me briskly back to the bike, supervised Jay as he refilled the tank, accepted a small gratuity, then strode home to confront the next crisis, a drunken quarrel over the misuse of a pool cue.

A mile further the bike quit again. "Gas?" I asked hopefully. Jay played with the starter until the battery was totally drained, and so were we. The herd of cows passed us again.

I set off once more, this time in search of a repair shop amid the rural huts and fields. The patrons of a nearby open-air bar poured out to offer inebriated advice. They swarmed over the bike, tugging at spark plug caps, jiggling the gas tank, and ordering Jay to start the engine while they drunkenly listened to it tick over. They pondered the situation and gave him their solemn verdict.

"Bike dead. You drink."

He wasn't in the mood. They put their heads together, even more baffled, while I passed around sugar cookies and slapped curious hands away from the zippers on our packs.

Finally they patted the bike and muttered *"keo"* under their breaths, the word leaping from one to the next like illicit whiskey. I whipped out my dictionary and looked it up. "Drag." Great word. Two dollars, they said, to haul the beast into town. I agreed, a little too quickly. They conferred. Five dollars, they said, per mile. We bartered for twenty minutes, while the mosquitoes alternated with the intermittent rain and one of the more inebriated pool players stumbled around, looking for rope.

I slid on the back of a pint-size Honda and watched them harness it to the beast. They wrapped the rope several times around Jay's handlebars and tucked the end under his fingers. My driver had just eased his bike into gear when a military jeep swooped down on us and came to a stop in a spray of gravel. Several soldiers jumped out and strutted, stiff-legged, over to Jay. They barked at us for our papers and circled the beast suspiciously, as though the breakdown were just an elaborate ruse to keep us out after curfew. Then they kicked the back wheel and told us to park it in the pub. We were under arrest.

Our newfound friends saw their windfall evaporating before their eyes and quickly went to work. They demonstrated the bike's many illnesses, shook the rope to emphasize the ingenuity of their solution, then invited one and all for a drink. Once the soldiers were safely inside, my driver started his engine and we wobbled off, towing the decidedly unsteady Jay like a water-skier at the end of a long rope.

All went well until we reached the cross streets on the outskirts of the city. It was pitch black, stoplights hadn't yet been invented, and the intersecting traffic simply wove through itself like the warp and weft of a loom. Without battery power to run his lights, Jay was nearly invisible, and no one could see the thin rope that tied us together. By the time we arrived at the hotel, he was several shades paler and I was hoarse from shouting at shadowy mopeds that swerved away in the nick of time.

We took the first guest house we found, a dilapidated warren of boxlike rooms, frayed wiring, and expiring fans. The reception area doubled as a karaoke bar, with rows of chairs lined up in front of a black-and-white television. "Passports!" the receptionist shouted over the blaring speakers. I handed mine over and staggered up three flights of stairs to fall onto the lumpy mattress and instantly sink into an exhausted stupor.

In my dreams the military had followed us back from the Hmong village, sniffing our trail like tenacious bloodhounds. They turned the corner of the karaoke bar and plodded massively across the cracked tiles. The building shook with their steps. . . .

I awoke to an insistent hammering on my door. The receptionist shouldered his way in. "You must pay now. I vee-rry busy in the morning." He stuck out his hand. "American dollars." Once he was gone I padded down the hall to the communal showers. The toilet bowl had been torn out of its foundation and cockroaches welled up through the hole in a steady, scurrying stream. The stench of raw sewage clung to the walls and water.

I waited for the icy trickle to warm up. The long hours in the rain had left me in no mood for a cold shower. After several minutes I turned off the tap and padded downstairs, the roaches crunching under my feet.

"You are making a joke," the receptionist said when I asked him to turn on the boiler. I pointed out that the room had included a surcharge for hot water. After several minutes of argument, he acquiesced gracelessly and waved me away from his interrupted card game. I crawled back up the stairs.

This time there was no water at all, just the faint clicking sound of endless roaches and the slow drip of an empty faucet. I wiped the grime off my face with the back of one hand and plodded back downstairs, thinking evil thoughts.

The first-floor stairwell was barricaded, the iron grate held in place by a rusty chain and lock. Beyond it I could hear a burst of laughter from the card table and the karaoke bar shifting into full swing. I rattled the bars. The receptionist's face appeared briefly at the end of the hall, cracked its first smile, and was gone.

133

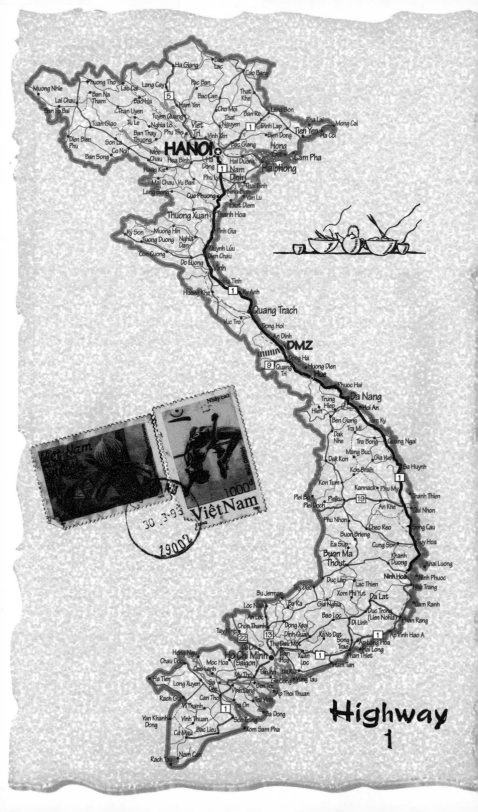

I 2

Dear Mom,
They all want to know what my relationship to Jay
is. I usually tell them he's my father. Jay is not
amused.

Sunshine

The trip was at a crossroads. On the map the thin strand of
Highway 14 continued directly north to Kontum and
beyond, deteriorating into a trail fit only for mountain bikes
and water buffalo. I stared at the wavy, dotted line and thought
of the tiny villages along the way, tantalizing but out of reach. I
thought of the beast that had thus far broken at least one of
everything and seemed in no danger of mending its ways; of
flashing white batons and dirty blue walls and unsavory guest
houses. It was time to face reality. The Ho Chi Minh Trail was
out of reach. All of my plans and preparations had turned into
an exercise in futility. I needed to get off Highway 14 if I
wanted to see more of Vietnam than police station walls and
rutted dirt roads.

But if not that, then what? I suddenly remembered the
grubby backpacker who had crossed over the border from
China and hitchhiked down to Saigon. What had he said?
*The police won't go near the tribal areas. They're afraid of the
minorities—think they're savages.* The minorities. They lived
in the Tonkinese Alps along the Chinese border. Hanoi was
the gateway to those mountains. From there I could jump off
and lose myself among the hundreds of tribal minority villages that lay scattered like rice seed in its fertile folds. I

wouldn't have to come out again until I had seen something of the real Vietnam.

"The Highlands aren't very user-friendly, are they?" I ventured to Jay. He didn't answer, his head buried in a map that looked suspiciously like Laos.

I checked my map again. A second, thicker line ran east from Buon Ma Thout to the coast. In my mind's eye I conjured up the blessed vision of the sun rising over the ocean. It had been raining without end for twelve solid days.

The next thing we knew we were barreling down the paved—paved!—road to the coast, scattering flocks of ducks and phlegmatic pigs sleeping on the warm tarmac. We swept past crumbling gun turrets peeping out at us from the undergrowth, and I felt a loosening in my chest. Even the beast, I felt sure, would no longer break down once it was out from under the city's evil influence.

The road was crowded, not with four-wheeled traffic but with the odds and ends of rural life. Dun-colored dogs stretched full length on the broken pavement, their ears carefully tuned to the difference between maneuverable Minsks and two-ton trucks. Long carpets of coffee, ground cassava, and unhusked rice lay drying in the sun, protected from trucks by chairs set at intervals along their edges. Old men sat with nodding heads, waving bamboo poles over the drying harvest to keep away marauding pigs and chickens. When the ancients roused themselves to laboriously sweep the crop into piles, we knew it was time to stop and put on ponchos against the coming rain.

And rain it did. It turned the packed dirt footpaths into silvery trails that slithered like snakes across gardens and fields. It saturated the colors until the new-sown rice and drooping leaves glowed a brilliant green. The cracked adobe walls smoothed out, and all livestock turned the color of mud.

We reached the intersection of coastal Highway 1 just in time to see the sun cut briefly through the clouds and disappear below the horizon. We were immediately surrounded by beggars and children hawking ID tags and inscribed lighters. A woman tried to wrap my fingers around a cheap imitation switchblade. Another hauled at my arm, shouting the charms of her private guest house into my ear. We were back on the tourist trail.

Although cratered with potholes and plagued with crumbling prewar bridges, Highway 1 was the only paved road that ran the length of the country. It had thus become the beaten track in an offbeat country for tourists eager to experience exotic Vietnam but unwilling to stray too far from English menus and traveler's checks. The standard two-week itinerary began in either Saigon or Hanoi and proceeded, via minibus or express train, through the familiar guidebook stomping grounds: Dalat, the cool, vacation mecca for wealthy Vietnamese and foreigners alike, with its freshly grown strawberries and swan boats on the lake; Nha Trang, a city of copycat Mediterranean beaches and old women plodding the high-water line, hawking rough massages and grapefruit halves; Hue, with its recently renovated Imperial Palace and dozens of lesser monuments and its brightly painted dragon boats cruising up and down the muddy Perfume River.

We had intersected the highway somewhat less than halfway to the DMZ, the demilitarized zone, the historical demarcation line between the old North and South. Jay seemed pleased to be off the Ho Chi Minh Trail, cheerfully leafing through his Lonely Planet guide for the coast's hottest nightspots while wolfing down the first fresh seafood we'd eaten since Saigon. I was in a blue funk. The trail had disappeared behind a curtain of rain that wreathed the mountains to the west. I had to decide whether to catch the bus back to Saigon or stay on the bike and follow the coastal route north. The problem wasn't Jay's incessant cigarettes, filling up my guest-house room with noxious clouds of gritty smoke. Nor even Jay's moods, occasionally as black as the thunderheads that gathered overhead every afternoon. It was the camera.

Jay's fascination with his new toy had quickly worn off in favor of hanging out and tinkering with the bike. My joy in finding an experienced cameraman had faded the first time I saw him turning the camera sideways to shoot. The advice I had been given before leaving—*Follow the action. Don't try to zoom, and don't pan. Take long shots*—seemed impossible to pass on in an acceptable format. My attempts to motivate by helping— "Here, let me get the tripod for you"—were studiously ignored. Suggestions—"The smoke from your cigarette is drifting across the lens"—resulted in a day of bad temper and a weeklong boycott of the camera. Worst of all, Jay virtually refused to film the one subject I needed most—me. "You're not interesting," he told me.

"I know I'm not interesting," I said. "But I'm necessary. Just a few shots here and there. Please." I had done the calculations. I needed two minutes of footage with me in it per week. Seventeen seconds per day. It wasn't happening.

I had taken my side of the bargain seriously. I was handling almost every interaction with the Vietnamese—getting gasoline, directions, finding soup stands, negotiating for guesthouse rooms—while Jay hung back and watched the bike. By evening I was exhausted, barely finding the energy to scrub my laundry on the bathroom floor, clean the cameras, fill in my journal, and tumble into bed.

In the end I realized that a reluctant cameraman was better than none at all. I would stay on the bike and look for a more enthusiastic travel companion once I reached Hanoi.

   ℮   ℮   ℮

The journey north swept by in a blur, a series of disjointed images interspersed with long hours on uneven tarmac and endless, driving rain:

Kilometer 900—The pearly beach and crystal blue water of Sa Huynth, a tiny fishing village off the express train line and therefore overlooked by foreigners. I walked down to the water, away from the boatbuilders hammering out their trade and the mob of two hundred children vying for the attention of an unexpected Westerner. Several pink baler shells lay just above the high-water mark, their graceful curves filled with flyblown excrement. I had stumbled into the village latrine. I picked my way past an old woman squatting in the sand, carefully averting my eyes from her morning's toilet. She grinned suddenly, made a thumbs-up sign, and shouted "America number one!" before sinking back into her reverie.

Kilometer 820—The rice seedling beds, a green so bright and concentrated that all other colors faded to gray. The wind blew through the six-inch stalks like a hundred burrowing animals, or gentle swells upon an odd-colored sea.

Kilometer 743—The young woman who stood outside an antique store in Hoi An, attracting customers to the fake antiques with her lilting voice and graceful gestures. She was unmarried and applied her meager income to supporting six younger brothers through school. Her father had worked as an administrator for the South Vietnamese Army, been re-educated into feeblemindedness, and now made rice paper for food stalls in the marketplace. Despite a quick wit and a clear aptitude for languages, she had been denied access to the university because of her family's sins. She forgave the communists their every trespass but one; in her schoolgirl days they had not allowed her to join a youth group, to earn the cheap plastic medallions given in reward for achievement in sports and communal activities.

She was a prostitute.

℮   ℮   ℮

In a back alley in Hoi An, on a hot and windless afternoon, I ran smack into the Syrian golden hamster.

139

He was generous with his advice and prodigious in his wrath at all things Vietnamese. He had apparently picked up a traveling companion in Saigon—a broken-toothed Swede who had agreed to an overland bus trip into Cambodia. Somewhere near the border they had been wandering the streets late at night when they ran into a gang of drunks, spoiling for a fight. With admirable forbearance they extracted themselves from the confrontation and hurried back to their guest-house lobby. The proprietor was just pulling down the heavy grate to secure the entrance when the drunks appeared, armed with machine guns. They were off-duty soldiers and they were hopping mad.

"One of them pointed his gun right at my chest and tried to pull the trigger," the hamster said, breaking into a sweat at the memory. "Luckily the clip fell out before it went off." The proprietor called the police, who arrived and immediately arrested the two Westerners for disturbing the peace. They were marched to the station and fined two hundred dollars, then ordered to return to Saigon. Too scared to spend the night at the guest house, they shouldered their packs and hiked out of town until they found a vacant lot, where they spent a miserable night in the rain. In the morning they found themselves sharing the local garbage dump with the rats.

"I've had enough," he declared loudly. "I'm outta here. And if you have any sense"—he pointed a stubby finger at me like the barrel of a gun—"you will too."

Kilometer 630—We carried on to Hue, the ancient capital of Vietnam and still home to a vast number of tombs, pagodas, and palaces. While everyone else was dashing from one monument to the next, I discovered yogurt. It had the sharp, biting flavor of unadulterated fungus and was served laced with sugar in plastic shot glasses. Soon I had accumulated a dozen empty cups on the table in front of me. Four men drinking beer laughed at my appetite and thereafter matched my intake bottle for cup.

The tomb of the emperor Duc Duc charged no entrance fee, largely because its outer walls had long since fallen to rubble in a field filled with cows. I thought the place deserted, a forgotten jumble of crumbling arches and scar-faced stone carvings, until a caretaker shuffled out and motioned me inside. He was sparrow-boned and stoop-shouldered, as old and rundown as the tomb itself. Two fingers of his right hand were missing, a reminder of his soldier days and the price of his guaranteed employment amid the ruins of the past. He described at length the lanterns, photos, and bronze knickknacks, and it took me several minutes to realize he was using the absent fingers to point at each object as he spoke. From time to time he slowly ran his hand down the length of his straggly beard, using those same fingers to untangle imagined knots in the five remaining hairs. I left him sitting peacefully on the stone steps, spitting into the garden, and hoped that when his time came, he too would be given a place beside the emperor as one of his more loyal servants.

ⓔ　　　　　ⓔ　　　　　ⓔ

Kilometer 585—The DMZ, once lined with barbed wire, minefields, and machine guns, now proclaimed itself with nothing more than a tiny plaque and a different-colored insignia on the lapels of the ever-present police. I had hoped to make a short detour to Khe Sanh, where there apparently was a plaque marking the head of the Ho Chi Minh Trail. Maybe I had just started from the wrong end. Maybe it was still possible. . . .

But the rain was coming down in solid sheets, and even the locals shook their heads at the thought of undertaking the sixty-kilometer journey to Khe Sanh along the slippery, washed-out road. Discouraged, we temporarily abandoned the chase and went in search of someplace warm to reconsider our options.

We found a comfortable cafe, and I stared moodily out the window, drinking coffee and trying unsuccessfully to browbeat the passing waiter into giving me a more hopeful weather forecast. An Australian overheard my conversation from a nearby table and said, "Khe Sanh? Forget it, mate. I just came from there."

"Was the road OK?" I asked hopefully.

"To hell with the road! It's the bloody coppers ya need to watch out for." He had hired a motorbike and guide for a day-long tour and taken along his camera and a few rolls of film. "I only took pics when my guide said it was right," he insisted, "then some copper started yelling and the next thing you know, I'm in the joint." The police had accused him of spying and insisted on destroying not only his used film but all his unexposed rolls as well. He was detained for over four hours, his camera threatened, and his guide given a hefty fine. "Just forget about going there. Nothing to see but mud anyway."

I wilted. Over half my pack was made up of film gear—ten pounds of batteries, twenty-five hours of videotape, forty rolls of film, two cameras, and a tripod. The police would have a field day.

"Head north," the Australian said with a shrug. "Everybody says its easier up there."

He was right. I would stick to my plan to disappear into the Tonkinese Alps. I had never been there, but somehow I was sure the mountain farmers would welcome me. After two years in a Filipino village, I had great faith in the generosity of the Asian villager, no matter how troubled the land or times he lived in. Their traditions of hospitality went much deeper than mere politics or skin color.

Somewhere in Vietnam I would find a place where I could live among the people, a place beyond reach of either the police or the Communist Party Machine.

℮   ℮   ℮

The government seemed intent on eradicating all traces of the former DMZ, and we left the zone with as little fanfare as we had entered it with. Although the political differences between North and South seemed to have been smoothed over, the road itself told another story. Not only had the northern highway to Hanoi once suffered intensive bombing, it hadn't been properly repaired in twenty years. Overuse by overloaded trucks compounded the damage. Potholes had developed potholes, and the beast bucked and jolted on the uneven tarmac. Highway 1 south of the demarcation line quickly became a cherished memory.

Kilometer 473—The landscape soon turned as bleak and oppressive as the weather. The soil was sandy, good for growing little other than the ragged gravestones that populated the hills. Piles of weathered rocks lay like washed bones at the edges of the fields. Here and there stooped figures spread armfuls of slimy paddy weed over their gardens to bolster the flagging soil. The road was edged with unnaturally round depressions. Some had become fishponds. Others, fringed with grass and filled with sand, looked like sand traps on a well-kept golf course. They were bomb craters, and they were everywhere.

A bent old man appeared on the road's edge, barefoot and wrapped in a thin sheet of plastic. He held out an inverted reed hat and bobbed it gently up and down, his fingers entwined in prayer. He was the first in a long line of beggars that scraped a living from the road. The central provinces were the poorest in Vietnam, so desperate that even interprovince buses responded to the entreaties of the inhabitants.

℮ ℮ ℮

Kilometer 352—The beast labored on, spitting out parts and inventing ingenious new afflictions at regular intervals. My vocabulary expanded to include "piston ring," "carburetor," and "accelerator cable."

We were on the road in another eight-hour downpour, pushing hard to reach Vinh, when the engine gurgled, coughed, and quit. I kept a careful silence while Jay played with the spark-plug wires, then took refuge under the eaves of a nearby hut. Despite my own hard-earned repair skills, I had learned to leave well enough alone when Jay fiddled with his fickle machine. There had been arguments; the repair bills were piling up, the cost in time and exasperation immeasurable. I lobbied to sell it to the first truly evil man that came along, or at least run it off a cliff and put it out of its misery. Jay, though grudgingly willing to admit that his classic machine had lost some of its original charm, stuck by it, less from a sense of loyalty than from the possible harm to his pocketbook. His lofty boast that he would drive it to Hanoi and sell it at a profit was in tatters. The best he could hope for was to make his money back, and then only if he spiffed it up, spackled over its cracks, and sold it to another unwitting foreigner with starry-eyed plans to cruise down Highway 1. For that he had to ride, push, kick, or drag it to Hanoi.

It looked like push this time. He turned it around and wheeled it past me, purposefully ignoring the hut I was standing under. I had already queried its agreeable inhabitants and knew there was a repairman living just down the road.

The old woman who came out to see what the dogs were barking at took pity on us, standing wet and miserable in the rain, and called her husband. He waved the bike under the extended eaves, put on a pair of Coke-bottle glasses, and inspected the beast. I knew that eventually the engine would dry out and probably start on its own, but in the meantime I was chatter-teethed with cold, my thin wet blouse conducting the chill wind directly to my bones. The old woman once again took pity on me, directing me to an empty back room with the banked remains of a fire. I stumbled about, struggling to persuade the dying embers to burst back into flame. The wood, stacks of twisted roots still damp with clinging earth, smoldered endlessly while I blew myself into apoplexy and the nearby pig slowly asphyxiated.

The family must have noticed the tendrils of smoke seeping through their woven kitchen wall because they sent their youngest daughter to check on the damage. She took over with consummate grace and in no time at all had a cheerful little blaze dancing among the ashes. Without waiting for a thank you, she was up and gone. I couldn't imagine what made her hurry so. It was still raining doggedly outside, and she was far too young to have a suitor. Curious, I forsook the fire and crept over to the living room to peer inside.

The entire neighborhood was sitting in absolute silence on the floor, staring slack-jawed at the smallest black-and-white TV I had ever seen. The picture, though riddled with static, was apparently a rural family drama set on an Australian cattle station. An unhappy little girl with flying pigtails and dirty petticoats raced on and off the screen, followed closely by a coolly sympathetic priest and her endlessly tearful mother. The voice-over into Vietnamese was all done by one female narrator, so the little girl sounded surprisingly mature and the priest a trifle absurd. The faint echo of the original soundtrack was recognizably German, though both the credits and the actors were English. By the time the last embrace had faded into a view of the windswept hills, I was equally slack-jawed and cross-eyed from trying to follow the snowy picture and unchanging monologue. I was completely unprepared for the general stampede that followed as three generations of extended family rushed to the fireplace to have a look at the second most interesting thing around—me.

They bombarded me with questions about the film. Why weren't those rolling fields being used to plant vegetables? Anyone could see they would support a fine crop of cassava or upland rice. Why did they not light incense after the little boy died, to help guide him to his ancestors? Did my mother also cry so much, and how many cattle did my family own? I struggled frantically to field the endless queries and impatiently tugging fingers, though I couldn't seem to understand a word from anyone except the little girl. Eventually an older auntie, frustrated by my apparent indifference, leaned forward and shouted *"Lao! Lao!"* into my ear. I looked to the little girl, who laughed and pointed at her grandmother. *"Kampuchea,"* she said, then indicated her aunt and various other relatives, *"Lao."* They were, she explained, all recent newcomers to Vietnam, having migrated from Laos after fleeing the killing fields of their Cambodian homeland. The grandmother, who still remembered the ripening corn left behind to the marauding Khmer Rouge, refused to learn Vietnamese and now wished only to be buried in the family plot, an impossible thousand miles away. The second generation had successfully mastered Laotian but did not have the energy to struggle with yet another foreign tongue. The little girl, after less than a year of local schooling, was their only mouthpiece to the outside world. She sat, immune to the shouted demands and pinching fingers, and simultaneously translated my sentences into both Laotian and Cambodian in one of the most impressive linguistic displays I had ever seen. When I fumbled too long in search of a word, she gently tugged the dictionary out of my hand, guessed at what I was looking for, found the word in Vietnamese, and showed me its English translation.

Jay wandered in, grimly bad-tempered from his hours with the nonfunctioning beast. They now wanted to tow us to Vinh, over sixty kilometers away. I encouraged them to keep trying to start the machine, but the novelty of jumping up and down on the kick starter had apparently worn off after several hundred attempts. I nudged the men aside and kicked it over a few times, and to everyone's amazement it roared to life with a loud crack and a long string of explosive backfires. The crack was the heavy kick starter, neatly split in two, lying in the dirt between the wheels. Never mind, it was running. I stuffed the pieces into my pocket, and we both leaped on board, calling out our good-byes to an unheeding audience. The next show had come on, and even the old man had disappeared to sit in front of a gray screen, to listen to a voice he didn't understand and dream up questions that had no answers.

146

@   @   @

We were just seventy miles short of Hanoi when we ran smack into one of the last things I ever expected to find in Vietnam— a national park.

At first glance Cuc Phuong was a disappointment, so over-poached that it had little left to offer other than biting ants and exorbitant entrance fees. We were on our way out the door when we stumbled upon the nearby German-funded monkey breeding program and its director, the laconic Tilo Nadler. He was a tall man and stoop-shouldered, with a tidy black beard and matching horn-rimmed spectacles. He had no use for the letter *w* and spoke in sentences that often drifted into silence before they ended. His assistant Manuela, the only other Westerner at the station, had gone to Germany for a month, and lack of company had made Tilo more amenable to tourists than was his custom.

He laughed bitterly at my desire to see some animals within the park. "You vant endangered animals? Go look for zem in ze illegal markets in Haiphong and Saigon," he told me, then quickly relented and offered to show me the endangered species he had collected at his station. We lingered by the gibbon cages, watching them swing from branch to branch on vinelike arms, and for the first time Tilo's forbidding face turned soft and gentle, almost fatherly. After two years and countless midnight raids, he had managed to confiscate six young gibbons, and the five that lived represented the last hope for the survival of their species.

The nearby langurs were in even more dire straits. "Zeir digestif systems are made only for a diet of leafs and ozer vege-tation, and zey deteriorate quickly when faced wiz bananas or man-foods," Tilo explained. The poachers who collected young langurs for the animal trade had little understanding of their special dietary needs and stuffed them full of cookies and fruit. They sickened within a day or two, and even if Tilo got his hands on them, he rarely managed to pull them through.

Tilo shrugged, his bitterness returning. "In five or ten years zey vill be all gone in ze vild. The Vietnamese and Chinese believe too much in monkey stew to cure zeir aches and pains."

We spent several days at the station, and on our last evening we came in for dinner to find Tilo deeply involved with his third bottle of beer. He had just returned from the local market-place, where he had spotted two six-week-old clouded leopard cubs for sale. He hastened back to the park to gather up several rangers for an official raid and confiscation, knowing that the cubs and their owner were disappearing in the opposite direction with equal speed. He returned in force to an empty stall and noncommittal passersby. "Zey are halfvay to China by now," he concluded morosely, and popped open another beer.

I wondered why he had even bothered to go back for them. Tilo stood a head taller than the average Vietnamese and sported the only beard for fifty miles. He was hard to miss. If he had seen the cubs, then the store proprietor had most certainly seen him. Why, I asked, didn't he just confiscate them on the spot?

"Ve must have official backup. It ees the law."

Useless to argue law with a German. I tried another tack. Why not buy the little fur balls?

"Ve must confiscate them. That vay ve teach them not to take ze animals in ze first place."

A laudable ideal, but with a thriving black market already in place, withholding the park's patronage wasn't going to create an industry-wide recession.

"Ez too late now," Tilo said.

The next morning I got directions to the local market, parked Jay and the beast at a corner soup shop, and set out to buy some leopard cubs.

The stall was empty and squalid. Several dirty orchids hung from the ceiling, and a badly stuffed turtle posed on a broken brick. I sat down to wait.

Eventually the curtain swung back and a stringy man stepped inside. He was as dusty as his orchids, with dark smudges highlighting the creases in his face and a frayed shirt whose cuffs had long since found a better use.

I told him I was a trader in opium, diamonds, and endangered animals, the only three illegal commodities I knew how to say in Vietnamese. I implied that he might have some interesting merchandise for sale.

"Opium?" he said, his eyes lighting up.

Damn. I rethought my strategy while he poured us tea. It started to drizzle.

Half an hour later I had weaned him away from opium and onto orchids, and was preparing to make the jump to leopards. The tea disappeared and homemade whiskey took its place.

"No," he told me, he had no clouded leopards for sale, but he knew where he could find some. Come back Monday.

By Monday, I said, I would be in China, making his northern neighbors rich with U.S. dollars.

"How many dollars?" he wanted to know.

This close to the park the two cubs had a market value of no more than a hundred dollars. I doubled the price, hoping to flush them out. It worked.

He jumped up and offered to take me to them, at a hut in the countryside a few miles away. "Where," he asked, looking around, "is your conveyance?"

The beast was still parked beside the soup shop, or so I hoped, fully loaded with two backpacks and running intermittently on only one cylinder. Jay had been less than thrilled with my plan to buy the cubs.

Of course, I told the trader, I would be happy to accompany him, and so would my companion. Did he have his own motorbike? No? Then by all means, we could take ours.

Jay was not impressed by my new acquaintance, nor was he thrilled at the idea of three on the bike. "If Tilo wants leopards," he told me, "then he can go get them himself."

"No problem," I said. "You can sit with the packs, and I'll take the bike and go after the cubs."

Jay took a long drag on his cigarette, crushed it out in the mud, and threw a leg over the beast. It started to rain harder. "You're gonna pay for this," he told me.

An hour later the road had become a gravel path and finally a narrow foot trail threading its way through rice paddies and between sodden huts. The trader remained stubbornly silent, waving his hand to continue whenever I pointed out a likely looking leopard hiding spot.

At last he signaled us to stop and disappeared inside a leaky shack. I found myself wondering if leopards could catch cold and if they would be small enough to stuff inside my jacket for the long ride back to Cuc Phuong and Tilo's toasty-warm nursery. The trader reappeared and waved us on.

Another hour passed. Several times the heavy bike sank up to its fenders, the twin mufflers disappearing completely under gooey mud. The trader hoped on and off like a hyperactive cricket, his voice getting progressively shriller as one set of solicited directions after another fell through. I sat sandwiched between the two men, feeling cold and soggy and perversely gleeful that another human being—a Vietnamese, no less—could fail to decipher the rural street addresses I had wrestled with for weeks. At last the trader recognized a particularly wretched hovel and dashed inside. When he reemerged his face was grim, and he ordered us to turn around with a single cutting sweep of his hand. He slid on board and stole Jay's last cigarette. "Sold out already," he snapped.

I felt an empty spot inside my jacket where two small furry balls were supposed to be. Instead they would be spending their short lives in tiny cages behind a Vietnamese repair shop or wind up suspended in dusty bottles of whiskey in a Chinese apothecary.

And on the spot I made a promise. Somewhere, somehow, I would do my part to save the few remaining endangered animals in Vietnam.

I left Cuc Phuong with a heavy heart.

13

Dear Mom,
Am I really blood type A? It's very important.

From Hanoi to the Hill Tribes

The final countdown had begun, the kilometer markers sweeping by as we zeroed in on Hanoi. In Saigon I had been warned that the northerners were a breed apart, that they had no sense of humor, they worked too hard, they ate weeds and dogs and were distinctly stingy. I had shrugged off the admonitions, assuming a cultural snobbery based on little more than which end of the egg they broke open for breakfast, or what color noodles they put into their soup.

I was wrong. Even before we reached the city limits, the differences had become obvious. We passed a crowded front yard filled with dun-colored dogs in cages and excited buyers waving money. Russian hats appeared, the thick furry kind with hanging earflaps. Vowels were hardening and intonations changing, and my hard-earned vocabulary was increasingly met with shaking heads and befuddled looks. Trees lined the highway—mature trees, their branches hanging over the road to provide shade for passing motorists. After Saigon's asphalt jungle I was astonished that they hadn't long ago been cut down. And everyone, from the potters stacking their wares on sturdy bicycles to the stall owners hawking small mountains of

First
Hitchhiking
Attempt

leafy weeds, was wearing army green. The men sported bulging headgear that looked disturbingly like Viet Cong helmets. The women remained loyal to their conical rice hats, the thick cloth straps tucked firmly under their chins.

There was something else, the last thing I expected to find in steamy, tropical Southeast Asia. It was bitterly cold.

                      ℮   ℮   ℮

The last five kilometers through city traffic was an agony of anticipation. Would we make it before five, when the General Post Office shut its doors for the day, forcing me to wait fifteen more hours for my mail?

Jay and I had been under way for several weeks by now. Although there were few post offices in the remote towns along Highway 14, I had continued to write home and send my letters via obliging truck drivers I'd met along the road. I knew how much my mother cherished every word from me and how much she worried when no mail came.

And she knew how much I needed to hear from her. She wrote often, long letters about brisk November evenings around the crackling fireplace, the silly antics of the family dogs, and a thousand other details of the people and places I yearned to see. Those letters, and others, had been accumulating at the post office in Hanoi, awaiting my arrival. I had thought about them almost daily and played over and over in my mind the moment when I might have them in my hands.

At last we turned the corner of Lake Kiem and I saw the words *Buu Dien* etched in granite over a huge gray building. I hopped off the bike, told Jay not to wait, and dashed through the post office foyer, to the slot marked *M* at the foreign desk. My fingers flew through the thick stack, plucking out the letters with my name on them. I wandered out the door, pretending nonchalance, to find an empty park bench somewhere along the lake. I tugged at the corner of a random envelope, then tore it open and raced through the letter in leaps and bounds. I read it again, more slowly. And again, savoring every word. At last, I put it aside and checked the dates on all the remaining envelopes, putting them in order. Then I stopped for a moment to take in the scenery, retie my shoelaces, and buy a soda from a nearby stand. When I could stand it no longer I tore open a corner of the second letter. . . .

It took two glorious hours to open all my mail. And then I read it all again.

℮   ℮   ℮

My first commercial act in the nation's capital was to buy a hair dryer. Not for my hair, which had long ago grown brittle with the harsh Vietnamese shampoos, but rather for my precious cameras, in sore need of drying out. And for my clothes, so long denied access to the sun that they had grown a greenish copper patina. And, to be honest, for my bed. I had developed a fantasy in the Central Highlands, and the endless progression of cheerless guest-house rooms and steadily worsening weather had turned it into an obsession. I wanted, just once, to crawl into a warm, dry bed.

I turned the dryer first on my clothes, slipping a damp sock over the nozzle and setting the heat on low. Within seconds it had become a flame thrower, shooting burning bits of rayon in all directions before committing suicide by melting its internal organs. The second dryer refused to run at all, beyond a short demonstration at the electrical stall. The third one purred along contentedly, provided I used only the no-heat setting, but by this time I was far too paranoid to point it at anything of value.

Hot water was a different story. In this I would accept no compromise, and when the guest-house owner regretfully informed me that my room's water heater was broken, I set to work immediately. The problem was simple—a missing fuse in the fuse box—and quickly remedied with a twisted foil chewing gum wrapper. Like a fool I gaily told the manager of my success as I swept past in search of a bottle of hair conditioner. I returned to discover that the lock on my door had been forced and my repairs permanently disabled with the help of a crowbar and a pair of pliers.

Conditioner wasn't the only luxury available in the big city. Hanoi was awash in Japanese computer games and pocket organizers that chimed in gentle reminder of meetings and deadlines in a country where most people judged the hour by the shadow of the sun. Or, if time was valued more as an accoutrement, Russian watches—huge, clunky fakes sold at very real prices.

I wandered around, blissfully scratching items off my shopping list and ogling the huge assortment of pastries and other sweetmeats. At the end of a long day at the market, I was as surprised by what I hadn't been able to find as what I had. Tiny rechargeable batteries, unique to my camera, were available on almost every corner, but tampons were not to be found, not even in the most sophisticated hotel in the city. The apothecaries could offer me gecko aphrodisiac and antler tonic, codeine and Valium at a penny a piece, but had never heard of sunscreen and, to my dismay, laughed at the mere idea that there might be that much sun. In a city that saw the temperature drop each year to close to freezing, there were no down jackets to be had, and not a hint of wool.

At least there were the foreign food stands. The government had grudgingly licensed a few dozen vendors to cater to Western tastes. The result was a long line of identical shops that sold SpaghettiOs and Campbell's soup, bottles of cheap wine, Swiss chocolate, and a wide assortment of dusty canned vegetables that could be had fresh at the corner market at a fraction of the price. They also offered a few condiments: ketchup, mustard, hot sauce, and soy sauce. I bought several items and scurried home with my loot tucked under one arm.

Later in the evening Jay stumbled in, footsore and disillusioned, grumbling about the value system of a society that imported Emmentaler cheese but not a shred of pot. I sat unheeding on my bed, the refuse of a small feast scattered around me. The chocolate was long since eaten, the smoked pork a greasy stain, and I was happily stuffing French baguettes with mustard. When the bread ran out I sucked the cheap yellow paste straight out of its plastic bottle. At last, after every shred and smudge was licked clean, I lay back with a bulging stomach and forgave myself my gluttony.

It was Christmas day.

℮   ℮   ℮

Hanoi was far more than foreign food and tourist trinkets. Its old quarter was a window back in space and time, a medieval landscape where entire streets had been dedicated to a single commodity and families handed down their secrets through generations. Dye street, with its brilliantly colored powders spilling over onto the crowded sidewalk and vendors who wore traces of their day's sales on their hands and faces. Herbal medicine street, a maze of sturdy paper bags filled with twisted brown roots and crumbling gray leaves. Music street and noodle street and sewing street and yarn alley . . .

Although the city's entrepreneurs clearly wanted to get rich as badly as their southern cousins, they were going about it quite differently. The Saigon crowd was right; northerners were more serious and perhaps a little thriftier, but the differences went well beyond nuances of character. Hanoi's streets hosted many fewer homeless, and begging had largely been replaced by some form of salesmanship, be it matchboxes, bananas, or a single pack of cigarettes. Even the two blind men I saw stumbling slowly around the lake each day were bristling like hedgehogs with all manner of brushes and brooms. One was always in the lead, and the other used his free hand to blow a whistle before crossing each street. They seemed to know every stall and cyclo stand, every bump and crack in the sidewalk, and navigated with unerring accuracy. I followed them for a while, determined to resolve a burning mystery: How did they know what they were being paid, in a land where the bills were all uniformly tattered and, more importantly, all the same size? After several blocks the shorter one turned and beckoned me forward. Embarrassed, I put the question to him. He laughed and offered me a clue: He knew I was a Westerner from the cadence of my footsteps, and a woman. He told me exactly where I had first seen him, that my camera was both expensive and heavy, and that my accent put me in Hanoi for less than a month. I offered to buy one of his brushes but he said no, I would have no need of it. In the end he accepted nothing but a handshake and left me wondering how long I would have to wander the streets of any city before I could see the world with such remarkable, sightless vision.

I had hung around Hanoi for two weeks, looking for a back-packer who might be willing to do some filming for me in exchange for a guided tour of the Tonkinese Alps—to no avail. Everyone was either heading down to Saigon, or on a whirl-wind tour of Asia with one week allotted to Vietnam, or aghast at the idea of living in mud huts and eating rice.

Mid-January found me restlessly rereading the notice board in a backpacker cafe, wondering if Chris—male or female?—might not be convinced to blow off his rendezvous with Stan in Hue in favor of a carefree jaunt among the hill tribes.

A Taiwanese businessman sitting at a nearby table waved me over to have breakfast with him. He was taken aback that I was wandering the world so far from the protection of my family and inquired, somewhat abruptly, about my blood type.

"A," I said.

He nodded knowingly. "You are being driven by your blood," he told me. Asians had long ago mastered the art of blood divination and applied it both to their politics and their social relationships. "Have you heard of the suicide squadrons of World War II Japan?" he asked. "They only took pilots with blood type A. They were single-minded and dedicated to their cause, even unto death."

With his verdict ringing in my ears, I packed my bags and set off to hitchhike a thousand kilometers in a great loop around northwest Vietnam, to the border of China, across the Tonkinese Alps, and beyond.

℘   ℘   ℘

Before leaving I stopped in to say good-bye to Jay. We had got-ten along surprisingly well—having spent twenty-four hours a day in each other's company for several weeks—given how little we really had in common. He was all for conquering the wilderness, starting with his home state of Alaska, while I was a dreaded tree-hugger. He disdained the Vietnamese and sought out the company of English speakers—preferably Americans and most preferably Alaskans. When I asked him why he returned to Asia year after year, he didn't hesitate: "It's warm and cheap."

Once we reached Hanoi we quickly separated, Jay to check out the city's nascent pub scene and I to find the latest news on the Tonkinese Alps and the tribal minorities that lived there. We rarely saw each other after that.

I found him in his room, bleary-eyed and still in bed. "The Alps?" he said. "How're you going to get there?"

"Hitchhiking." If others had done it, then by God so could I. I just wasn't planning on telling my mother.

"So when do we leave?" Jay asked with sudden breezy confidence.

That caught me by surprise. Jay didn't seem the type to suffer the indignities of the outstretched thumb. Against my better judgment, I thought about it. It would certainly be safer, but I wasn't really worried about that. Vietnam, with its Confucian history and Buddhist leanings, seemed eminently respectful of women, and I had yet to experience an indecent word or gesture of any kind.

Wait a minute. What was I thinking? I had come to Hanoi to get rid of Jay. I shook my head. "I'm doing this one on my own," I said.

"Who," Jay asked with studied nonchalance, "is going to film you?"

The documentary. Damned if that camera wasn't holding me hostage. It was time to make up my mind—to dedicate myself wholeheartedly to capturing what I saw on tape, or leave the equipment behind and travel a great deal lighter but with no eventual proof of my conclusions.

It didn't take long to decide. Whatever I found out there, I wanted to bring it back to America with me, to show that long-ago mechanic that he was wrong—or right. And for that I needed Jay. "OK," I said. "We'll give it another shot."

We agreed to catch a bus the following morning to the out-skirts of Hanoi and dutifully arrived at the station in the predawn darkness. The bus was already bloated with passengers and cargo, heavily biased toward the front. I chose a convenient pile of rice sacks behind the last seat, unslung my pack, kneaded myself a spot, and went to sleep.

I awoke with my eyes bouncing inside their sockets, amid the thunder of an artillery battery and a swirling cloud of dust. The bus slalomed wildly back and forth, chattering over the washboard road like a runaway jackhammer. A bag of sawdust had apparently burst under the onslaught of several dancing wooden planks and filled the interior like a desert sandstorm. I crawled forward to the last tier of passengers, sitting mute and expressionless, their hands clasped over plastic carryalls to shield them against the dust. An elegant young woman slid over a fraction of an inch in invitation and immediately began bombarding me with heavily accented English. "How many creatures are in your relative family?" she asked, then without waiting for an answer, "When do you drink whiskey?" Long before she reached "Do you dance without pants?" I recognized the outlines of a grade-school grammar book. We finished her long-overdue homework and got down to business.

No, she wasn't married. Nor, she told me proudly, was she gainfully employed. She had just spent the day visiting her "darling," an unemployed postal worker living in the city. They planned to marry as soon as he found the money to purchase himself a job. At present she was living with her retired parents on a tea plantation in the countryside, waiting.

"What do you do all day?" I asked.

"Nothing," she replied, carefully tucking her callused hands into her lap.

Word spread of our discussion, and the moment she disembarked the conductor called me to the front and cleared a space for me. He had silver-rimmed incisors that overlapped his lower lip in a serene Buddha face. It was a disconcerting combination. He asked me where I was from and laughed maniacally at my response, then clapped a heavy hand on my shoulder to keep me in place.

"Before, I VeeCee," he said in pidgin Vietnamese, loudly enough to include several rows of openly eavesdropping passengers. "I kill two Americans in war. Bang bang!" He laughed, cocked an imaginary trigger, and fired twice. Before I could react to his story about once being a Viet Cong guerrilla, he reached into a plastic bag, pulled out a fresh baguette, and tore it in half. "Different now," he said, "Welcome back!" He handed me a piece. He settled down beside me, munching on his bread, and regaled me with stories of his years in the jungle, of carrying his ration of rice in a tubular sock, of the feast when a hapless village cow stepped on a hidden mine and of the famine that followed.

When he heard that we had no clear destination in mind for the night, he chose a picturesque village and insisted that the bus driver take us directly to the guest-house door. He wasn't trying to make up for the two dead soldiers; his own family had lost three sons, and he still carried heavy shrapnel scars in his elbow and calf. For him the war was over, its sorrows laid to rest, and he accepted an American tourist with the innocence of a child.

It was indeed a lovely village, nestled against the serene and muddy Red River. Water tumbled merrily along bamboo aqueducts and fell into mossy barrels. An old woman walked behind her buffalo, picking up wisps of hay that dropped from a wood-wheeled cart. Jay and I ducked inside the guest house to drop off our packs. I snatched up my camera to capture the last few rays of sunlight and ran smack into three policemen drinking whiskey in the sitting area behind the receptionist's chair. Despite my recent experiences on the bus, I backed away. The forgiving conductor was retired. These young men were not. They saw me at the door and waved me over, and I was trapped.

They were bachelors and had only recently been assigned to the tiny village. They lived on the second floor of the guest house and had their tea every morning with the lady of the house. They jostled and muttered among themselves, then decided to entrust me with their carefully kept secret. "We are learning English," they whispered solemnly. When I offered my services they broke into huge smiles and whipped out three dog-eared texts, all unintelligible rejects from the Czechoslovakian school system. We spent the next two hours laboriously enunciating a string of b's and v's and k's the likes of which my tongue had never encountered. By the time I finally escaped to a shower and some food, I was sure they would never learn English with the resources at their disposal, and they were equally certain that I had never spoken it in the first place.

Jay and I were up early the next morning, having learned the simple truism that all experienced hitchhikers swear by: It's not who you are or what your destination, but when and where you are. We planted ourselves at the appropriate intersection in the gloomy predawn hours and squatted down to wait.

Several hours later a nearby soup shop opened and was soon doing brisk business. The aromatic trail of bubbling broth drew us like hungry strays. The woman who poured our soup asked what on earth we were doing sitting on the corner like that, laughed at my shamefaced reply, and pointed at a man eating on a mat in her back room. "My husband," she explained. He would be leaving shortly, and we were welcome to travel with him. We accepted gratefully and sat down to breakfast.

When her husband's meal was done, he carefully patted his lips with a napkin, put on his Vietnamese Army officer's cap, and climbed into the driver's seat of a two-ton Russian Army truck. We followed with considerably less enthusiasm.

He was a lieutenant from the stars on his lapels, and one of the most handsome men I had ever seen. Try as I might, I understood not a word he said, and he in turn just shook his head and smiled at my attempts at conversation. Our front hood seemed to stretch forever over a massive engine, but the truck was nearly thirty years old and had long ago lost its shocks and Grand Prix aspirations. We bumped along at eight miles per hour, stopping frequently while road crews shoveled large piles of stones out of the way to allow us passage. The landscape turned lush and wild, with handmade aqueducts gathering water from the road before snaking down the mountainside to unseen villages. Barefoot men in homespun clothes appeared, carrying long, handmade rifles and necklaces strung with leather bags of powder and bird shot.

We weren't the only hitchhikers on the windy, one-lane road. Time and again our heavy vehicle rumbled to a stop, the lieutenant climbing down to help load a group of village women and their baskets of market produce into the back. Each time he returned with an armful of tangerines from his grateful passengers, and I passed the time peeling and handing out wedges of the juicy fruit.

After three hours the language barriers began to tumble down, in six hours the misunderstandings were nothing more than a vague memory, and by dark he insisted we share dinner with five of his friends at a roadside cafe. They ordered a veritable feast—roast pork and dog and steaming cabbage, rice and soup and whiskey and tea. We ate until we bulged, and then sat holding our stomachs while they took turns choosing succulent bits of meat and laying them delicately in our bowls.

They were all army lieutenants and had made the thirty-year commitment to soldierhood on the same day. They were from the city of Viet Tri, had risen in the ranks together, and eventually had been sent to Moscow for six years to learn mechanics and driving skills. At first they seemed quite sure that Russia was a fine place to live, but as the whiskey made its rounds, so did their second thoughts. "It's too cold," they said, and added, "The Russians, they never smile." They seemed to enjoy good-naturedly plying Jay with whiskey until he was quite drunk, although they drank sparingly themselves, and the two drivers not at all. They spoke often and longingly of their families. Their work took them away from home for several days each week, and my handsome driver in particular missed his year-old son. His wife, he told me proudly, ran a restaurant single-handedly. His boast sparked off a round of playful competition as each man held his wife's profession up for inspection. "Teacher!" one called out, and another "Doctor!" The fourth and fifth men were married to tailors, and the last was unmarried, although he apparently won the game by sending me a sideways glance and saying, "I wait for an American wife." To my surprise, not one of them had more than two children in a land that valued family above all else, the larger the better. My driver reminded me of the billboards I had seen in almost every town, proclaiming the new government policy in favor of small families, with captions reading "Have one or two children!" Army doctrine apparently took a more active role, and soldiers were demoted one star for every child more than two.

We eventually took our leave, waddling back to the truck cradling our bellies like bowling balls and laboriously clambering over the massive wheel and into the cabin. I liked these men for the way they scrupulously washed their hands before they ate and the loving way they spoke about their wives and children. I liked the lifelong friendship they had forged among themselves and the enormous calluses on the palms of the drivers, each an officer. They seemed not at all the stereotyped soldier, nor the crafty North Vietnamese fighter, nor even the patriarchal Asian man. Things were "different now," as the bus conductor had told me, but I wasn't quite sure how. Perhaps it was the whiskey, or the overindulgent meal, or the last forty miles of rugged roads in the pitch dark, but the answer didn't come to me until we were standing on the roadside, saying our good-byes. The driver climbed back into his cabin, reached down to shake our hands one last time, and said "friends." He was right.

A week later we arrived in the provincial capital of Lao Cai, a stone's throw from China and the jumping-off place to the minority villages scattered like grains of sand across the nearby mountains and fertile valleys. Splashes of color in the busy marketplace confirmed the presence of the shy tribespeople in their incongruously vibrant headgear and embroidered skirts. We shouldered our packs and set off on the last leg, the narrow feeder road that wound its way high into the mountains to the tiny market town of Sapa.

The corner was already crowded with Hmong men in homespun hemp, all waiting for a ride. I shook off a swarm of Hondas-for-hire that were trying to earn a month's wages off the two-hour ride up the mountain, dropped my pack, and sat down on top of it.

The first truck went by, causing barely a ripple among the torpid would-be travelers. Another thundered past, then another. No one even looked up. I watched six, then eight, potential rides slip past before standing and waving my arms when number nine appeared. This did nothing but rouse the persistent swarm of Honda owners to another round of lobbying. By midafternoon the warm sun, the drone of grass-hoppers, and the dust had conspired to end such foolish antics, and Jay and I were as prone as the rest. Another truck, identical to all its predecessors, appeared in the distance, and there was an instant flurry of activity. Bags were packed and duffels stuffed. By the time the truck rumbled to a stop, we were all standing in line, ready to board. I threw my pack into the wrought iron bucket above the cabin and climbed up after it. The driver's concerns about my safety were soon eased when so many Hmong men climbed up after me that I was wedged solidly in place by friendly, smoky bodies. We lurched off and quickly picked up speed, the heavy truck swaying dangerously on the steep mountain switchbacks. When I stood to film, I was instantly supported by a scaffolding of muscular arms. The Hmong were as worried about my falling off as the driver had been, and after a short conference one of them bribed me with a dirty white radish to sit back down and enjoy the ride. Even then I occasionally felt a callused hand push my head down from behind, to protect me from the overhanging bamboo groves with their lethal three-inch spikes.

I passed around some peanuts and a bottle of Pepsi, and everyone added what they had in their pockets for an impromptu picnic of wilted cabbage leaves, butterball candies, and a well-kneaded ball of cement-colored rice with bits of lint in it. They drank the cola with gusto and snorted in surprise at the unaccustomed carbonation. When it was gone one of the men asked to keep the plastic bottle for hauling water and tucked it carefully into his backpack.

I eventually fell into conversation with the only man who spoke Vietnamese, an apple farmer from the tiny township of Bac Ha. He was visiting his brother in Sapa to help plan an elaborate funeral for their father. The old man, far from dead, was playing a vital role in the upcoming affair and would be arriving within the week to check on the arrangements.

I had yet to see an apple for sale in Vietnam, and although the farmer had none with him, he proudly showed me several blurry photos of his orchards. He was convinced that he would recognize one of his apples in any fruit stand in the world and asked me to send him photos of an American market day so that he would know if they were still in good condition when they arrived. In return he offered to tie a bit of string around the stalks so that I would recognize them as his. I took a second look at his photos. The apples were round and red, and not entirely un-American. For the price of a piece of string and a stamp I could make him a happy man, so I took down his address and promised to do as he asked. He in turn invited me to his robust father's funeral.

14

Dear Mom,
If you ever go hitchhiking through rural Asia you
should make a point of learning what the stars on
the soldiers' lapels mean and the accompanying
form of address in local dialect. It makes a
fabulous impression.

The Hazards of Hiring a Horse

Sapa was awash in concrete construction, mostly catering to the tourist trade. Everyone was getting in on the act: The main street alone sported a Bank Guesthouse, a Fansipan Mountain Hotel, a Waterfall Lodge, and even a Post Office Hotel, where rooms were available but stamps were not. Along with the building boom had come a glut of entrepreneurial, nonethnic Vietnamese who not only looked down on the minorities, but also by now outnumbered them.

The town itself had once been a French resort, perched high on a mountainside in the cool and comfortable Tonkinese Alps. An old, browning photo in the neglected museum showed wide streets, well-spaced houses, fancy fifties cars, and a central green for communal sporting activities.

Present-day Sapa was somewhat less idyllic. The larger grassy areas had deteriorated into grazing land for skinny packhorses. Cars had been replaced by flocks of motorbikes for hire, the gaps between houses filled in with pigsties and food stalls, and lawless chickens scratched among the street-side trash. A general air of boomtown money and shoddy, hurried workmanship hung over the piles of homemade bricks and construction materials that littered the sidewalks and backyards. Worst of all, every relationship seemed adversarial. The guest-house owners disliked each other, the Vietnamese disdained the minorities, and everyone was trying to wring the last dollar out of the transient tourists before sending them back to Hanoi. Even the dogs were uniformly mean.

But just beyond the edge of town, a mere five minutes' walk from the busy marketplace, a rugged mountain landscape took shape. It was a land of bamboo groves, of gentle breezes and sinuous terraces, their careful geometry cut by tiny streams.

As twilight fell I reluctantly retraced my steps to town and intercepted the first likely looking man I found to see if I could hire one of those scrawny horses for a monthlong trek into the mountains. His name, he told me, was Cham. He immediately squatted down into a comfortable, long-term bargaining position and arranged his face into an expressionless mask. He motioned for a suitable prop, a cigarette. I didn't have one. The corners of his mouth sank half an inch and he fell into a moody silence.

The horses, he said after considerable thought, were far too delicate to carry a big-boned foreigner.

I had seen them plodding into town with several hundred pounds of rice lashed to their wooden saddles. I hastened to assure him that I had no intention of riding the wretched beasts. I wanted one to carry my pack, a trivial item to say the least, a veritable feather on the back of these fine steeds.

He plucked a piece of grass and chewed it thoughtfully. How were they to know that I wouldn't just steal it and disappear over the nearby border into China?

I imagined myself wandering about the Chinese hinterlands

with nothing but a bony stallion. No currency, no language skills, no visa. I pointed out that a foreigner with a horse would leave behind a superhighway of gossip and that I couldn't "disappear" if my life depended on it.

He thought some more, his eyelids drooping in an effort to focus his concentration. I suspected, uncharitably, that he might be dozing off, if that were physically possible while bent into such a tendon-snapping squat.

His eyes popped open with a sudden inspiration. Perhaps, he said, he should accompany me as interpreter and guide, as the Hmong horse owner would almost certainly speak no English and would insist on chaperoning his steed on such a hellish trek.

I studied Cham's face. His features were pure lowland Vietnamese, and he wore not a shred of native garb. I was willing to wager he spoke no Hmong, nor any other ethnic dialect. Since we were conducting the conversation in Vietnamese, I knew his English was nothing to boast about.

A man wearing such fine clothes, I exclaimed, indicating his wilted T-shirt and tattered shorts, shouldn't stoop to sleeping in mud huts and washing in the river. As much as I aspired to his services as guide and mentor, perhaps he would content himself with a hefty finder's fee and my eternal gratitude.

"You know check?" he asked with unexpected abruptness.

Check. Traveler's check. Chekhov. Checkers. Checkmate. I had no idea.

"Czech language," he said impatiently.

"No, I don't," I said, feeling a little ashamed of the fact.

He had apparently spent five years in Czechoslovakia, studying construction and women. He had managed to acquire no less than three girlfriends, all tall, plump, and European. They had convinced him that Asians would someday rule the world because, try as he might, he failed to impregnate a single one of them, despite fathering six spanking infants by his Vietnamese wife in as many years. The Western world was dying out, he told me. Their women were barren. In a few generations it would all be over, empty houses and fancy cars with the keys still in the ignition, and the sturdier Asians would simply move in and take up where they left off. He himself had his eye on a fine three-story house in Brno, if all went according to plan, for his grandchildren.

He looked at me with pity, and seemed surprised at my lack of concern.

"Fine," I said, "but what about the horse?"

℮   ℮   ℮

The next morning was market day. The sudden appearance of hundreds of Hmong and Zao in their Sunday best was enough to temporarily banish all thoughts of mountain hikes and scrawny steeds. The minorities in their turn attracted dozens of itinerant traders, who set up their wares on long mats at the bottom of the market and did their level best to relieve both tourists and tribespeople of cash and kind.

The Hmong women all wore indigo-dyed hemp clothes embroidered with inhumanly intricate designs. The Zao held their own with elaborate stitchery and enormous red headcovers, layered and twisted into pillowlike pads that hid their shaven heads. Small knots of teenage girls ventured arm-in-arm among the food stalls, simultaneously attracting attention with their lovely costumes and rebuffing it with waving hands and averted faces. I saw infants less than three weeks old, their mothers having walked as much as fifteen miles to attend the market-day activities. The children slept endlessly, or looked upon the world with wide, attentive eyes. I never saw one cry.

Almost everyone was barefoot, their soles as hard as rhino skin. Those who could afford footwear had but one choice—a cheap Chinese sandal, sold for the forbidding sum of ninety cents. I watched a bent old woman try on one pair of plastic sandals after another, enviously fingering the rigid straps and then shuffling away, unshod.

Everyone arrived with their purchasing power in hand—a

couple of carefully padded eggs woven into a tiny reed basket, a string of gnarled mushrooms, or a bulbous sprout of mountain orchid. It was the middle of winter and the life-giving earth was hard as iron. Planting wouldn't begin for several months, and attic stores of unhusked rice were already running low. Many families bolstered their meager resources by foraging in the forests for tubers and roots, bamboo shoots, tender leaves, and edible insects. They sold the excess and used the money to buy salt and medicines, blankets, kerosene, and a few iron cooking pots. If anything was left over, they wandered down to the traders' mats to pore over the latest gadgets and tempting trinkets.

Market day was clearly more than just a shopping trip. It was a time where villagers could meet and chat, where romances were kindled and conflicts resolved. It was a day without the usual burden of chores, a time to temper the rigid daily discipline with a few minor luxuries. Stalls advertised peanuts by the tinful, tangerines, balloon-size cabbage heads and tiny, prepared pineapples on a stick. Hot food vendors sold sizzling tofu, rice gruel, deep fried batter, blood soup, and fully developed chicken embryos, cooked shortly before hatching and served with fresh basil and a dash of chili.

Market day had functioned this way for centuries, filling the meager needs of its feeder population. New products occasionally appeared and traditional items faded away, but the market itself continued, unchanging.

Until now.

The tourists arrived in white minibuses, dazed and stiff-legged from twelve cramped hours on the winding, wretched road. Other, more courageous souls flooded the train to Lao Cai and got fleeced by the bus conductors on the long ride up the mountain. They arrived late Friday night and filled the rapidly expanding guest houses to the bursting point. They left Sunday afternoon, their film duly exposed, each clutching some piece of intricate embroidery a tribal women had labored over for many days. They left behind a small mountain of banknotes that was turning the economy on its head and affecting everything from dowries to death rites.

Virtually every Hmong woman carried a basketful of embroidered clothing on her back, ready for sale. They descended upon the tourists brave enough to forsake their balcony rooms for a ground-level view of the bustling market. They spoke not a word of English and only a smattering of French, enough to say *"Jolie, jolie!"* as they clustered around the towering white strangers, tugging on their sleeves and reaching up to slip indigo skullcaps on bare heads and tunics over broad shoulders.

Oddly enough, the clothes they sold looked nothing like the clothes they wore, lovely tunics with multicolored stitchery and delicately sewn seams. The tourist garments were a patchy shade of purple and made of poorly matched panels that puckered and sagged. I snagged one for a closer look and realization dawned. They were reworked secondhands. The women had torn the collars out of old jackets and cut the broad, embroidered edge out of their tattered skirts, then stitched the pieces hastily together. The sacklike jackets were then immersed in homemade dye to disguise the battered embroidery and clashing colors. The same was true for the popular skullcaps made exclusively in foreign sizes. The bumpy embroidered patch across the front was really an old collar, baptized in a vat of dye and stitched to a piece of plain blue cloth.

The Hmong did brisk business selling their grungy clothes to grungier tourists who seemed to welcome the secondhand look. I wondered how they kept themselves supplied with used clothes. Surely they had cleaned out their own rag bins months ago.

The answer arrived in the form of several men with bulging sacks who set up shop outside the apothecary. They were immediately inundated with native women who snatched up the best pieces, squinted at them briefly in the sunlight, and tucked them into their bodices before they could be seized by other dye-tinted hands. It was all over in minutes, the women drifting away from the tattered remains. I wandered over to have a chat with the frazzled-looking men.

They were from a hamlet on the far side of Lao Cai, they told me, and business was good. They had long since emptied the surrounding villages of old clothes and now traveled 200 kilometers on horseback through the mountains in search of new sources. Some of the skirts were fifty years old, having been passed on from mother to daughter. The traders were getting desperate, and rich. Dwindling supplies had pushed prices up sixfold, and even the most ragged clothing now found a ready buyer.

I asked if I could go with them on one of their treks if I brought my own horse and gear. They turned pale and shrunk in upon themselves, shaking their heads like angry buffalo and insisting that my mere presence would spoil business. Not even an offer to pay my way with tobacco and rice wine could bring the color back into their cheeks, and they didn't look healthy again until their bags were packed and they were safely on their way.

I slunk off, feeling rather unwanted, and tried to lose myself in the boisterous crowd of Hmong and Zao that gathered around the traders' mats. A close-cropped Hmong man squatted near a pile of small-animal traps, wistfully opening and closing their rusty teeth. He stood and shuffled off and another took his place. This man clutched several bills and motioned to a stack of razor-thin saw blades wrapped in twine. For the next thirty minutes he examined every single blade, testing each tooth with the ball of his thumb until his fingers were bloody and he had finally found one to his liking. He paid and was quickly pushed aside by the next eager customer.

Few of the items for sale were basic necessities. This, then, was the disposal area for the newfound wealth from the embroidery trade—I had wondered where the money went. Certainly not for dental work, since most of the women had only a few token teeth and those that remained looked like they would soon be on their way. I wormed my way forward to inspect the mats.

An entire section was devoted to bangles and strings of plastic beads. Tiny bottles of dragon oil and hand-rolled pills were also quite popular, the brighter the better. The hardware section was exclusively male turf, and here the traders outdid themselves in their effort to introduce gadgets indispensable to every village household. A Hmong man picked up an old pair of barbershop clippers with interlocking blades. He played with them for a moment or two, then grabbed a friend's head and cut a broad swath of his hair to the crown. He seemed quite pleased with the result and immediately sheared off one of his own sideburns. His friends were saved from further impromptu barbering by the trader, who snatched away the clippers, shook them clean of hair, and shooed all but serious buyers away.

The market was winding down, the sellers packing their supplies onto lethargic horses and the buyers hurrying home with their new purchases secured to their backs or dangling from their fingers. I was retracing my steps to the guest house and a cold shower when I heard an imperative hiss from the corner of a chicken stall. Cham, my Czechoslovakian builder, gestured me urgently into the shadows. I followed, and we huddled like spies exchanging top-secret information.

"The horse," he said, and nodded impressively.

I didn't know whether to agree or not. "The horse," I said.

The formalities over, he pulled out a rumpled piece of tissue-thin paper with many eraser marks and a few holes. It was a bill, or rather a wish-list, for an overly optimistic Hmong. I scanned it and handed it back. He assumed that I hadn't yet acquired the basics of arithmetic and squatted down to walk me through it, line by line.

The horse itself, a virile young stallion, would run me 300,000 dong a day, about fifteen times the going market rate. By comparison, the horse's owner was a bargain at a mere 40,000 dong. Pound for pound, he was worth less than a third of his steed. My Czech friend, however, was a prized commodity, valued at ten strong Hmong men per day, or one and a quarter horses. The two companions he had chosen to accompany him would accept no less than 100,000 dong each, plus—a penciled-in arrow led me to the small print—thirty cigarettes and a bottle of whiskey, per man per day.

Of course, Cham added casually, a few important extras, like food and gratuities, hadn't yet been calculated. He looked at me expectantly.

Yes, I agreed. Food certainly was an important extra.

The list bore an astonishing resemblance to the Saigon Youth League requirements for my Mekong journey. I reinspected my young friend. He was even starting to look like Fang. Perhaps they were cousins.

Cham tapped the total impatiently with his index finger to keep me on track. I reevaluated the list.

"About the horse," I said. Three hundred thousand dong a day seemed a bit steep. And this virile bit was somewhat disconcerting. What if he should lose himself in the presence of a young filly and make off with my expensive camera gear?

A mare, he promised quickly. He would procure me a young female. Obedient and pliable, as all members of the gentler sex should be. He gave me a pointed look.

And then, I added, there was the small issue of his salary. Did he really think he was worth more than the horse? How much did he intend to carry?

He snatched back the bill and stared at it for a moment, then motioned for a pen. I found one and handed it to him. He carefully scratched out the 300,000 price tag for the horse and wrote in half a million. Then he stuck my pen in his pocket and handed the paper back to me. An ingenious solution.

I could see nothing else wrong with his arithmetic except the extra zero on the end of each number. I stood and wished him a good day. He called after me, insisting that I owed him a finder's fee, since he had spent an entire day writing up the list. I thought for a moment, then offered him a few token bills, but I was off in his estimation by at least two decimal points and so even that negotiation fell through, a victim of incompatible arithmetic and the vagaries of human nature.

15

Dear Mom,
The Four Minute Rule: No matter how far off the
beaten path you trek, no matter how well you hide
behind rocks or inside bamboo thickets, the
children will find you in four minutes or less. This
means that when lunchtime rolls around I have just
enough time to either answer the call of nature (in
relative privacy) or gobble down the bulk of my
meal. One or the other. I just can't bring myself to
do both at once.

Eldercare

J ay had all but disappeared once the tourist buses arrived
Friday night. I eventually tracked him down to tell him of
a trail that we might follow up into the mountains for a week
or two, overnighting in villages along the way. He made it
clear that he was disinclined to go slogging into the wilderness
in search of people who had yet to discover either English or
electricity. I didn't even try to talk him into it. With so many
intrepid travelers already here in Sapa to see the tribal markets, I was confident I could find someone else willing to take
a weeklong trek.

By Sunday afternoon I wasn't so sure. The weekend market
was winding down, the tourists preparing to board their dirty
white minivans back to Hanoi, and I had yet to find a soul
interested in a once-in-a-lifetime opportunity to spend a week

among the mountain tribes. Most had strict itineraries taking them down the coast. The few that didn't blanched at the thought of sleeping on mud floors among the chickens.

I had some hope that the weekday crowd, though perhaps a bit thinner, would offer up a more die-hard stock of backpacker. Monday and Tuesday were devoid of foreign faces. Wednesday dawned gray and soggy. I went in search of a bowl of hot soup and found myself sitting next to a pair of miserable French people. They had arrived in the rain, spent several damp days in a cheerless hotel room, and were leaving in the rain. They had poorly timed their visit and missed the all-important market days. I pointed out that a short hike down the mountain would not only bring them to a string of gem-like villages, but also drop them down into the sunlight below the cloud cover. And that the next few days would see another market weekend, not entirely unlike the last one. They turned their backs to me and hunched more deeply over their coffee and baguettes, determined to make the most of their sour moods and their universal condemnation of all things un-French, particularly Americans and soup for breakfast.

That night I climbed onto the flat guest-house roof to watch the mist roll across the valley below and swirl around the moonlit paddy terraces. It was time to get to know the tribal minorities, not on the paved streets and sellers' market of Sapa, but in their own villages, living their ways and beliefs. If I couldn't find a travel partner, so be it. I would go alone. It was time to trek.

(e-   (e-   (e-

The trail sloped gently down the mountainside, past scattered huts wreathed in cooking smoke and early morning mist. I was truly alone for the first time in days. The fields above me undulated with sunny yellow mustard seed. Down below, shiny buffalo lay half submerged in shimmering paddy fields.

A woman appeared ahead of me, her parasol angled over

one shoulder to shield her from the early morning rays. Further still, two older matrons, leaning heavily on each other as they tottered over the uneven boulders. I turned another corner and saw six more hikers, then eight, all dressed for Christmas dinner and struggling to negotiate the rutted road in an assortment of completely misanthropic shoes. The grim, foreboding beat of a drum heralded doom ahead.

I hurried past the stragglers, hoping to get to the bottom of the mystery, or at least outrun the crowds. A distant oboe wove its tuneless wail around the gloomy drumbeat. Three small boys squatted in the dirt, filling their already bulging pockets with stones. Their white headbands stood out in sharp relief against mops of black hair. I knew before I saw the bobbing altar and the elaborately ornamented box that this mournful group would soon be turning off the path to find a place along the windswept knoll above us, already studded with a dozen listing gravestones. I stood aside to let them pass. A frail old woman looked up as she went by, returned my smile, and bade me with an outstretched arm to walk with her.

The deceased had just turned sixty-eight, she told me, and had left behind a wife and eight children, who mourned him well. He had died of rotting stomach, but had lived to see the birth of the generation beyond his children's children and would have long tales to tell when he stood among the ancestors.

We clambered up the hillside to a red-clay gash in the pastured slope. The men set to with frenzied, ritual digging while the women plucked randomly at weeds that grew on nearby graves. The drummer lay down his instrument and took up a bottle of whiskey with a satisfied sigh. The three little boys plopped down into the grass, their legs outstretched, mightily enjoying the cigarettes they'd cadged from an old man assigned to pass out such tokens to the spectator-crowd. When the grave was clear and the coffin safely lowered, the digging resumed for real. Those without shovels pushed clods of earth into the hole with their bare feet. The immediate family, all wrapped in tattered mourning veils, crouched down and pressed their hands against the reddish dirt, and rocked and wailed, while others filed by with incense sticks. Soon the grave was barely visible inside a swirling cloud of scented smoke. An old woman led forth an almond-eyed child of such stunning Venus-beauty that it took my breath away. He handed her a dozen smoldering incense sticks and, one by one, she pushed them into the dirt beside a wreath of paper flowers.

The drum began again, and the yellowed banners unearthed themselves to begin their weary march back up the hill. The old woman plucked my arm and invited me to a lunch feast in town but I declined, unwilling to intrude into their suffering with my camera and my questions. The long caterpillar of mourners straggled away, to feast and celebrate and retell their tales, just as they had told me he would now be doing, standing tall among the ancestors.

With startling suddenness I was alone amid the graves, watching the playful wind pick up the clouds of incense and whirl them around the lonely red-clay mound.

A shining river ran along the valley far below, fed by paddy fields that rippled up the mountains on either side. Below me the zigzag footpath bore the round footprints of a plodding buffalo and the occasional slashing scar where a tired farmer had let slip his plow.

I descended through dry fields scooped out of the boulder-strewn earth, with stone walls holding back the soil like cupped hands against the mountainside. A stringy Hmong, his face just taking on the lines of age, worked patiently to pry loose a stone and build another wall. I put down my pack to help him, and together we heaved it clear.

We never spoke a word. Occasionally he pointed with one dirt-stained finger when I used my eyebrows to ask what to do. We shared his rusty crowbar, sometimes pausing to smooth the holes out of the thin gray earth where the heavy stones had been. He worked with the timeless deliberation of one who has no train to catch, no lover's tryst, no quota, and no boss. Once or twice I urged him on with an impatient gesture or a strangled sound. We could finish the field so much more quickly, I was thinking, if only he would hurry up. He stopped from time to time to stand back and survey our work.

An hour later I was tired and he was not. I sat and watched him deliberately choose a wedge of rock to lever out a larger stone, and finally I understood. He would be here until dark, and tomorrow, and beyond. Progress—to arrive sooner, leave earlier, and produce more; to buy more complicated tools to create greater output to earn more. These things had little meaning amid the timeless fields. From where I sat, overlooking a bubbling river flanked by ancient walls of hand-placed stone, such ambitions made no sense. He worked the fields as his ancestors had. If his father had time to sow and harvest the crop, then so, in the end, would he.

(e   (e   (e

By early afternoon I was blister-toed and pack-sore. I found a small knoll on the side of the trail and had hardly unslung my pack when six children materialized and settled down to watch. Kids were as common as crickets, and it was rare to sit for more than a few minutes without acquiring a miniature, wide-eyed audience. This time they were followed closely by an older woman with a basketful of paddy weed and exactly one half-mouthful of teeth—the left half, top and bottom. She compensated for the slightly lopsided look with a birdlike tilt of her head. She watched in silence as I fed the kids some rolls I had brought with me. She spoke no Vietnamese, and I no Hmong, but when she offered me a place to spend the night with the universal sleeping sign of both hands pressed up against her cheek, I understood immediately. Soon I was following her up and up the mountainside to her mud-hut home.

The weather was unseasonably sunny and cast a ruddy tone

over the near-naked children that flocked the fields. They used their parents' tools as props and handled them with such ease that I felt like I had stumbled into a munchkin universe, where pint-size farmers hacked the earth with absurdly elongated hoes, and tiny girls swung giant infants onto their slender but capable backs. A five-year-old plowman in need of a buffalo slung a rope instead around his little brother and called him to task. Together they dragged a hoe around the field, the child-buffalo snorting and tossing pretend horns while its owner bellowed out commands and kept a steady hand upon the reins.

The old woman's hut was surrounded by a field of blooming mustard seed, the yellow so bright that it paled the reddish earth around it to gray. Two little girls arrived from the nearby river, bent under the weight of rattan baskets overflowing with straggly paddy weed. At dinnertime they nipped the long, crisp stems into shorter pieces and boiled it for both people and pigs. The old woman retrieved two eggs from the bottom of the water trough and fried them in lard, carefully squirreling one away in an empty beer bottle and dividing the other among three adults and five children, to lay over the rice and weeds for supper.

The trail had long since deteriorated into a tangle of softened footpaths through endless paddy fields. After four hours of sudden dead ends and impassable wallows, I looked behind me to see my starting point barely half a mile away. I thought back to the Hmong farmer, patiently prying stones out of the rocky earth. He would have laughed at my impatience. Since I had no clear destination in mind, what was my hurry getting there?

My home that night was impressive: a two-story Giay hut with massive, fifty-year-old beams and a towering pyramid of unhusked rice stored in the attic. The house held four generations of extended family, from the old man who sat motionless before the fire to the newly mobile toddler, negotiating with difficulty the lumps and bumps in the packed dirt floor.

Mia, a lovely round-faced woman with a cheerful smile, was the backbone of the family. She was my age and had five children and managed the entire household with a firm and unhurried hand. When evening came she showed me to a cubbyhole where I unrolled my sleeping mat. I retired early and luxuriated in the unexpected privacy until the rest of the household shuffled off to sleep. I suddenly discovered that a scant half-inch of rotting plywood separated me from the grandfather's bed. He hawked and spat until his coughing fits merged imperceptibly with his saw-toothed snores. Several times that night I heard him try to rise, followed by the sound of patient footsteps as someone came to help him to his feet. In the morning he shuffled over to his rattan stool beside the fire and spread his knees to dry his pants. A young woman brought him a toothbrush, hand cloth, and a basin of warm water. He methodically scrubbed his face along the hairline, inside his nostrils, and across his teeth. He used the battered toothbrush to groom the wispy hairs protruding from his chin and swab out his ears. When his toilette was completed, he rinsed his mouth with a handful of basin water and spat it into the corner. He shuffled past the family altar and swiped the cup of lukewarm tea set there for the spirit ancestors.

He was seated first at mealtimes, served the tastiest tidbits from the table, and given pride of place beside the fire. He had little to his name except a lifetime of service to his family and this, apparently, was enough. They begrudged him nothing they had to give and offered him respect without a hint of obligation. I thought of the wealthy elderly back in America with their retirement accounts, their lobbying clout, and their empty, echoing homes. For all their financial independence and health insurance coverage, their lives seemed a poor shadow of the twilight years of this old patriarch, idling poking coals under the cooking wok with his cane.

One evening, on our way back from a day spent in the paddy fields, Mia and I passed a hut wreathed in strips of white paper. When we got home Mia bade me change into my best clothes and said she would do the same. I gathered together an armful of toiletries and picked my way down the steep path toward the river, attracting the usual crowd of pint-size onlookers along the way. My body was as white as milk after the many months of layered clothing. I was toweling dry when a young girl of five or six approached and reached out a tentative finger to touch my arm.

Was everyone in my country the color of cooked rice? she inquired politely, before scampering back to the safety of her friends.

I returned home to find Mia waiting for me. We walked over together in a chilly downpour to find the hut filled to bursting and resonating with a monotonous chant. Blue-and-white banners covered in ancient Chinese script hung on the walls around the altar, and every flat surface was covered with bottles of homemade rice whiskey with paper corks. An ancient shaman sat under the altar, dressed completely in black but for a sagging crown of brightly embroidered thread. The table in front of her was laden with offerings: stalks of dried herbs stuck haphazardly into a bowl of uncooked rice, murky bottles of unidentifiable liquids, and a wobbling mound of pig fat. The old shaman laid a callused hand upon the head of a young Giay girl kneeling in front of her and began another round of tuneless chanting so deep that it reverberated in my chest like an overamplified guitar. As she sang she tied a black thread around the girl's wrist, weaving the ends over and under each other in a complicated knot. When she was done the girl backed away, head down, and a wrinkled grandmother crawled forward to take her place. This time it was a bag of clothing that needed to be blessed, the items coming out one at a time for their bit of string and heavy-handed chant.

An older Giay man slid onto the bench beside me and translated into horrendous French. It was a funeral, and the threads were to keep the spirit of the dead man at bay. They would work only if they were worn until they broke off of their own accord. The tying-on ceremony had been going on since early afternoon, and by now everyone in the room had their requisite bit of string. I asked if I could also kneel to receive the protective blessing, and a lively discussion ensued among the forty highly opinionated Giay. The women were nodding, the men shaking their heads. The old priestess beckoned me with one gnarled finger and inspected me from head to toe. Satisfied, she bade me kneel. The big-knuckled hand lay on my head, the rough-edged chant washed over me, and out of the corner of my eye I could see two dozen giggling Giay watching me over the top of a sacrificial chicken, its head pulled back, blood dripping steadily from the gash in its throat.

I was the last, and they proceeded quickly through the ceremony. The sacrificial table was cleared, and the women moved into high gear, bringing out borrowed stools and jury-rigging benches. Everyone sat according to their age and gender, the old women in black taking the privileged place under the altar and the men setting up near the fire, where they could drink and smoke in peace. I found myself at the young ladies' table, being served heaping bowls of rice topped with horse meat and snowy white pig fat. I dug into my portion of the feast with plastic-smiled determination, smearing layers of rice onto the gobs of fat and swallowing them, surreptitiously fishing around in my mouth for stray bits of horse bone. I discovered the bottom of my bowl with infinite relief, and looked on with paralyzed horror as the woman beside me used her chopsticks to dig several pieces of glistening fat from the center platter and lay them into my bowl. She smiled at me and topped it off with a tablespoon of fish sauce. I ate. I ate the horse meat that slipped onto my plate when I wasn't looking. I ate the seventeen-day eggs, crisscrossed with bluish veins and shedding sodden feathers, that appeared magically on my plate whenever I looked away. That evening I ate for the rice-white population of the world.

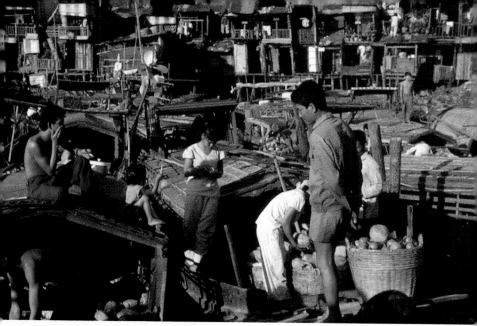

Life along Saigon's waterfront

A Saigon produce market

Ahn Tam

A canal in the Mekong Delta

The patriarch in the Mekong

A relic of the "American War" in a southern village

Jay and the camera—and the everpresent children

Sapa valley

The darker side of life in Halong Bay

A cyclo driver takes a nap between customers

Sapa town on market day

A slow afternoon at Bac Ha's Sunday market

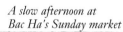

AIDS posters were everywhere

A Hmong child gets a ride home

Opposite: *The two faces of Vietnam*

A rice-drying platform—and its intrepid guardian

Blood? Strawberry Jam!
A specialty of Dalat

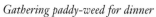
Gathering paddy-weed for dinner

Near the border of China—where it
sometimes snows

A typical eatery—pig heart, cooked chicken, blood soup

Capitalism comes to Sapa

Not as easy as it looks

The embroidery identifies both her Zao village and her clan

Driving the Unification Express!

The night market in Dalat

The matriarch in Tafin

A Zao villager with an unusual accessory

The deadly animal trade

A bedraggled leopard kitten after a much-needed bath

My most flattering portrait

Escaping the animal market with our menagerie

Jochen falling in love

A Hmong woman

Opposite top: *On the road to Dien Bien Phu*

Opposite bottom: *The tedious uphill task of watering the rice paddy*

Mai Chau—an island village in a sea of emerald paddy

Stockings of mud

Scarecrows were everywhere—but the birds had long since been eaten

A moment's respite from cutting wood

A glimpse of modern technology

And I drank. My tiny teacup was an endless fountain of milky rice whiskey, powerful enough to light a fire. At last, with my head swimming and worse still to come, I covered the cup with my hand and begged them to stop. Eight pairs of eyes fastened themselves to my face. "Don't you like it?" they asked. The dreaded question. I thought fast and hazily. Loved it. Fantastic. Only, I was—what was that damned word?—pregnant, and whiskey wasn't good for the coming child.

They sat back, smiled, and nodded knowingly. I sagged with relief. They talked briefly among themselves and then began to ask me questions.

My mother had always warned me that one lie requires two to uphold, and those two need four. That night, under the incessant, grueling curiosity of my hosts, I built a pyramid to rival the Egyptians. I grew an elaborate family tree, contracted and cured illnesses, won and lost fortunes. By the time the tables were pulled back and the fire stoked, I had lost track of the details and knew only one thing for sure—that I had best not return to this place until my face was long forgotten and I might have the chance to start over again.

I rose to find the hostess and bid her good-bye. She turned out to be a tiny woman, bent into the shape of a question mark with age and wear. She smiled gently as I took her hand in mine.

"I'm so sorry about your loss," I said, feeling close to tears as I thought of the twilight years of her life, sad and lonely without her mate.

"No problem," she replied, and gave my hand a shake to buck me up. She shrugged her shoulders, asked if I had eaten my fill and bade me stay a while longer and warm myself by the fire. My mournful sympathy clearly made no sense to her. This was a party to celebrate the memory of her husband. I should eat until my legs could no longer support my belly, drink until I staggered, and honor the old man with merry words and joyful tales. Unless, of course, I was carrying my own, private burden of sorrow. She took my hand this time. Was something wrong?

185

I thought it over as I negotiated the slippery stones by moonlight and tried to remember which of the identical huts along the path was hiding my sleeping mat. I knew the death of an elder Giay called for a funeral and an immediate party, one that sometimes lasted for days. The family members, particularly the widow or widower, were responsible for the well-being of their guests. They were made to rush around, continually supplying drinks, slaughtering chickens and any other livestock foolish enough to come within cleaver-reach, and generally working themselves to exhaustion just when their pain and sorrow must have been at its peak.

And yet it made sense. During the first critical days after a death, those left behind were surrounded by family, laughter, and friends. Their elaborate duties left them no time to wallow in grief. When the party was finally over and the guests took their leave, the widow was ready to tumble into bed with exhaustion, to slip into a deep and dreamless sleep. When she finally awoke, the healing process had already begun.

I returned to my hut to find my host family poring over the *Life* magazine I had left lying on my plywood bed. They were unapologetically insistent that I sit down to translate the impossible photographs—a Greek fisherman pulling a 1,300-pound fish; a Miata, shiny red and voluptuously curved; and a supersonic jet punching through the clouds. They were particularly interested in the photo spread about the Damms, a poverty-stricken family in the Midwest. I tried to field their excited questions.

"Not all Americans are wealthy," I explained.

They tapped the old pickup behind a portrait of the sullen family and marveled at its size.

"Some people in America don't have enough to eat," I added.

They showed each other the half-empty Coke bottles lying around the filthy bedroom.

I pointed out the picture of the Damms all sharing a single bed. Several Giay reverently stroked the edge of the mattress, marveling at its thickness. We were having separate conversations. When they had thoroughly discussed the ramshackle house, the kitchen, the dogs, and the useful trash lying around in the yard, they turned their attention to the family members. Why were their clothes and hair so dirty, their faces so unhappy? Perhaps their water supply was far away and they couldn't do laundry or wash. Maybe their fields were suffering a drought and there was no harvest. Or they had lost a loved one and did not have the resources to provide a grand enough leave-taking ceremony.

I left my hosts with another magazine and retired to read the article myself. Why *were* the Damms unhappy? Their welfare check was late and they had made a fruitless visit to town to pick it up. The mother was addicted, on and off, to methaqualone, and the father was abusive, overweight, and unemployed. The article was gently sympathetic. I tried to conjure up a suitably sensitive explanation for my infinitely poorer and endlessly hardworking hosts, and failed.

I took my leave a few days later, without my magazines but clinging obstinately to my immensely popular Velcro sandals. The family stood outside to see me off, the greens and pinks of their native costumes impossibly bright in the sharp early morning light. My final, lasting impression was not the swirl of colors but of the old man sitting up against the pigsty in his worn black tunic, carefully paring his toenails with a large pair of rusty scissors.

16

Dear Mom,
The lovely, lightweight bags you made me have long
since lost their original purpose—the map holder
(I no longer need to know where I am) has become a
wet laundry bag. The book satchel is great for
keeping mud and maggots out of my food. . . .

Bride-price and
Embroideries

The path wound its way through one village after another,
often through the individual huts themselves. No one but
the dogs took offense as I opened courtyard gates and ducked
under clotheslines, or skirted pigsties and buffalo sheds.
Everyone seemed to be outside taking full advantage of the
uncommonly bright sun. The farmers made virtually everything they needed to live; tightly woven baskets with hammered
bark headstraps, snares carved entirely of wood and looking
only marginally strong enough to break a chipmunk's leg,
incense, plowshares, ashes, paper, and beeswax.

Eventually the path took me to the river's edge. I could see
it pick up again on the other side and zigzag up the hill, but
the rushing water in between was thigh-deep and filled with
slippery, moss-covered stones. Under the amused eyes of several small boys I dropped my pack, took a camera in each

hand, and waded in. It was steep and treacherous, the water tugging at my legs and the rocks shifting underfoot. I thought to ask for help but didn't really trust the boys with either the heavy pack or the expensive cameras. Halfway across my sandal caught on a rock, the Velcro tore open, and I watched helplessly as the current whisked it away. The kids went after it like bloodhounds, their feet barely touching the stones as they hopped, cricketlike, from one boulder to the next. They returned it to me in less than a minute, their teeth flashing in impudent grins. I surrendered my bags, far safer in their competent hands, and watched them scamper to the far shore.

Evening found me clambering up a gash in the hillside between two rice fields. Bamboo groves rose on both sides, snaring tendrils of the incoming mist and deepening the gloomy shadows inside the narrow gorge. I had just given up hope of finding a hut for the night when I stumbled upon a run-down shack with a rat-tailed, deeply obnoxious dog. After several moments of feinting and parrying, I was rescued by an aged grandmother who came out and motioned me inside. The family shrine, just inside the door, held nothing more than a month-old orange, half deflated and hard as leather. Blackened cobwebs hung from the drying racks over the fire and the customary second-floor reserve of stored rice was nowhere to be seen. The children were thin-faced and slunk around in the shadows with hopeful, wary faces.

The old woman bargained poorly, and I gave her more than she asked for. It was a sad place where the children cried often and silently. All of the resident adults—with the possible exception of the grandmother—were addicted to opium. I shrugged off my pack and escaped the cheerless hut for the only marginally brighter garden. A middle-aged woman stood among the mustard greens, aggressively weeding out the leftover vegetables to make way for the new years' planting. She unearthed two white radish roots, hairy with fibers and tough as wood. A nearby shaven-headed girl immediately dropped her hoe and snatched them, depositing one into the hands of her younger sister and gnawing on the other without bothering to wipe the dirt off first. Her smaller sibling sat on a rock and clung to her grubby treasure, occasionally rubbing it against her cheek or nicking it with her nail and then sucking on her finger.

Dinner was pickled banana heart and cooked weeds, same as the pigs. I ate with the children while the family's unmarried sister prepared the opium. She had a beautiful, thin-boned face, the luminescent smile of an addict, and the wracking cough of a terminal tubercular. She lit a kerosene lantern and carefully lowered herself to the thin, woven mat to begin her preparations. She kneaded the brown paste into a long tube, then cut it into balls with the meticulous precision of a watchmaker. By the time she had filled her bong and taken her first puff, the others were ready to join her. Only the grandmother stayed apart, holding a tiny infant between her knees and poking at the fire with a stick for warmth. I was given a bed of straw laid perilously close to the flames and a brick for a pillow, and fell asleep to the flickering kerosene flame and the sad, old eyes of the woman cradling her starving grandchild.

The next morning dawned gray and dull. The sounds outside were curiously muted, the voices wrapped in cotton wool and even the yappy dog less abrasively shrill. I peeked out to a watery world of viscous mud and solid sheets of rain.

The path down to the Zao village of Tafin wandered through rolling hills sculpted into terraced paddy. My horizon was the edge of the heavy fog no more than a dozen feet away. Misty monstrosities only gradually solidified into deserted French ruins and tall stands of gray bamboo. Two women materialized, walking fast and flat-footed, their heads down. They both splashed barefoot through the puddled red water, on a day cold enough to turn each breath into wispy puffs of fog and make me wish I had brought gloves and wool socks.

I followed them on little more than a nodding acquaintanceship along terraces lipped with hardened clay and filled with the stumpy stalks of long-dead rice. Scattered houses appeared from time to time, heralded by the muffled bark of a dog and the steady thump of a rice thresher. The women never faltered, their legs churning under heavy baskets bulging with a week's supplies. The fourteen-mile trip to Sapa was obviously nothing to them, nor was the steep, slippery trail that led up to their forest home.

They lived in a typical Zao hut—massive, dark, with leaky cathedral ceilings to accommodate the rising smoke from several fires. It was made entirely of rough-cut, overlapping planks, the cracks stuffed with old rags, plastic, bits of grass, and mud. There were no windowpanes, and the fire did little to combat the icy mist pouring in through the open doors.

She led me to the guest fireplace and deposited me there beside a sedate old man. The old Zao roused himself and leaned forward to collect the blackened kettle from the fire. It was already stuffed with sodden tea leaves, and he searched briefly for a stick to act as a makeshift sieve. He filled the first tiny cup with tea, swished it around, and poured it into the second cup. When all the cups were rinsed of ashes and old tea, he handed one to me. He settled back, his water pipe in one hand and his teacup in the other, and began to talk.

He was the patriarch, the head of a clan that extended well beyond the walls of the hut. Four of his five sons were married and two had begun their own households no more than a stone's throw away. His daughters still lived at home, though one would soon be wed and leave the village for her husband's clan. An indeterminate number of barefoot children scurried in and out, invariably stuffy-nosed and carrying a younger sibling on their backs. In all he was directly responsible for nearly two dozen people under his own roof and was titular head of a dozen more. Most would return home with the fading light, the women having gone off in search of wood for the fire and the young men taking advantage of the poor weather to pay social visits around other, similarly smoky fires.

Dinner arrived, in the form of a table with six-inch legs and a long procession of women bearing boiled leafy greens, a one-egg omelet, and a huge pot of steaming rice. The old patriarch and his sons sat on three-inch wooden stools while the women disappeared to eat the leftovers in the kitchen with the children, as was their custom. One of the men unplugged a bottle of homemade whiskey and filled everyone's teacup. We sat in royal silence while I cocked my ears to catch the lively laughter and mysterious thumping noises coming from the other room. When several neighboring men showed up with additional water pipes and a worn pack of playing cards, I retreated thankfully to the women's fire.

The kitchen was a beehive of activity. Several girls plucked kernels off a mountain of dried corn. Another hacked away at knotted roots and piled the split pieces against the wall. A woman with an infant on her back stepped endlessly on a see-saw rice pounder, husking rice for the next morning's meal. The smaller children ran around the fire, feeding it with corn cobs, and the older girls held embroideries inches from their faces as they stitched by the light of the dancing flames.

I joined them, wringing the pebbly kernels from the dried cobs and tossing them into the fire. Weevils ran up my arms as the kernels they had gutted turned to powder between my fingers. Sticky spiderwebs hung from the cobs, sometimes cocooning them completely. I took a turn at the handmill— two heavy round stones that rumbled as they rubbed the corn to gritty dust between them. Everything went into the blend, including weevils and a few unfortunate spiders too slow to scramble away. The resulting flour seemed uniform enough, but I still hoped the household was one of the wealthy few that used its homemade cornmeal exclusively to feed the pigs and chickens.

The conversation turned lively, and after much coaxing they translated their native Mien dialect into broken Vietnamese. The problem, they told me, was love and family finances. Apparently a young Zao man couldn't just fall in love, sweep the lucky lady off her feet, and live happily ever after. He had to purchase her, in the form of a bride-price, from her former owner, her father. The payment was substantial, since the father had taken great pains to raise his daughter well, only to lose her labor and childbearing capacities to another clan. This particular family had been blessed with four sons and three daughters, an almost perfect balance, since sons were more welcome but daughters brought in the money to pay for wives. Therein lay the present difficulties. Two of the family sons had recently married at great expense while none of the daughters had yet brought in a bride-price to defray their costs. In addition, both grandparents had died within a year of each other, requiring elaborate funeral ceremonies and the sacrifice of much-needed family livestock. The result was an imbalance in the family's human portfolio—too-frequent purchases of wives while the unmarried daughters sat around and depreciated. It all sounded like a rather cold-blooded game of human chess, but was really just a form of enforced savings. The bride-price calculations were based on the cost of the groom's mother, with upward adjustments made if the young lady came with one or more children.

But what, I asked, if the husband were to die shortly after the wedding? As long as the father had been paid off, shouldn't the young woman then become a free agent, beholden to none?

They looked at me with horror. "Of course not," one said, and elaborated slowly, as to a child. "She still belongs to the family of her husband. They paid money for her." She might become the second wife of her husband's brother, which would keep the bride-price and children in the family. If she chose an unrelated suitor, then the negotiations began all over again, since the new man's family now owed her father-in-law a settlement—less a discount for wear and tear. Should the bride be unhappy with her husband's family and run home to her father, then the bride-price had to be returned, or else a certain number of her children given over as payment. In that case she was free to marry again, though who would want a woman who had willfully abandoned her husband and his clan?

They spoke and stitched, and beneath their nimble fingers the most extraordinary wedding garments took shape—elaborate embroideries in five colors that completely covered a pair of handwoven pants and a tunic, turbans and bags and boots. It wasn't one wedding they were stitching for, but two. In expectation of the coming bride-price, preparations had already begun for one of the remaining sons to wed. He had chosen a girl, several members of his family had visited her family with the gift of a rooster, and negotiations were well under way. It seemed a pretty risky move for even the most entrepreneurial dad. If the young son-in-law-to-be broke off the engagement . . .

They laughed again. Of course not. "No wedding," one girl said, "lose down payment." If it was the girl who changed her mind, however, her family owed the groom's father twice whatever had been received.

The young lady in question sat closest to the fire, laughing with the rest. Was she sure now? I asked. Was this guy really *it?*

She lowered her head demurely while her sisters poked fun at her in dialect. Apparently he was already sharing her bedroom, a practice they didn't entirely approve of. It had nothing to do with Zao propriety or her father's wrath. As a matter of fact, her bedroom had been built close to the kitchen door just to allow convenient access to suitors. The only demands placed upon a young woman choosing her lover was that he be from another clan and that his birth date, matched to her own, should signify a good omen.

But, her sisters admonished, if she gave him a place in her bed every night then he had no reason to hurry the wedding. This would be a discourtesy to both her father and her unmarried brothers.

"Absolutely," I agreed. That made perfect sense.

"Then it must be the same," they asked, "in America?"

"Well," I mumbled, fumbling a bit. The bride's parents might not understand if the groom showed up with a set of scales and a shopping list of silver jewelry and precious stones. And the guests would be somewhat taken aback if they received a packet of salt in lieu of a wedding invitation, and a hunk of raw pork when it came time to go home. And even the most liberated father probably wouldn't build his daughter's bedroom with her lover's best interests in mind.

"Why not?" they asked.

"I'm not sure," I replied, and decided not to ask my dad.

I had brought along several photos of my brother's wedding in the hope that they would provide some common ground. I dug them out of my pack, and the corn was momentarily forgotten. Why on earth, they exclaimed, was the bride wearing white? It was the color of mourning. Was my brother such a terrible mate?

"No," I replied, "he . . ."

And why was there not a stitch of embroidery on her plain white dress? Was her family too poor to give her time off from the fields to make a proper wedding garment?

"Not really," I said, "but . . ."

And she looked positively old to be getting married. Had her first husband died? How many children did she bring with her to this union?

"None. But you see . . ."

"And what," they said, turning their searchlights on me, "about you?"

I excused myself and scurried back to the men's fire.

Several more young men had arrived, and a serious game of poker was under way. They slapped their cards down angrily, shouted, drank moodily, and won and lost a great deal of money. The old patriarch sat off to one side, methodically roasting peanuts for their pleasure. Perhaps the old suitor-in-the-bedroom trick wasn't such a bad idea after all. It certainly cut down on whiskey consumption, and saved a bundle on peanuts. And if a baby came of it, that was almost as good as a new buffalo, or several piglets and a goat.

The windows had long since been shuttered against the chilly night air, and the smoke from the fires and tobacco pipes descended like a thickening fog. The six-inch tables and tendon-twisting, three-inch stools suddenly made sense. They were built low enough to allow some breathing space below the fumes. Everyone seemed immune but me; my clothes already reeked of ashes, and my nose stung so badly that it bled.

The women finished their chores and retired to their cubbyhole rooms. The pigs were bedded down in their sties, the buffalo in his pen, the hens roosted comfortably in their woven baskets. Even the rats had their place among the eaves.

I crawled away and spread several sheaves of rice stalks for a bed and lay down amid the raucous laughter of the card game and the rustle of roasting peanuts. In the darkness, away from watchful eyes, I pulled out my tiny pocket flashlight, pad, and pen. There was something that I needed to do, something so secret that I didn't want anyone to see the look on my face. A fantasy had taken shape during the last few days spent hiking across the valley. It was the image of my mother, *walking beside me*. At first I had dismissed it. I missed her terribly, but that was nothing new. I'd wanted her to share my trip since the Mekong and had written to her almost daily to make up for her absence. She was the reason that I loved to travel in the first place: her bedtime stories, her curiosity, her enthusiasm whenever I came home with another crackpot idea to see the world. Of course I wanted her to be here with me.

But then one dreamy afternoon, a sudden thought took shape. Why shouldn't she be here—at least for a visit? I knew the language and the terrain. I could protect her, carry a pack for both of us, make sure she ate well and had a comfortable place each night to sleep. She certainly was no stranger to this kind of lifestyle. I could already see the look on her face when she caught her first glimpse of the marketplace. . . .

The idea, once allowed to take shape in my imagination, grew like a weed inside my head. For days I had been looking for a quiet moment when I could frame my thoughts and write them carefully, persuasively. Now that the time had come, the words spilled out in an eager scrawl. The Alps . . . babbling brooks and mustard fields . . . pick you up in Hanoi . . . a train high into the mountains . . . bright red headgear and blue-dyed hands . . . shiny buffalo . . . lazy afternoons . . .

When I was done I folded the letter carefully and tucked it into my pack. I would wait to mail it until I got back to Hanoi. This letter was too important to get lost along the way.

      ℮   ℮   ℮

It rained for a solid week. The mist lay dense and heavy over the fields and poured in through open windows. Clothes hanging from the beams sagged with moisture, and my tiny cassette deck squealed and died, despite several attempts to warm it over the fire and vigorous shaking on the part of several frustrated sons. Everyone got restless, and smoked more, and tracked mud across the packed dirt floor. Only the matriarch, a tall woman with a smoothly plucked forehead, high cheekbones, and thick pair of reading glasses, seemed immune. She sat motionless for hours but for one flickering hand, embroidering a pair of wedding pants.

On the third day they brought me a tiny baby, less than a year old, that had somehow stumbled into the fire in a neighboring hut. Her arm had ballooned and turned an ugly shade of purple around two deep craters, already floating with pus. The wounds were filthy, wrapped in old rags, and the infant cried endlessly. Every time I approached, her wails redoubled and she urinated in fear on the six-year-old girl who carried her in a back sling. Too cowardly to do it myself, I told the girl to wash the burns in soap and warm water and asked the old man what medications he was using. He reached into his tunic and extracted a tube of cream, handling it as gently as if it were a tiny bird. It was athlete's foot medication, donated by the Red Cross. I slathered triple antibiotic on the little girl's burns and promised to repeat the procedure every day if they covered her arm with a clean cloth. They brought her to me religiously, and I came to dread the distant wailing that always preceded her arrival, the smell of fresh urine, and the terrified, tear-filled eyes that widened at the sight of me.

The rest of the children darted in and out of the house like hummingbirds, the boys roughhousing and the girls stepping lightly, one hand behind their back to settle the infants that invariably peeked over their shoulders. They played in groups of two or three and seemed to have the run of every house in the village. Having grown up in a highly segmented Western grammar-school world where seventh-graders wouldn't be caught dead playing with sixth-graders, and smaller siblings were about as welcome as the mumps, I was surprised to see that age and gender seemed to make no difference to these kids. From oldest to youngest, their protective custody of each other was endlessly endearing. When I offered a four-year-old a box of cookies, she accepted it with open mouth and unblinking eyes, made a beeline for the other children, and opened it in their midst. It passed from hand to hand, each child taking only one, and was then returned to me, still half full. When I gave one cracker to a nine-year-old, it immediately went to the infant on her back. I gave her a second one and that, too, went to the baby. I had to give her two at once, and even then if the infant tugged on her earring, it got both cookies, until it had eaten its fill. Apparently no one had told the teenage boys that they weren't supposed to like small children, and any toddler who ventured near the men's fireplace was likely to be scooped up into a pair of brawny arms and nuzzled, or swooped about like an airplane. Apart from infrequent accidents and poor teeth, it seemed like an ideal life for a youngster. They had no more than two sets of clothing, and both were dark enough to hide a great deal of dirt and wear.

They had only to wash their feet in the evenings and were never told to wipe their noses. They slept with their parents, peed into the corners, and if one ventured to pour small piles of rice husks on the heads of several aunts, he was scolded with nothing more than laughter. Perhaps best of all, when their parents went out to work or play, they were always welcome to tag along.

And so, apparently, was I. When the rain finally let up, the patriarch shook himself, as though from a long hibernation, and motioned that I should follow him outside. I spent the day watching two dozen men raise a hut, and when I returned home I looked at our house with new appreciation. The entire structure was built without a single nail. The main support beams were massive—I could barely encircle one with both arms. There were certainly no trees of that diameter left anywhere in the neighborhood. The roof shingles alone weighed several tons. Yet wood was so scarce that the women were laboriously digging up roots to feed the fire. Where, I asked, did all the lumber come from?

The patriarch looked around and nodded his head, then slowly refilled his pipe and began to scratch some numbers into the dirt floor. The house was over thirty years old—ancient, by Zao standards, and so well made that not a single wood borer had yet dared take up residence in its beams. The massive foundation posts had been dragged no less than fifteen kilometers from a secret place near the border of China. Ten men and four buffalo worked twenty days to haul in a hundred tons of building materials, and then two dozen clansmen had labored through the winter to complete the structure. All the proper sacrifices had been made before the house was raised, and as an additional precaution the posts and beams had spent three years immersed in water to discourage insect infestations. This house, he promised gravely, would still be here to keep his great-great grandchildren safe and warm. It suddenly seemed more than a muddy floor and smoke-stained walls, filled with wet laundry and sniffling children. It was one man's legacy to his family and clan, a foundation upon which to build the future, a home.

And despite his present wedding dilemmas, the old man was already planning improvements. In a few years he would buy a hydropump and sink it into a nearby stream to power a ten-watt lightbulb for a few hours each day. Several piglets were committed to taking part in a merit-making ceremony that would appease both spirits and the ancestors and bring luck in all future endeavors. He even had hopes of buying a small stereo system and one day filling the room with scratchy tunes and disco beat. That would have to wait, however. He was afraid the batteries would be a continual drain on the family's resources, and the younger generation might be inclined to sit and listen rather than going out into the fields to do their work.

An outhouse, running water, a refrigerator and ice; they were dreams only his children would realize, or perhaps his children's children. He didn't seem to mind. Sitting there, shuffling a place in the fire for his teakettle, surrounded by a small stampede of bare-legged progeny, he looked like he already had it all.

I shared one last meal and shouldered my pack. They seemed almost not to notice when I took my leave, accepting a discreet gift of cash with barely a nod, their hands never faltering over their chores as I said good-bye. Only the children followed me down the trail, leaping like young fawns and laughing at my clumsy steps. I hiked back up the path to Sapa with the comfortable feeling that this was the proper way of things, and if I should return in ten years they would greet me with a similar nod and offer me a cup of tea.

I returned to Sapa to find red flags strung across the street and a clutch of old men adorned in army uniforms and old medals. It was the twentieth anniversary of the fall of Saigon, and the government was living it up with martial music and telecasts of mile-long parades of tanks and soldiers along the streets of Ho Chi Minh City and Hanoi.

That evening the sky flickered and glowed with the repeated flashes of a lightning storm behind the mountain, an unusual-enough event to bring the local population out into the street. The power blinked out, and we were each issued a two-inch candle stub to help us to our rooms. By the end of the second day we still had no electricity, and rumors were running rampant. The Chinese had launched a major attack on Lao Cai, and we were cut off and surrounded. The government had turned off the power to remind everyone of the privations of the war. Someone had gotten electrocuted stealing electricity from the high-voltage wires, and his fried body was twisting slowly in the breeze halfway down the mountain. Most people in Sapa had never been to Ho Chi Minh City and knew little of the circumstances surrounding its fall. They were well versed, however, in the art of the triumphal parade. The endless centuries of occupation and warfare had provided the government with a smorgasbord of victories to celebrate, and the people expertly twirled their three-inch Communist flags and bowed to the beribboned old men. Only the minorities had no idea what was going on and stood off to one side with bewildered faces or used the flags as hankies for the infants on their backs. I wondered if it was an omen, and if the mountain way of life would ever be the same.

17

Dear Mom,

. . . so I found this tourist agency that said they could get me a visa extension for thirty days. An hour later they called back and said they could only do fifteen. Ten minutes after that they said five days. Apparently the anniversary of South Vietnam is coming up and the government wants to rid the country of Americans and cockroaches.

Later I was looking at my visa date and realized I could make the "3" into a "23" — which I did. I then took my passport to a little old man in the old city who does Chinese wood carvings. I asked him if he could duplicate one of the rattier provincial extension stamps. "Two dollars," he said.

Isn't life grand?

A Parting of the Ways

Sapa, perched near the top of a good-size mountain, seemed permanently enveloped in an icy cloud. It was late in the week, the market-day tourists had come and gone, and the guest-house owners were once again clamoring for customers. I had brought back with me a cold of head-popping proportions, so I dug out the fourth incarnation of my Vietnamese hair dryer, stuck it up my nose, and retired under a Vietnamese blanket that had the consistency of a sack of potatoes.

By the time Jay found me I had long since stuffed my head into a hot-water thermos filled with dragon balm. In my absence he had met a young Australian woman named Melissa, a cheery Australian who had divorced her husband, cashed in her half of the house, and spent the last four months in an Indian ashram studying levitation under an enlightened guru. She missed her dog, she told me, and was considering returning to her ex if he bought another house. She was tired of living out of a backpack and scrubbing her laundry on the bathroom floor.

She carried several business cards, and when her cash ran low she plied whatever trade would best remedy the situation. In this case it was masseuse and Jay was the lucky client. We splurged on a room in the only guest house that offered both a fireplace and a hot shower. Melissa dug up several vials of herbal extracts, and I cruised the local eateries in search of coconut oil to mix them with. One cook after another wiggled her hands in the direction of China and the coast. We were far too high for palm trees, and vegetables were difficult enough to come by—why squeeze them into oil? The woks they cooked with were all filled with great congealed lumps of pig lard. I returned to the room empty-handed and was immediately sent out in search of butter. When I got back the second time, Melissa was so pleased with what I'd found that she generously offered to throw in a second massage for me.

We lit the fire to ward off the bitter night air. Five minutes later we were standing out on the balcony, coughing up the smoke that had taken over the room rather than escape up the poorly ventilated chimney. We eventually reached an unhappy compromise—a tiny fire and open windows—and sat shivering on the bed drinking cups of hot green tea for warmth. It wasn't the most conducive environment for a relaxing massage and despite Melissa's best efforts, my relief at being allowed to cover up sections of buttery, goose-bumped skin outdid the joy of her handiwork. I dashed for a hot shower as soon as it was over.

I stripped, holding my long hair away from my greasy shoulders, and turned on the hot-water tap. Nothing. I experimented with the other tap. A stream of icy water blasted by, accompanied by a swirling cloud of arctic mist. I bit my lip, climbed into my clean clothes, and slithered down the stairs to get the proprietor.

He personally checked out the hot-water tap, clicking his tongue and rapping the pipe with his knuckles. He pointed out that the tiny sink still had hot water and suggested that I use it to bathe, as it was too late in the evening to fix the shower. I reluctantly agreed, wanting nothing more than to climb back out of my now grease-sodden clothes and wash my skin clean.

I showed him to the door and stripped, then turned on the sink's hot-water tap. Nothing. I tried rapping the pipes. Still nothing. I struggled back into my clothes and plodded down the stairs.

The entryway was barred, effectively locking us onto the third floor. I hammered on the glass panes until the proprietor showed up, his face twisted into an angry scowl.

"What do you want?" he demanded.

"Hot water," I said.

"Too late tonight," he informed me. He would look into it in the morning.

"NOW," I said.

"No," he told me.

I looked over his shoulder at the line of circuit breakers along one wall and saw that my room had been switched off. I marched over and flicked it on, and as I walked away I heard him slam and lock the door behind me. I sat on the bathroom floor and waited twenty minutes for the water heater to work its magic, then turned on the tap. Nothing. I marched back downstairs. This time the door was locked and all the lights were out. After several moments of dedicated rapping, another guest appeared and let me in. He chuckled when I apologetically told him of our predicament. "I was in your room last night," he told me. "I moved because it was too smoky and the hot water didn't work."

This time when I switched the circuit breaker on, I dabbed the connectors with Krazy Glue. Twenty minutes later, nothing. Jay offered to confront the proprietor with his more imposing six-foot frame. He returned somewhat sheepishly with four thermoses of hot water he had managed to snatch from the kitchen. I found a bucket for a sponge bath, decanted, and began to pour. The liquid was dense and black and had the unmistakable odor of coffee. In the end we rinsed out several soda bottles, filled them with water, and nudged them up against the dying embers, hoping they wouldn't explode. Jay washed with diluted coffee, I with diluted ice water. We had just extinguished the last of the fire when we noticed smoke rising through the wooden floorboards in front of the fireplace. I pried off the metal strip fronting the stone chimney and discovered that the flames had already wormed their way several feet into the room. The landlord had locked us onto the third floor when he went to bed, and there were no smoke detectors. I soused the floor with buckets of water and crawled into my lumpy bed, still sticky, cold, and smelling like a cross between a New York deli and the wrong end of a cigar.

The next morning Jay and I agreed privately to ask for a discount on the expensive room without either hot water or a properly ventilated fireplace. The proprietor, a straight-backed French-Vietnamese, completely lost his temper when we made our suggestion, stamping the ground like Rumpelstiltskin and accusing us of bad customs, dishonesty, and outright theft. We pointed out that he had charged us for a hot-water heater that he knew wasn't going to work. He ordered us to leave.

When we returned to our old hotel, the manager was so angry that we had gone elsewhere for the night that he refused to take us back. It was the height of the weekend market, and all the other hotels were overbooked. Homeless, Jay and I sat in a soup shop and discussed our dwindling options. He was all for heading back to Hanoi. I tended to agree. The chilly night and cold shower had taken its toll—my head cold had blossomed into a full-blown flu. Sapa, with its frigid guest-house rooms and perpetually damp weather, was no place to be ill. I didn't really mind leaving. Like the Mekong, my scouting trip into the tribal areas had been a resounding success. I knew that somewhere in these mountains was a village where I could settle for a month or two, learn the dialect, and get to know the people and their lives. But first I would return to Hanoi, recuperate, and gather up my equipment for a much longer trek.

I would be back.

18

South to
Nha Trang

The train to Hanoi filled up quickly, four and five passengers layered like canned sardines on seats meant for two. Just as the final whistle blew, a dozen Hmong clambered on board. They squatted in the aisles, holding hands and chattering breathlessly among themselves.

All went well until the conductor came through, loudly demanding tickets. Every Hmong turned to look at the patriarch, who carefully loosened an animal-hide pouch and pulled out the flimsy tickets. The conductor snatched them away and examined them with an evil eye, then tossed them back and demanded an additional eight cents. I held my breath as the old man unfolded a pitifully small wad of bills and slowly counted out four fuzzy two-cent notes.

The conductor stomped off, and the Hmong let out a collective sigh of relief. It was short-lived. The food cart appeared, piled high with exorbitantly priced candies and fruit and pushed by a Vietnamese boy. He used the metal-edged cart as a battering ram, shouting obscenities as he prodded the Hmong out of the way. I watched him conduct business up and down the aisle. With Vietnamese passengers he was polite, with

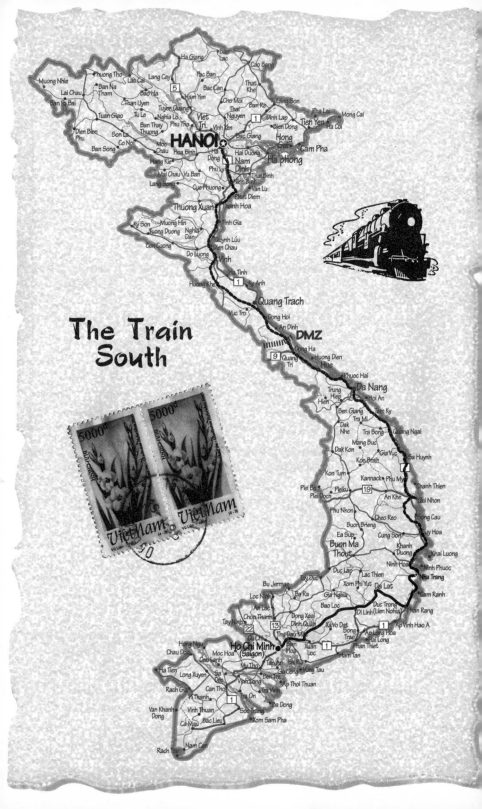

Westerners obsequious, and with the minorities imperious and rude. I began to understand why Vietnam's ethnic population kept themselves apart, refusing to learn the national language and customs or even to use the public transportation system. Apparently the minorities saw foreigners as an extension of the Vietnamese; when I offered a Hmong woman with two infants my seat, she refused with a quick, grateful jerk of her head and stayed squatting on the floor.

℮   ℮   ℮

Later, unable to sleep, I wandered out into the corridor and sat at the window. An ivory moon was rising over the Red River. The train swayed gently to the rhythm of the sixty-year-old tracks. A conductor came by on patrol and ordered me sharply to close the window grate. Just as he was leaving he turned abruptly and asked, *"Sprechen Sie Deutsch?"* When I answered yes he returned with two cups of coffee and another stool and sat down for a chat.

His name was Pham. He had spent six years in East Berlin, learning to weld pipes and work with iron. He spoke a soupy, soft-edged German that must have raised the neck hairs of his stiff-tongued hosts in the fatherland. He carried an ugly scar on his leg from shrapnel that had left him with a permanent, shuffling limp. Both he and his father had spent four years on the Ho Chi Minh Trail, fighting against three uncles who had chosen the south. The losers had migrated to Munich and Los Angeles; the winners had disappeared behind the Iron Curtain. As the years passed their ideological differences faded away, but the physical ones loomed taller as the family tried to reunite itself across the impenetrable Berlin Wall. His dream of visiting them had faded with a thirty-dollar monthly salary that couldn't begin to cover the airfare, let alone the four-thousand-dollar bond required for an overseas trip. "And for this," he shrugged, his laughter gone, "we fought a war."

I returned to my seat to find a Himalayan wind blowing through the open window and my blankets all wrapped around sleeping children. By the time we crossed the bridge into Hanoi my joints ached with fever and only a depth charge could relieve my permanently stoppered sinuses.

At five in the morning the guest houses were still sound asleep, their entryways shuttered against the night air and early risers. I sat on a stone bench in the narrow strip of green that ringed Hoam Kiem Lake and watched the city rouse itself to another day of honking horns and roving peddlers. As the horizon paled, a silent crowd of thick women in thicker jackets gathered on the pavement beside me, shuffling themselves into exact rows to begin an endless series of indifferent Tai Chi exercises. They called the count with military precision, but always ended inexplicably on the number fifty-seven. In a fever mist, my eyelids grainy with lack of sleep, I wanted to leap up, wave my arms, and finish the progression to a final shout of sixty.

"Fifty-five! Fifty-six! Fifty-seven! One!" They carried on, unheeding. I finally drifted off to the slap-slap of joggers shuffling around the lake and awoke to the honor of being the only one of Hanoi's teeming masses to have been allowed to fall asleep on a park bench under the willow trees of the lovely lake Kiem.

The fever came and went, and came again. I found myself resting on every third step of the endless climb to my second-floor room. One morning I awoke to bleeding gums, and for a week could bear nothing more solid than yogurt and old bananas. With no end in sight, I resigned myself to the care of the much-maligned Vietnamese medical system.

Medical establishments, like eateries, worry me when they have no patrons. I always wonder if I'm missing some important bit of news. I seemed to be the only one sick in the whole of

Hanoi that day, and after an hour at the International Hospital I began to worry that a recent epidemic had wiped out not only the patients, but the staff as well. At last a nurse appeared and beckoned me to follow her. We tramped in silence down endless halls, past doors labeled Endocrinology, Radiology, and Neuropsychology, all opening into empty rooms.

The doctor, a brisk woman in a reassuring white coat, poked around inside my mouth and nodded knowingly. She handed me a pack of vitamin C, a bottle filled with tarry black traditional medicine, and a dose of motherly advice; "Gargle two times each day with saltwater." West, east, and old-fashioned. She had covered all the bases.

I was disappointed. I wasn't, after all, some backwoods farmer, ready to be cured by anything that came packaged as a pill. I knew that vitamin C was no miracle drug, and gargling with saltwater seemed about as useful as slurping chicken soup. Perhaps the unmarked bottle had some secret ingredient that would make me well.

Later, after an application of the black paste had sent me careening off the guest-house walls in excruciating agony, I took the time to decipher the label. It was, to my relief, meant for teeth and gums. It was, to my horror, made with snake venom. That's it, I thought. It was time to bring in the big guns. I called my mom.

Somewhere between growing up in Africa and marrying my father, my mother had found time to earn her medical degree in Switzerland. With the birth of her two children, she had given up practice in favor of sand castles, tie-dyeing, and fresh bread twice a week. Nowadays she rarely mentioned her medical degree to anyone and had long since given up the honorific "Dr." Her training became apparent only when one of us got sick. "Conjunctivitis," she would say, pulling back my eyelid, or "probably another ear infection; let me get my otoscope and have a look."

Her biggest fear for me when I went overseas wasn't rape or robbery, or even murder. It was parasites. By mutual agreement my letters home were peppy and free of any references to diarrhea. She returned the favor by filtering out all other worries before reading them to Dad.

She was home, thank God. At four dollars a minute to make the call, I got straight to the point.

"Mom, I've got bleeding gums, intermittent fever, mouth ulcers, and my skin smells like I've died already."

She was immediately all doctor. "Sounds like scurvy," she said.

"Scurvy? I thought that went out with Captain Cook."

"It's a vitamin C deficiency. Have you been eating enough fruit?"

"It's winter here. There's nothing but bananas."

"Bananas won't work. Can you get your hands on some tablets?"

I looked sheepishly at the pile of pills on the dresser. "Yeah, I think so."

"Get some rest," she instructed, "and gargle with saltwater, that should help the ulcers. How are you otherwise?"

We chatted for a while, and it wasn't until I'd hung up that I realized what I'd done. That calm and collected doctor was my mother, probably frantic by now, helpless and half a world away.

She'd told me once that my endless trips had finally taught her to let go, to enjoy my travels vicariously without the crippling fears of motherhood. I knew with sudden certainty that she was lying. And I'd accepted her words because I wanted to, because it absolved me of guilt and allowed me to share my joys and sorrows with her unconditionally, like a child. But I was twenty-nine, well past the age when I should know to censor what I said and wrote. The letters! What had I written? I tried to remember. Had I told her about those truck-top rides along rotting mountain roads? Probably. And those raw snails, filtering every parasite out of the cesspool of the Mekong? No, I couldn't have been that stupid.

I wanted desperately to call her up, to tell her that I wasn't really sick, but I knew it would only make things worse. My relief had become her burden. What a selfish idiot I'd been.

℮   ℮   ℮

Hanoi was still cold and gray, and daily swept by bitter winds that rolled off the Tibetan mountains, screamed through China, joined forces with the Northeast monsoon, and came howling down the coast, carrying with it vast quantities of rain dust that settled like powdered sugar on camera lenses, drying laundry, and shivering tourists. I swallowed my yogurt with hands wrapped in T-shirts, my teeth chattering against the tiny tin spoon. What better place to gargle saltwater, I thought, than the lovely seaside town of Nha Trang, a tourist mecca a mere thousand miles south of Hanoi, delightfully located in an entirely different climatic zone? I packed my bags.

Jay watched the proceedings with a jaundiced eye. Vietnam had not lived up to his expectations, offering none of the beach-and-bungalow lifestyle he fled Alaska's icy winters for. Moreover, our off-the-beaten-track itinerary had given him few opportunities to ply his admittedly excellent storytelling skills to a wonder-filled traveling audience. Although he tried to make up for this lack with nightly expeditions through the pubs and clubs of Hanoi's burgeoning nightlife, he was clearly ready for a dose of the beach scene. He decided to come along.

℮   ℮   ℮

The train wound south at a leisurely thirty miles per hour, stopping every few hours at tiny stations where peddlers hawked tangerines and rice cakes through the carriage windows. The weather gradually warmed, the sun shyly revealed itself after months in hiding, and my sinuses began to crackle and pop, like a frozen river during a spring thaw. On a whim I dashed forward at one of the stops and called up to the engineer, asking if I could join him. He cheerfully reached down a hand and hauled me on board.

His name was Anh Lac, and his partner, Anh Thuy. They shared the forty-four-hour drive from Hanoi to Saigon, taking turns at the helm and sleeping in the green army hammock that hung between the doorknob and the gearbox. They spent their southern stopover on board to save the thirty-cent hotel fees. Their feet touched solid earth only every seventh day.

They both had families back in Hanoi and admitted to the hardship of their frequent absences. Anh Thuy had missed the birth of all three of his children and, worse yet, his father's sudden death. Anh Lac worried about his young wife's safety and her aging parents. They were both silent for a moment, lost in their thoughts. As quickly as it had come, their momentary sadness left them, replaced by a cheerful resignation. "It is life," Anh Thuy said. "One must work to eat." I wondered, though I didn't have the words to ask, what gave them the strength to accept their fate. Was it their Buddhist faith? Or their farming ancestry, with its yearly monsoon rains? I remembered Ho Chi Minh's long-ago promise to his men, to fight thirty years if need be, until the North prevailed. The VC heading down the trail had signed a pledge not to return home until the war was won. They couldn't know that they would need as much grim courage to survive the peace as they had to win the war.

Anh Thuy offered me a cup of tea from a thermos lashed to the gearbox, and we drank while Anh Lac drove. Both men knew the tracks like Mark Twain knew the Mississippi, and could tell me to the year how old each section was and what gear best suited the coming gradient and curve. Their route took them through some of the most enchanting landscape in the whole of Vietnam, and I had a ringside seat. To the east, the sand dunes fell away to a turquoise sea, and to the west the rolling hills climbed ever higher until they became one with the rocky mountain chain that ran, unbroken, to the roof of the world. The tracks themselves seemed a magnet to all manner of wildlife, from blue-winged birds to local boys with rocks and hideously accurate aim. The dogs, too, seemed to relish playing chicken with the oncoming locomotive, lingering between the humming rails until they all but disappeared under the wheels.

I slipped through the side door and leaned against the front railing and suddenly understood the unusual attraction the gravel embankment had for bird and beast. The stench of raw sewage that I had associated with the train's latrines really came from the tracks themselves. The open sewer fed hungry strays and chickens. The train, I was told, dispatched at least three roosters on every run and the occasional crow that stopped to feed on them.

We approached a small station, and Anh Lac called me back inside. He hung a heavy metal ring on a hook outside the train window and proceeded full speed ahead. With a loud crack it disappeared, and another took its place. Anh Thuy hauled it in, unwrapped a handwritten note, and read it carefully. "S3 approaching," it said, and indicated time and station number. Anh Lac looked at his watch, did a quick calculation, and poured on steam. Seven minutes later we pulled off the single track at a bypass. I had barely taken three breaths before S3 came barreling by. I was impressed—and appalled. The trains had no way of communicating with each other except by passing notes via the stationmasters, who kept each other posted in a complicated game of chicken that went on night and day along the busy single track.

Once the danger was past Anh Lac retired to the hammock, while Anh Thuy tapped out another cigarette and poured himself a cup of tea. I gathered my courage, sidled over to him, and whispered in his ear. He grinned and thought about it for a moment, then nodded slowly.

For the next hour I was allowed to fulfill a childhood fantasy, something that I've wanted ever since I was six years old.

I drove the train.

19

Dear Mom,
. . . I traded some of my antihistamines for Tampax
yesterday. What a relief.

Conversations on the Beach

N ha Trang could have been the Riviera, but for the occasional Vietnamese fruit-seller picking her way between slack and well-oiled Europeans. The shoreline was entirely devoid of Vietnamese bathers, and even the beachside cafes seemed devoted to Western tastes and white faces. It was a comfortable place where one could get by without a single word of Vietnamese and never have to speak directly to a native beyond the occasional waiter or receptionist. The locals were quick to see the merits of so many well-lined pocketbooks in such a confined space and had set up beach chairs for rent along the high-water line, a dollar a day. The glut of sleek and overfed bodies laid out like drying kindling had spawned an entirely new industry, plied principally by wrinkled older women with brawny arms and callused fingers. They offered brisk, gritty massages at four dollars an hour, three at a pinch.

I listened to them surveying their torpid clientele from a convenient perch on the crumbling seawall above the beach. Although they worked alone, they sat together every morning, deciding who should pitch to which potential clients and where to concentrate their energies. This required a consummate eye for the nuances of cultural tastes and a deft understanding of the delicate underbelly of human nature.

"The Germans," Fe said, "They stink." She wrinkled her nose up into her forehead and shook away the imagined smell. "Even after they come out of the water."

The Israelis, though aspiring to a higher level of personal hygiene, were apparently guilty of an even more heinous evil. They were stingy, and often tried to renegotiate the agreement after the service had been rendered, a habit the Vietnamese regarded as their own cultural prerogative.

"What about," I asked in my best Euro-Kazak accent, "the Americans?"

To my immense relief, they nodded approvingly. "Number one!" they agreed. "You tell them you're hurt, they always think war. Then they're sorry. The French too." Fe pulled up the back of her blouse to reveal a horrifying peach-size bulge at the base of her spine. I cringed. She laughed. "My husband," she said, and swung her fist. "Thwack!" She drummed her bare feet against the seawall. "He died in Cambodia. I was so glad."

An older women examined me with sun-swollen eyes. "Where are you from?"

I considered the various options. Stinky, stingy, or stupid. What a choice. "Italy?" I ventured.

They shook their heads in unison. "Not soft enough," one said, and drilled a bony finger between my ribs.

I tried repeating what the children had shouted at me all through the Central Highlands, where Westerners hadn't been seen for nearly two decades. *"Lyn So."* Russian.

"Cretins! Insolent knaves! Mangy curs!" They were quite beside themselves and took it in turns to heap invective upon their unhappy allies until one woman topped them all with a single sentence: *"They are Russians."* Everyone fell back into moody silence.

I explored the issue as gently as one would a throbbing tooth. What was it, exactly, about the insolent, mangy knaves that they found so unappealing?

To my surprise, they had no ready answer. They muttered vaguely about Russian men bringing their Vietnamese girlfriends to the beach and how they sometimes kissed and fondled them in public, but this was nothing worse than I saw every afternoon on the sand, and far less than a typical evening's entertainment under the secluded beach umbrellas.

The problem, when they eventually got around to it, revolved not around a stolen kiss or two, but the much more serious issue of national pride. The Russians had replaced the free and easy Americans but had not done their duty in outspending them. Quite to the contrary, they had turned Vietnam into a cheap vacation getaway, arriving in droves to sample the women and bask in the unfamiliarly balmy air and returning home with most of their rubles intact. An unforgivable sin.

Back to work, they said suddenly, and slapped the sand from their lower calves. The time had not been idle. They had been watching the beach scene and were ready to stake out their turf. They sketched it out as carefully as a Super Bowl play. The round and rather blubbery American beneath us was now or never, before the sun roasted his fish-belly-white skin to the color of raw meat. The young couple—an English teacher spending a year in Tokyo and his Japanese girlfriend—were in the midst of an ongoing tiff that wouldn't be resolved until midafternoon, if the past three days were anything to go by. He might take an hourlong massage now, to make her jealous, and she would almost certainly retaliate in kind. That was good.

I pointed out an uneven row of hirsute Spaniards, their fingers spread to blend the tan between their knuckles. A veritable gold mine.

The women were not impressed. "Them! They get their rubbing at night, from the pretty girls." Without another word they picked up their woven mats and tiny bottles of dragon oil and marched off to do battle with rolls of excess flesh and sandy buttocks under the burning southern sky.

℮   ℮   ℮

Tet arrived rather unexpectedly, while I was still reveling in my first few meals of solid food. It wasn't the Vietnamese New Year's Day that caught me by surprise, but the entire week that preceded it: seven days of such profound importance that they required a month of preparations. Long flotillas of cyclos plowed through the burgeoning traffic, their padded seats blooming with pots of miniature orange trees. Public transport unraveled, and even the most helpful tourist agents simply shrugged and offered their desperate clients small gifts of candied fruits. Visiting took on a whole new dimension, and overindulgence became a form of good manners.

It was the day everyone turned a year older, regardless of their individual birth dates. It was Christmas and Thanksgiving all wrapped in one. To the joy of the hundreds of vendors that set up their stalls along every sidewalk, in every nook and cranny, it was the season for indulgences, large and small.

In a land of tiny inventories and multigenerational customer relationships, the very idea of a holiday sale was utterly foreign. "Spend," not "save," became the national byword as stall owners made the most of the skyrocketing demand. I wandered out to buy a soda from my favorite street-side vendor and found that prices had doubled since the previous day. When I returned a few minutes later with another bill, they had doubled again. The muted, tinkling background noise resolved itself; it was the sound of piggy banks being shaken to excess, and grinning shop owners counting their coins. Money had suddenly become cheap and spending it a matter of national pride.

The marketplace, already working overtime, outdid itself once the sun went down. Shoe stands became soda stalls and apothecaries sprouted handmade roulette wheels as the entire city emptied into the streets to join in the fun. Colorful numbered wheels spun ceaselessly while bets were won and lost, coins tossed and darts thrown. On every corner, rickety stages showcased aspiring singers, their sequined dresses glittering in the glaring lights.

I bought a slice of salted pineapple and wandered over to a nearby gaming stall. A decidedly unenthusiastic hamster sat under an inverted basket in the middle of a table. When the basket was raised, the noise and lights were supposed to send it bolting for shelter into one of the twenty numbered huts nearby. Prizes ranged from tiny plastic bags filled with a half dozen roasted peanuts to cereal box toys. Several excitable young ladies stood clutching shopping bags filled to bursting with such trinkets, while their knights-paramour sauntered in deadly earnest from one table to the next, exchanging fuzzy bills for an endless stream of darts and betting slips.

The next morning—New Year's Day—seemed unusually quiet after the weeklong fuss. For the first time I saw Vietnamese appear en masse on the beach, the little girls dressed in their best print frocks and clinging to each other as they teetered across the sand in dressy heels. They played tag with the surf, scurrying after the receding waves like sandpipers until the water turned, then scrambling away, then dashing back again to retrieve the sandals the sand had sucked off their feet. Professional photographers congregated around the public fountains and soon had long lines of customers waiting to pose, stiff-backed and unsmiling, for their yearly snapshot.

I had been scouring the official bookstores for days, looking for a trashy English novel to reward myself after months of tedious grammar texts and pocket dictionaries. I had come across nothing but a Vietnamese translation of Jack London's stories and had spent a sweltering week on the beach, adding *snow bank*, *sled dog*, and *icicle* to my already lopsided vocabulary. Western books and magazines, I was told, were potentially corrupting influences on the national psyche and therefore banned to the public. I resigned myself to a few more months of barren reading and returned to my dictionary, opened to the letter *R*.

Once again the indomitable Vietnamese entrepreneurial spirit rose to the occasion, this time in the form of a little old man with a tattered handbag and a big floppy hat, plodding slowly down the beach.

He paused at my towel and offered me an elegant bow. "Excuse me," he said in almost perfect Voice of America, "would you be interested in a novel or two? I have titles in several languages. . . ."

Unconstrained by the finer points of social decorum, I almost toppled him in my haste to get inside his bag. Danielle Steele, Kurt Vonnegut, Ken Follet, he had them all, and a healthy dose of Danish and German works as well. He spent his days wandering the beach, buying, selling, trading, and reading the worn paperbacks he garnered from sun-baked travelers. He had followed Dante through the Inferno, shared thirsty days and nights with *The Old Man and the Sea*, and was hoping to someday come across some of Orwell's works, to understand the mysterious references to Big Brother and the Savage.

After much coaxing he sat on the edge of my towel and told me his own history, a tale worthy of Dickens at his best.

It began in the South Vietnamese Army and followed a path depressingly like Tam's. He had, in the years since the war, been an itinerant sign painter, a balloon seller, and Popsicle maker. "That was the job I liked best," he said with a chuckle. "Riding my bicycle around the city, blowing my horn. The children were always so happy to see me. . . ."

He looked back over the city and smiled for a moment in private reminiscences. He told me without rancor that there was hardly a menial job he had not been forced to take since the defeat of the South. For fifteen years he had listened to the American broadcasts in secret and smuggled censored Western books into his tiny shack. When the government finally relaxed its restrictions on foreign contact, his secret hobby become a vocation. He had been roaming the beaches ever since, finding joy in every new title that came his way.

The books had brought him more than a love of Shakespeare's sonnets. His language skills had blossomed while others were busy forgetting their Western ways. He now spoke a haunting, lyrical English that rivaled some of his most cherished authors. I wondered why he didn't migrate to Saigon and accept one of those sought-after positions as translator for a foreign firm.

He shook his head and directed my gaze out over the frothy white surf and cloudless blue sky. He was quite content, he said, and enjoyed the freedom of working to his own rhythm and in his own space. He seemed sincere, but a lifetime of diet books and car commercials had made me suspicious of such pure and unambitious contentment. There must be something, I insisted, something that he wished for but did not already have?

He hesitated for a fraction of a second. "A house perhaps?" I prompted quickly. "A small motorbike? A steady income?"

He shook his head. "A library," he said at last. A place where everyone was free to browse, to sit and read and drink a cup of tea. It had been his dream for years. Lately he had even found the perfect space for it, above a tailor shop and overlooking a tiny corner of the harbor.

He cocked his head and smiled again. For now I was welcome to borrow any of his books, he said, and could even return them by mail from Saigon or Hanoi if my travel plans took me elsewhere. We spilled his bag onto the sandy towel, and I listened while he put a gentle finger on each crumbling binding and explained why one was good, the other not. Eventually he rose to continue on his pilgrimage, leaving me with four of his favorite titles and the feeling there was more to life than making money, and that he had found it somewhere between a child's hopeful smile and the pages of Shakespeare's greatest works.

(e   (e   (e

It seemed an eternity since I had first met Jay and agreed to explore the Ho Chi Minh Trail with him. When we left Saigon on the motorbike I had put the bulk of my possessions in storage, naively assuming that one could actually make plans in this topsy-turvy country and that I would be back within two weeks to pick everything up.

Two months had passed since that fateful day, months filled with longing for my sorely needed spare socks and plastic bags. Now, unexpectedly, I found myself less than 200 miles from Saigon. I suddenly realized that with a bit of luck I could head south, collect my things, and be back in Hanoi within a week.

The very next morning I was on my way, by motorbike, in the company of a young German named Jochen.

Jochen had taken a year off from his studies in Stuttgart and come east on the trans-Siberian railway in search of adventure. The thermometer had fallen with alarming velocity as his train approached the frozen tundra, leaving him shivering in his bunk. He had been saved only by the happy confluence of his birthday and the arrival of his girlfriend, who managed to knit a pair of wool socks entirely without his knowledge, despite sharing a sleeper only marginally larger than a coffin. He had enjoyed the Chinese to distraction, mourned his girlfriend's return to Germany, and left himself less than a month to dash down Vietnam's backbone in a hideously reliable Minsk. He arrived in Nha Trang with his boots full of rainwater after thirteen days of nonstop driving, spent two days wincing under the hands of a firmly therapeutic beach masseuse, and saw no earthly reason why we couldn't be in Saigon by the end of the week.

His determination carried us there in three bone-shattering days. The city was everything I had remembered: the smog, the double-weave gridlock, the high-volume beggars and tenacious cyclo drivers. Nothing had changed, I thought, until I dropped off my pack and sprinted over to see Tam. His door at the end of the alley was locked and bolted, a heavy chain wrapped around the knob. Inside were my duffel bag, my traveler's checks, film, spare cash, and plane ticket—everything I need to survive . . . and get home.

My impetuous arrival had created a stir among the alley's doorstep-sitters. I was soon surrounded by a silent crowd of Tam's neighbors. Eventually his niece stepped forward and gestured to the bolted door. "He's gone," she said. "To America."

I was thrilled by his good fortune and appalled that my checks and all my money might have gone with him, leaving me temporarily as poor as the silent faces around me. I waited anxiously while the key was fetched and the rusty chain undone, and stepped inside to face my own unfounded suspicions. It was all there, with an apologetic note on top. He was sorry that he would not be here to greet me but his name had come up. . . .

And I was sorry to have so little faith in a trustworthy friend. I wished him Godspeed in the land of computers and bright yellow taxicabs.

20

Dear Mom,
There are four leopards under my bed. I'm rather
afraid to put my bare feet on the ground. . . .

Only a Miracle . . .

My initial weeks in Saigon yielded unexpected dividends as I steered Jochen flawlessly through complicated streets and interconnected alleyways. Our first stop was the extension agency, to humbly beg the privilege of another thirty days to enjoy Vietnam's hospitality.

"It's lunchtime," the doorman snapped. "Come back at two."

The afternoon siesta. A delightful custom, we told each other, characteristic of an easygoing people and a refreshing independence from the hurried pace of the modern-day world.

We returned on the dot of two. At three we were reluctantly permitted entry. At four we were allowed to speak to an office boy who was diligently straightening paper clips for no apparent reason. "Mr. Tuan's not here," he said without looking up. "Come back tomorrow."

A busy man, we remarked, no doubt essential to the smooth operation of the office. We made a note to call ahead.

The next morning we were there when the gates opened, hoping to be allowed to make the acquaintance of the busy Mr. Tuan. He didn't seem overjoyed to see us but was grudgingly pleased with the bottle of Johnny Walker Black Label, a small token of our appreciation for his coming efforts on our behalf.

He led us into his office and immediately claimed our passports. His face darkened as he leafed through my provincial extension stamps and read the handwritten caveats and cautions penned in by suspicious officials. I nudged the whiskey into a more prominent position on the table.

He closed my passport with an audible snap and rearranged his face into the universal expression of all third-world government officials: half-lidded eyes that could spot a guilty stain on the left wing of a housefly, lips compressed and sagging at the ends. "You must provide copies of your plane tickets," he told us at length, "to prove that you are returning to your home of origin in thirty days."

Very understandable, we assured him, only Jochen wasn't leaving by plane and my ticket was open-ended.

"And," he continued implacably, "official registration forms stamped by every hotel you have frequented since your arrival in Vietnam, signed and countersigned by the manager and owner."

I squeaked a little on that one, thinking of tire shops and sugarcane fields, until Jochen stomped firmly on my foot.

Mr. Tuan returned to his desk and slipped our passports into a drawer in case we should attempt to flee the country without his permission, and handed me a thick sheath of papers. "You must fill out three copies of each form," he announced. "Typed." I ran my eyes down the headings. They were all in Vietnamese. We gathered up our paperwork before he could invent any further requirements and left, promising to return on the morrow with his every wish fulfilled.

The plane ticket was easy. I penciled in the appropriate departure date, photocopied it on a wheezing prewar copier, and touched up the results with a smear of cornstarch. With a few minor corrections, Jochen became eligible for a coach-class flight to America, although upon closer inspection his seat looked a tad crowded with both of us in it.

I next tackled the paperwork and spent a tedious afternoon battling my way through a convoluted morass of bureaucratic officialese. The first page slyly requested my passport number in six different places in the hopes of catching me in an outright fabrication. Scattered throughout the forms were cleverly worded questions intent on tricking me into revealing several different nationalities and dates of birth. It proceeded like a well-rehearsed interrogation, at first deceptively simple (name? date?), then gently sympathetic (parents deceased? when?), becoming overtly incredulous (if parents deceased, living where?), and ending with a brilliant coup de grace (overt purpose of visit? covert purpose?) designed to take full advantage of several hours of logic deprivation. It was an unmistakable masterpiece of obfuscation, and I made every effort to make my responses equally obscure.

Jochen, meanwhile, had been wrestling with our final obstacle, the nonexistent hotel registration forms. The answer was unexpectedly straightforward. He suggested that we simply approach our present guest-house owner for a stamp and signature, then change the dates to include our entire stay in Vietnam. Problem solved.

The owner was not impressed. "Of course such a stamp exists," she told us, "but I don't have one." Such luxuries were available only at official foreign hotels, places that were willing to fork over half their foreign revenue to the government. She operated a simple, unofficial pension, had come to an agreement with the local law enforcement agency, and never advertised. That was why she took people like us, she sniffed, cheap travelers who did their laundry in the bathroom sink and found their lodgings through word of mouth. She looked us over suspiciously. If we were having paperwork problems then she would thank us to pack our bags and take ourselves elsewhere until our business was resolved.

We escaped with our room reservations barely intact and retreated to a nearby soup shop to discuss our options. Jochen was by this time reconsidering his plan to visit the Mekong in favor of a quick getaway to user-friendly Malaysia, but misery loves company, and I begged him to put off his decision until I had prevailed upon one of the fancier hotels to donate a moment of their stamp's unofficial time and a smear of ink. I chose the New World Hotel, a two-hundred-dollar-a-night extravaganza of chandeliers and layered doormen. The staff, who had never before met a white Vietnamese speaker, gathered around. I decided to come clean with my problem, throw myself upon their mercy, and trust the national addiction for exploiting yet another government-inspired niche market. They commiserated with my predicament, expressed astonishment that so clever a solution could come from anything as foolish as a foreigner, and cheerfully handed over the stamp in return for a crisp five-dollar bill. They were happy. I was happy. The government got the paperwork it wanted. Problem solved.

The next morning we returned to the extension office weighed down with photocopies of every aspect of our lives, both real and imagined. I had taken the precaution of falsifying an international driver's license and marriage certificate and felt prepared to meet any reasonable request head on. Mr. Tuan merely frowned, took our papers and a brick-size stack of local currency, and told us to come back in three days to pick up our extensions. It was almost a letdown. We trailed out the door.

On our way home we inadvertently motored past the exotic animal market. The cavernous, gloomy shed brought back a flood of memories. A tiny leopard cub with tufty ears clinging to a pint-size baby macaque. A blue-winged bird, perched on the verge of freedom, dragged down to cage-bound eternity. That hollow, empty feeling, watching bedraggled animals pace back and forth behind filthy bars.

But this time things were different. I wouldn't have to wander helplessly among the cages wishing there was something I could do—because there was. I could buy them and take them to Cuc Phuong.

Jochen argued, rightfully, that purchasing endangered animals would only encourage the black market trade. He had a point, but I thought the situation in Vietnam had moved beyond the possibility of educating the population before there were no longer any animals to protect. Even Tilo agreed that their only future was extinction in the wild, with possible repopulation from captivity once the poaching pressure was removed. Shouldn't we be siphoning away as many animals as we could, to increase the captive gene pool and their ultimate chance for survival? A flourishing animal trade was already in place. We weren't encouraging it as much as we were depriving one more wealthy Chinese gentleman of a placebo tonic for his unfortunate arthritis.

Jochen agreed to accompany me inside but repeated his objection to my crackpot scheme. I didn't try to change his mind. I simply hoped, when the time came, that he would help me load a few orphans on the train before he rode south into the Mekong.

The market was as dark and dirty as I remembered it. I trolled for gibbons, ducking behind hide-filled counters and muttering discreetly to perspiring proprietors, and eventually a tiny infant appeared. It was snowy white and soft as a merino lamb, with large round eyes and implausibly long arms and legs. Jochen put aside his camera to come and see. The gibbon extended a tentative arm and wrapped his tiny hand around Jochen's equally cautious finger. In a moment they were snuggled in a corner, the infant clinging to his shirt with all its might while he stroked its head and murmured gentle German endearments.

I wandered over. "Does this mean you'll help me put them on the train?" I asked.

"I'm going with you," he said softly. "We'll take as many as we can."

I scoured the market for more gibbons, without success. I returned to the stall where Jochen had finally torn himself away from the clinging baby. Too late. The owner had noted the entire interaction with an appraising eye.

"How much?" I asked. Two hundred was the going rate. "Two thousand dollars." She smiled sweetly. "Cash."

I banished Jochen to the stall with tiger hides and snakeskin belts, a safer place for his soft heart, and negotiated in earnest. The price dropped in painful fits and starts, and lodged at $260. She had other buyers, she said, five Chinese businessmen who were happy to pay what she asked. I conferred with Jochen and we agreed to play it safe and check our visa status one more time before buying the infant. Besides, if we called her bluff on the Chinamen nonsense, then she would have to lower her prices.

We left with heavy hearts.

(e   (e   (e

The next morning Jochen and I were both up early and prowling the streets around the visa office long before it opened its doors. Mr. Tuan was, as usual, delighted to see us. He nodded stiffly. "They will be ready this afternoon," he said, and shut the gate firmly in our faces. We raced back to the market.

The infant gibbon was nowhere to be seen. Its former owner shrugged and wiggled her hand. "The Chinamen came back," she said. She waited for the disappointment to sink in. "But I have another . . ."

It was indeed a different baby, younger than the first. It sat in the middle of its steel cage, its long arms wrapped around itself, sucking mightily on the wrinkled skin just above its elbow. It whistled in terror when the proprietor tried to drag it out, its eyes widening and its arms clinging tightly to its own body. It made no effort to grab hold of Jochen's shirt, and I noticed a bloody spot on each arm where it had chewed off its fur in psychotic distress.

I left Jochen to check out the rest of the market, and this time met with more success. Four gibbons were expected in the city that afternoon and would be China-bound by freighter the following morning. We could have them if we paid cash up front. I returned to find Jochen trying to coax the downy infant into sucking on the end of a banana, and began the tedious process of negotiating. The implicit competition from the incoming gibbons brought down the price, and soon we were offered the bargain-basement deal of $180 for one of the last remaining Vietnamese gibbons in the world.

"We should wait until we have our visas," Jochen insisted as he rocked the frightened infant. I went through the motions of arguing with him, knowing that an infantry platoon couldn't pry him away from his tiny charge. Turnover in the marketplace was so quick, I pointed out, that if we waited another day, this one would probably be sold. Jochen agreed.

"In that case," I said, "I'll be back." I dashed off and returned a few minutes later with my own arms full of three young leopard cats and a two-month-old clouded leopard cub. Leopards eat gibbons, Jochen pointed out. We reluctantly purchased two of the hateful steel-bar cages. Then we looked at our small mountain of cages and animals and wondered how on earth we were going to get them back to our guest house.

Jochen slalomed expertly through rush-hour traffic while I balanced precariously on the back of his bike, trying to look nonchalant with four restless leopards stuffed inside my jacket and a gibbon under one arm. I closed my eyes and gritted my teeth against the casually gripping claws and tried to savor a unique moment that might never come again. A catfight erupted under my breasts.

We smuggled them up the guest-house stairs and into my room. The leopards quickly disappeared under the bureau. Jochen left for the post office to call Tilo and ask just what a baby gibbon might be expected to eat. I stayed behind to turn an old sock into a protective covering for its swollen arms. He returned with a tin of baby formula, an armful of bananas, and instructions to administer both by eyedropper every two hours, day and night. We fed them until their bellies were round and they gurgled with contentment. Once they were comfortable—the monkey lying among a half dozen soft toys and the leopards curled up like hairballs under the bed—we snuck away to visit Mr. Tuan and retrieve our passports.

The gate was locked and the windows shuttered. The office boy eventually responded to the rattling chain by sticking his head out the door and squinting into the sunlight. He approached, flourishing our passports, and handed them to us through the narrow bars. "No visa," he said loudly. "Reject."

"You're kidding," I said, flipping through the pages.

"That's not possible," Jochen managed.

"Reject! Reject!" the young man shouted and waved his hands about in illustration.

Our old visas were due to run out in twenty-four hours. Neither Cambodia nor Laos would accept us on such short notice. I tried pointing this out.

"One day! You leave! Good-bye!" He walked away, still windmilling his arms. We stood behind the gate and stared at his retreating back. The door closed firmly behind him.

We wandered into a small cafe and sat in silence over several cups of coffee. "It's not possible," Jochen said again. Vietnamese ingenuity had clearly exceeded the orderly limits of his mind. I wasn't much better off. Our circular thoughts were temporarily derailed by Jochen's budding maternal instincts when an internal alarm reminded him it was time for the gibbon to be fed. We hurried back to the guest house.

The leopards were still tucked into the darkest corner of the room, sleeping off their first good meal of milk. The gibbon had shredded everything within reach and returned to her favorite pastime, chewing wrinkly holes in her arms. With great difficulty I convinced Jochen to put the smallest leopard cub, barely the size of a fluffy softball, into the cage with her. I remembered the similar pairing I had seen in the animal market; the mismatched orphans had been a comfort to each other.

Not so with these two. Sabine, as Jochen had christened the baby gibbon, seemed determined to take revenge on the hapless kitten for the predatory habits of its entire species. She made full use of her long arms, rapping the leopard on the nose and tweaking his ears and tail. When this didn't make enough of an impression, she pushed him against one wall and leaned on him with all her insubstantial weight, trying to squish him through the bars. This time I was the one who objected, though Sabine seemed quite pleased with her new toy. The kitten went back under the bed, and Sabine was given a knotted rag to torment.

We climbed wearily back onto the motorbike to make a run on the Cambodian embassy for an entry permit. When we arrived the embassy guard smiled and opened the door for us. We were immediately called into an office, where we were introduced to a smiling Buddha in a coat and tie who bade us sit and politely requested our passports. He leafed through them, asked a few questions, then pulled out some paperwork and began to fill it out. It can't be this easy, I thought as I watched his pen race across the page. It was almost a relief when I saw his brow wrinkled with concern. "The Vietnamese government has assigned you Ho Chi Minh City as your port of exit," he informed me. "Have you already bought a ticket? The flights are often full."

I shook my head. His hand hovered over the phone. "I would be happy to call the airline," he said, "and make sure you have a seat." My jaw dropped open.

"I plan to go by bus," I told him meekly. "I'll change the exit point to the overland border before I leave."

He considered for a moment. "What should I write?" he asked, then brushed away the problem with a flick of his wrist. "I'll just leave it blank, and you can fill it in at your convenience." My jaw fell another notch.

In five minutes he was finished. He stood to hand us back our passports. "Your visas will be ready in two hours," he said. "You may collect them anytime." My jaw hit the floor with a solid thunk.

We thanked him and left in a daze, wondering whether the Cambodians were from a different galaxy than the Vietnamese. The mystery was cleared up by an Englishman awaiting his turn in the foyer. "Some Westerners just got shot by Khmer guerrillas," he told us. "The Cambodian government's trying like hell to get the tourists to come back."

Time was running out. We raced over to the nearest Vietnamese tourist agency to change my exit stamp. The wait was endless and the chairs were hard, and the woman who eventually took my passport was indifferent to my pleas. To change the stamp would take a week, she said. I asked for the heavy-duty, no-holds-barred, extortionately priced rush service advertised on the wall. Five days, she said.

We rushed back to the visa extension office, to appeal to their previously untapped altruism in the hopes that they might provide us with a five-day extension. After all, if the damned Mr. Tuan hadn't kept our passports for so long, we wouldn't be in this predicament in the first place.

The office boy slouched out to see who was pleading at the gate. "Closed now!" he said through the bars.

"But it's only three o'clock," we argued.

"Closed!" he shouted, cranking up the volume once again. We begged.

"Passports," he said, and held out a hand. We fled.

It was time to feed the gibbon. On our way home we passed a Western woman in a long skirt, stiffly upright on a one-speed bike. Jochen throttled back and cruised along beside her.

"Excuse me," I said. "Do you like cats?"

She seemed taken aback. I swallowed my pride and explained our predicament, playing down the mischievous claws and midnight feedings, while Jochen swerved around pedestrians and ice cream carts to keep pace. "Would you be willing," I concluded, "to take care of a few very tiny leopards for a week while we arrange for a new visa in Cambodia?"

"*Certainment pas!*" she said, her body stiffening on the already unstable bicycle. "I work for the French Embassy. Such a thing would be illegal!"

"So is the animal black market," I pointed out, "which nevertheless is advertised in your tourist guidebook." But the Embassy was no longer listening. Head held high, skirt swishing, she pedaled off in a straight, matronly line. We returned home to our unwanted orphans.

I left Jochen to pre-chew a quarter-pound of meat and mix up a tasty banana and baby formula shake and sped off to Vietnam Airlines to buy a ticket to Cambodia. The line was long, the ticketing agent brief. "We're booked out," she said. "Nothing until next week."

I dragged myself up the stairs, stupefied with exhaustion and gritty-mouthed with city soot. I unlatched the door and two pint-size kittens launched themselves at my ankles. As I stooped to scoop them up, a hearty voice call out from inside the room. "Karin! Good to see you!" It wasn't Jochen. It was Jay.

He had decided to come south after all, he told me, as he stretched himself out on the only comfortable piece of furniture in the room—my bed. "Aren't you glad to see me?"

"Where is Jochen?" I asked, wondering whether the gibbon had been fed.

"What *is* all this garbage about the animals?" He brushed imaginary hairs off his shirt. "You know I'm allergic to cats."

I sat down to mash some bananas into monkey food. "I'm afraid I won't be around for very long," I told him over my shoulder. He listened to my visa dilemmas, and their conclusion, with rising indignation.

"But what about me?" he demanded, sitting up abruptly. "I come all the way to Saigon and you tell me you're leaving in the morning?" He shook his head. "Don't expect me to follow you to Cambodia. Or hang around waiting for you to come back." He leaned back to see what I would do.

I left. I ran into Jochen parking his motorbike in the courtyard. He had just returned from the home of a Vietnamese professor from Hanoi, a woman of thoroughly Western ways who had given him carte blanche to call on her if he ever needed help in Saigon.

"Not a chance," he said. She had agreed, albeit reluctantly, to store the animals in her garage provided they didn't need to be fed more than once a day. We had to find a Westerner. Perhaps, Jochen suggested, Jay would be willing to take care of them until we got back.

"Not a chance," I said. There were Westerners and there were Westerners. But I, too, had a connection, even more tenuous than his. I knew that Mobil Oil had an office on the second floor of a nearby hotel. If we could get an introduction into the expatriate community . . .

The office was far too posh for our bedraggled clothes. The doorman protested with every muscle in his face when he stepped aside to let us in. The president was intimidating in his starched shirt and shiny shoes, but his handshake was strong and he made us welcome. I suddenly didn't know where to begin.

He listened in silence as Jochen spun our tale, then scratched his chin thoughtfully. "Now if you'd just come for money it would've been easy," he said with a small laugh. "How many leopards did you say you had?"

He gave us the names of a few likely expatriate hangouts and promised, with another chuckle and a shake of his head, to ask his wife if she would be willing to take on our orphan charges.

We split our forces, Jochen plying his golden tongue among the upper-crust expats while I cruised the backpacker hangouts in the forlorn hope of finding a generous spirit willing to take charge of our menagerie.

Kim Cafe was overcrowded, the chatter of a dozen languages mingling with smoke and unwashed bodies under the harsh fluorescent lights. Everyone, it seemed, was discussing tours and travel plans. The few conversations I dropped in on weren't promising. A Danish nutritionist on her way to Dalat by minibus the following morning, giving detailed advice to a pair of shaggy Australians who planned to take a slow boat down the Mekong. A French couple in a tight huddle at the end of a crowded table, exhaling clouds of smoke and wanting only to be left alone. I stood and tapped my glass with a spoon. No one paid the slightest attention. I sent a brief prayer for forgiveness to the gods of the jungle and pulled the smallest leopard kitten out of my pocket. All conversation stopped. Even the French couple lent a covert ear.

They heard me out in utter silence, every eye fixed on the ball of fur nestled in the palm of my hand. Then, like an auction, people raised their hands with dates and places, and had soon forgotten me to pass the leopard kitten from lap to lap and organize its social calendar for the next few weeks. A brawny German was utterly captivated by the tiny kitten nestled in the crook of his bulging biceps and immediately canceled his intended visit to the famous Cu Chi tunnels, or "ze dirty, veasel holes in ze ground," as they had suddenly become. An English carpenter was returning from a Mekong tour in three days and would be happy to host the little dust mops for the weekend. If his guest-house owner didn't approve, she could jolly well find a new boarder. Two unkempt Canadians promised the orphans a permanent home in their awesome new digs, available a week hence.

I sat off to one side and watched a miracle gradually unfold. People who would haggle for hours over a fifty-cent discount, who had scrimped and saved for years to see Vietnam, were fighting for the opportunity to give it all up on behalf of a sleepy ball of fur.

"It's not so surprising," a voice said in my ear. "You've given them the opportunity to do something extraordinary. That's worth a few tourist traps." He was American, scraping by teaching private English classes while he looked for more permanent work. "Will you be buying more?" he asked, and handed me a hundred-dollar bill.

My room was momentarily silent. The gibbon lay fast asleep, its long arms wrapped around a pillow twice as large as itself. The two youngest kittens were quiet after hours of entertaining antics. Unlike their older brethren, they actively courted human contact, lying in wait until I came out of the shower and playing Tarzan with my bath towel until I gave up trying to hold it in place. For the first time in my life the monsters under the bed were real, and when I put my bare feet down a playful set of claws wrapped itself around my ankle. As I drifted off to sleep, I felt a feather-soft tail across my face and four tiny paws kneading a depression on my pillow.

I floated up through layered dreams to the rapid pitter-patter of rats running across the roof beams. I awoke to find that they had turned into leopards, dancing on the carpet. I watched their shadowy forms slither around my pack and burst into a pool of moonlight, where they pranced and sparred. I fell asleep to the cottony thud of velvet paws and dreamed of jungle nights, of braided vines and dark green leaves, and mottled shapes that flowed from space to space.

The next morning—a wild, worried rush to the airport, standby on an empty flight, and I found myself sitting next to two sleek businessmen from another planet. They chatted loudly about the stock market, the NBA results, and their favorite ski resorts in Aspen. I looked out the window at the earth-brown Mekong flowing smoothly toward the sea and tried to remember why I had been so afraid when I first flew over this strange and complicated land.

I heard the man beside me say, "It's an opportunity, there's no doubt about that, but it won't be easy." And I thought, *You have no idea.*

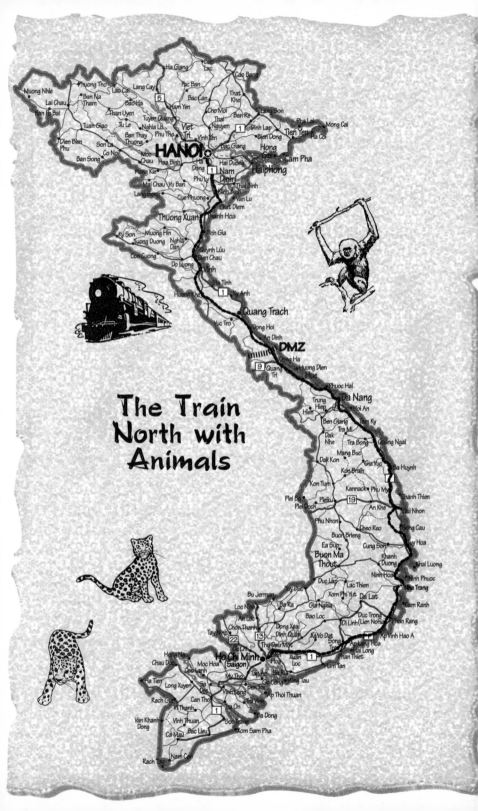

The Train
North with
Animals

Dear Mum,
The eagle's talons pierced my thick leather gloves
like tissue paper. His wing feathers are completely
tattered from scraping against the sides of his cage.
If you had ever been in a hang glider you would
understand why it was necessary to buy him.

The Traveling Menagerie

Jochen and I returned to Vietnam in the most incongruous
of vehicles—an ancient, wheezing taxi. They congregated
like vultures around the bus station, waiting to take up the
slack when buses were crammed full. We bargained hard for a
place on the torn plastic seats and congratulated ourselves on
the final price—until the driver cranked his engine to life and
five Cambodians crowded in beside us. The driver cheerfully
munched on roasted baby birds at all the ferry stops and
inhaled endless homemade cigarettes. In all ways he was a
fine, upstanding fellow . . . until he got behind the wheel. He
drove as though he wanted wings for Christmas and was quite
prepared to earn them, either by a spontaneous breakthrough
in rocket science or via a more traditional path, bestowed
upon him by the good St. Peter.

We arrived in Ho Chi Minh City thick-witted with eight
hours of airless heat, abraded from gritty dirt and delighted, in

the most shamefully parental way, to see our animals again. We immediately examined them for signs of growth, character development, and most importantly, whether they were glad to see us.

The gibbon had acquired a new tailor and looked quite dapper in her protective shirt. The two youngest kittens were slowly losing their octopuslike gait from calcium deficiency. The oldest leopard, subjected to six long weeks of black market abuse, was still most comfortable under the bed. He now felt confident enough to defend his space, and when I took the liberty of scooping him up, he let out such a reverberating roar that I immediately set him down again. Since he was small enough to fit inside one of my larger pockets, his newly voiced opinion was as surprising as an elephant's bugle emerging from the depths of a medium-size mouse.

Jochen left to spend the day negotiating for gibbons and returned to tell me that he was expecting a substantial payoff the very next morning. We agreed to make a clean sweep of the animal market and be on the train by nightfall, heading for Cuc Phuong.

The following morning we arrived well prepared, our pockets stuffed with thick bricks of Vietnamese currency, bananas, and baby formula. The turnout wasn't quite what we had hoped for—one gibbon with a badly cut hand—but we were repeatedly assured that seven more would be available by early afternoon. We could afford only five, maybe six if we bargained well. We reluctantly agreed to reject the damaged infant in favor of more healthy stock.

I gave the baby gibbon back, but not before an older man with a gray-streaked beard had snapped a dozen photos. He was, it turned out, the director of the Berlin Zoo and his name was Wolfgang. He was on a whirlwind tour of Southeast Asia, and his itinerary had already included a visit to Cuc Phuong. He seemed pleased that we were bringing Tilo animals and assured me that they would find a good home in his breeding program. I drifted back along the cages, hoping for another clouded leopard. A piercing whistle stopped me dead. My feet followed my ears, and I found myself once again looking into the unblinking yellow eyes of a serpent crested eagle. It was the same bird I had seen so many months ago, its wings still impossibly tattered and its tail a ratty stump. The cage was also the same, although the eagle had grown and now had a bald spot on its head where it rubbed endlessly against the top bars. It stared at me defiantly, then returned to tearing at a strip of beef held in its two-inch talons.

I sidled up to Wolfgang. "How would Tilo feel," I inquired casually, "about taking on an eagle?"

Wolfgang shrugged. "Ah, Tilo, his heart is so big, he vill never say no."

Ten minutes later the eagle, in a substantially larger cage, was waiting to be transferred to my guest-house room.

Jochen was back with the gibbon, his face clearly indicating his second thoughts about leaving it at the mercy of the marketplace. I pulled out some money.

An agitated wave swept through the stalls. It had no apparent origin but created a sudden burst of activity. Snoozing owners leaped to their feet and began plucking animals out of cages and removing bear galls from display cases. The proprietor snatched the gibbon out of Jochen's arms, popped it into a rattan bag, and quickly lashed it to the back of an already departing motorbike. "Police!" she hissed at me and shooed us away from her stall. Within minutes the market had undergone a complete animal turnover, replacing toucans with sparrows, gibbons with dog-faced macaques, and a long-tongued bear cub with a full-grown porcupine.

The rumored raid never materialized. The market gradually settled down, like a flock of seagulls re-alighting after a passing shark. The gibbon proprietor bore down on me with murder in her eyes. "Your friend!" she hissed, "The old man! He from newspaper! Take pictures! Call in police!"

I tried to assure her that Wolfgang had no connection with either the police or the local press, but the damage was done. The injured gibbon had disappeared, hidden somewhere in the bowels of the city. The other seven infants were no longer "under way." I asked her when we could continue negotiations.

"Come back at four," she said, somewhat mollified by the thought of a future sale. "They be here for you then."

Caretaking up to seven gibbons, an eagle, and four leopard kittens was more than our tiny guest-house room could handle. We were determined to be on the evening train, to minimize the amount of time the vulnerable infants had to spend between the market and the breeding program. We split our forces once again, with Jochen gathering our gear while I headed for the train station to purchase tickets.

The station was an enormous chamber wrapped in layer upon layer of satellite industries: women hawking processed food, hotel agents scaring up new customers, motorbikes for hire, and a few scattered taxis.

I examined the daily schedules and approached the nearest teller. Half an hour later I was still wandering from one window to the next, never quite being allowed to buy a ticket. At last I was directed to the tourist desk, where they would know to charge me the official foreign price of three times the published rate. The woman behind the counter was brisk.

"You will take train S-3," she said in English, pulling out a pad of blank tickets. I checked the schedule. S-3 arrived at Cuc Phuong in the wee hours of the morning. I objected.

"S-6 then," she said, annoyed but still polite.

S-6, I pointed out, had left an hour ago and wouldn't be returning for another run until next Thursday.

"There are no other trains," she snapped.

S-8 was leaving shortly after dark, I suggested, and had the additional advantages of being fast and relatively cheap.

"Military train," she snarled. "No foreigners allowed."

Then why, I asked, were the S-8 rates quoted in U.S. dollars under headings written in English?

"That train is always empty," she insisted. "It would be dangerous for you to travel in it unprotected."

My heart leaped. With our illegal cargo, an empty train was exactly what we were looking for. I assured her I would be well protected by my two strapping young male companions and an assortment of well-armed acquaintances.

"S-8 doesn't go every day," she said.

"But today," I said, waving the schedule, "it goes."

"It's very slow."

Only twenty minutes slower than its brother the express train, a trivial difference over the course of a forty-four-hour trip.

"It doesn't stop at Cuc Phuong," she insisted. "You will have to go on to Thanh Hoa."

I thought it over. Cuc Phuong was indeed on the schedule, but if it made her happy we could buy an extra stop and jump off early. I agreed.

She seemed nonplused, but rallied quickly. "You will not be allowed to disembark until the train has reached its final destination in Hanoi," she said. We could then reboard for Thanh Hoa when S-8 made the return trip, twenty-four hours later.

I shook my head. She glared at me. We had reached an impasse.

"I must have words with my boss," she said, and started to rise. I knew she wouldn't come back until I had given up and left the station.

"Yeah, me too," I agreed, and stood up with her.

"He does not speak English," she informed me smugly.

"No English? No problem," I shot back in Vietnamese. She stared at me in surprise, then sat. "Passport?" she asked, holding out her hand. I had won.

I tried to be gracious. "Three tickets please, and thank you for your help."

"Three?" Her plastic smile turned feral. "Three passports please."

I had only mine. It had never occurred to me that we might need passports to travel from one city to another within Vietnam.

"No passports? No tickets." Her ticket pad closed with a snap and was quickly locked back in its drawer. "Come back later."

There wasn't time to cruise the city in search of Jay and Jochen. With no options left, I got loud. When that failed I resolutely climbed the steps to the second-floor offices.

"It's lunchtime," she called after me. "No one home."

I didn't even hesitate.

"I sell you tickets," she said in a defeated voice. I was back in my seat before she had unlocked the drawer. "You write the other passport numbers," she insisted, pushing a large ledger toward me.

I nodded and began to scribble random combinations. Jochen got my Nissan license plate and my phone number, Jay my mother's birth date and my bank personal identification number. She pulled the heavy binder back. "You must return before six o'clock to present your passports," she told me curtly. I nodded in deference to the face-saving ritual. She wrote out the tickets and handed them to me. Two were in one six-bunk sleeper, the third two cars away. I objected.

"Nothing to do," she said, and closed the ticket book a final time. "We only sell two seats per sleeper. The others are filled in Hue."

Hue, I thought, is halfway there. I can make a deal with the conductor long before then. I rose to go.

Jochen and I met at the animal market on the dot of four. Not a single gibbon had made the rendezvous. A full-blown police raid had swept through an hour earlier, and the market was in self-imposed lockdown. "Come back to-morrow," one of the stall owners said, and waved us away. We huddled. Our train tickets had cost hundreds of dollars and the possibility of a refund was looking grim. In desperation we inquired after the injured gibbon, hidden somewhere in the city.

"Far away. One hundred kilometers," the woman said. "Come back tomorrow."

Tomorrow was too late. We sadly packed up our animals and left Saigon.

The six-bunk sleepers had shrunk enormously since my last encounter with them at Lao Cai. Four cages, backpacks, and two days of food for nine hungry mouths filled almost every available space. A passing conductor bent over to peer through our torn curtain and came roaring through the door, spoiling for a fight. I froze and scanned our gear. The cages were well camouflaged but emitting the curious scratching sounds I had come to associate with leopards in need of entertainment. If the eagle let rip one of his shrill whistles, the entire train from end to end would know what we were carrying. Despite the permission papers I'd had made up, complete with fake official stamps, we were still smuggling illegal contraband. If the conductor discovered our animals, he would either confiscate the lot or simply dump them out the window.

We talked loudly. Jochen hummed the German anthem under his breath. I crumpled and uncrumpled a letter I had been writing. The conductor inadvertently helped our cause by shouting and pacing back and forth in front of us. Why were there three people in the compartment with only two tickets, he demanded. The odd man out, unfortunately, was Jochen. He was quickly made to disappear.

Could we, I asked cautiously, switch Jochen's bunk for Jay's for the duration of the journey?

Absolutely not.

Could Jochen return to visit us from time to time if the other bunks remained unfilled?

Completely out of the question. And further, where were we planning to sleep ourselves? The top two wooden slats, our assigned bunks, were lined with gear.

The other four bunks were empty, I pointed out. Perhaps we could make use of . . .

"Forbidden," the conductor snapped.

The floor, I suggested quickly. We could spread a blanket . . .

"Forbidden."

If necessary, I lied, we could share a single bunk . . .

It would most certainly break under so much weight, the conductor insisted with painful candor. He left us with orders to condense our yards of gear into a few square feet and store it in the alcove over the door. I spent the next hour experimenting with new iterations of the ancient corn-fox-duck game, trying to fit a gibbon, eagle, and leopards into a tiny space without allowing a razor beak to make contact with a careless tail, or curious fingers to pluck feathers from an already balding crown.

The hours passed to the swaying rhythm of the tracks and frantic, covert feedings in the dead of night. The leopards, responding to their healthy diet, developed surprising energy. The infant gibbon needed as much love as food. With Jochen banished from our carriage, the task of feeding, cleaning, and entertaining an increasingly unruly crowd fell to me. I hung towels from the middle bunks to create a kitten jungle gym and discovered, way too late, that eagles instinctively direct their streams of excrement outside their nests to keep from soiling their own space. The compartment gradually shrank as eight unwashed bodies competed for both space and air. The growing stench of uncouth cats now added to our risk of getting caught. From time to time I experimented with an open window, but the memory of Tilo's tales of baby gibbons catching cold at dusk and dying before dawn kept us largely sealed in tight.

Halfway through the second day we crossed the DMZ, and the sun abruptly disappeared. I glanced out the window and saw a landscape grim and dreary. During my southern month in the liquid heat of Ho Chi Minh City, I had conveniently forgotten the cold and wet I'd left behind in the north. The temperature dropped twenty degrees in as many minutes, and the compartment went from hot and airless to frigid and damp. Nothing dried, not the towel I had rinsed and hung out the window overnight nor the bedraggled kitten who had fallen into her water dish and now lay snoozing like a soggy ball of yarn against my ribs.

I woke up the final morning to find the eagle shivering in the bitter cold. The last of my socks were sacrificed to make overcoats for the kittens. The gibbon took up permanent residence in a sling around my neck. Six more hours. The final countdown had begun.

We were just thirty kilometers short of our destination when a furious hammering signaled yet another visit from our unfriendly conductor. This time he was flanked by two evil-looking army types. I could hear him through the door, loudly cataloging our orphan cargo, their market value, and our apparent destination. I panicked, whipped off several layers of clothing, and let them catch a glimpse of one bare shoulder through the curtain before calling out that I was still sleeping, could they please return in half an hour? Bless their Buddhist hearts, they withdrew gracefully and the race to Cuc Phuong began. I realized they were expecting us to disembark at Thanh Hoa, a half-hour's ride beyond Cuc Phuong, due to our unexpectedly helpful Saigon ticket agent.

Cuc Phuong station pulled into view and we exited with military precision, tossing packs and cages out the window and clambering out behind them. When the train pulled away my relief was quickly replaced by a growing sense of unease. The station was deserted. We stood shivering on the grassy embankment, grainy-eyed with lack of sleep and surrounded by far more baggage than we could carry.

At last we heard a distant hail and there was Tilo, standing by his Mekong van, with Manuela by his side. I nearly fell into his arms. He nearly knocked me into the gutter in his haste to see which cage held the infant gibbon. She disappeared at once inside Manuela's jacket while Jochen watched, a helpless look of displaced motherhood etched across his face. Tilo glanced at the other cages, picked them up, and walked away without a word. The two were halfway back to the van before it occurred to us that we were being left behind. We scooped up our packs and gave chase and caught them just in time to be grudgingly offered rides into the park.

I listened to them discussing the fate of my beloved bird and kittens in their muttered German. Wolfgang had been somewhat optimistic in his assessment of Tilo's willingness to take on strays. The eagle he had no use for. The leopard kittens would go to a convenient new arrival, a Ph.D. student by the name of Sheila who was doing research on civets and had some experience with wild cats.

We helped unload. As I put the eagle down, he let out an inquiring squawk that sent the nearby langur cage into a frenzy of activity. Tilo immediately ordered the unruly bird back into the car. I scooped up my unwanted cargo of cats and made off in search of the mysterious Sheila, in the forlorn hope of a less wintry reception.

I knocked on her guest-house door, the leopard cage behind my back, wondering what on earth to say. In the end there was no need for words. Her eyes opened wide at the sight of the little kittens, and next I knew they were disappearing inside her zipped-up jacket. She rummaged through her things and emerged triumphant, flourishing a tiny baby bottle complete with rubber nipple.

"It's been too long since I've shared my bed with cats," she said as she fished a kitten out of the depths of her bosom and applied the bottle. I glanced over at her single bed and wondered where *she* was going to sleep once they grew up, but wisely kept my questions to myself.

To my surprise another Westerner soon plowed through the door. She was a plump young London girl called Emma, who had been hired to teach English to the staff. She took one look at the bedraggled eagle and immediately took possession. Her first act as eagle owner was to sit down with pad and pencil to come up with a suitable name—Polonius. That done, she dashed off to write to several friends about her exotic acquisition. She returned at feeding time to undertake a death-defying attempt at handing him some meat, having first donned a pair of heavy motorcycle gloves and helmet. She didn't strike me as the best caretaker the world had to offer, but my plans to lodge the eagle in the unfinished monkey cages had been dashed by their proximity to the langurs. I hoped to build a small but comfortable cage for the two remaining months of cold and then return to rehabilitate him in the park come spring.

Emma was all business, dividing up the sleeping space on the floor for Jochen and Jay, reserving me for her room in case her eagle, henceforth to be referred to only by his given name, should need my services in the dead of night. As to the cage I planned to build—the staff adored her, she informed me briskly. She had only to snap her fingers and it would be done, complete with heating lamp and self-feeding tray. I was impressed.

The next morning I bid Jochen farewell. His flight departed Saigon a few days hence, and he had yet to sell the motorbike that had transported him so faithfully from Hanoi. He went to say a last good-bye to his tiny gibbon but found the way solidly blocked by the implacable Manuela. The infant, she said, was not to be disturbed.

It was a sad good-bye.

I returned to my room to find Emma eyeing the eagle cage with ill-concealed distaste. Polonius had, as all well-brought up birds are taught to do, declined to soil his immediate environment. A ring of well-aimed excrement splattered the tiled floor. Since Emma had not yet snapped her fingers, the outdoor cage was nowhere in sight. She was also clearly regretting her impulsive decision to claim the bird and roundly chewed me out as I cleaned up the mess. Who was I, she demanded hotly, to show up uninvited, upsetting schedules and disrupting delicate relationships?

The relationship in jeopardy, it turned out, was her own. The park director had taken her aside and made it clear that hosting me was denying the park hotel some income. Threatened with the loss of her privileged status, she bid me pack my bags. The eagle, though allowed to keep his name, was included in the expulsion order. "I have no time to build a cage," she told me airily. "You'll have to release him right away."

I pointed out that her beloved Polonius wouldn't survive his first cold night and probably couldn't fly with any accuracy, much less hunt, but she stood firm in her decision.

I wandered out into the chilly night, the eagle cage dangling from two fingers, feeling as unwanted as my orphans. The hotel charged larcenous rates for an unheated wooden cubicle with one malfunctioning bulb, no shower, and a toilet in another building. I couldn't afford to stay until spring thaw, and Tilo seemed unwilling to open the spare room reserved for visiting colleagues. I poked my head in Sheila's doorway and asked if she might keep the eagle warm for the night while I found a place to sleep. She kindly offered me her floor, with the whispered warning that Emma was not to know as she really did wield power among the staff and was therefore dangerous to cross. The eagle, she said, could spend the night in the heated storage shed nearby. We passed the evening sharing steaming bowls of chocolate and feeding the voracious kittens.

Sheila had arrived less than a month ago. She planned to stay for two years, doing research on the territoriality of a subspecies of the local civet population. Her meager grant money stretched just far enough to purchase a dozen radio collars. She showed me a carefully drawn plan detailing the construction of live traps. "I'm having them built nearby to help support local industry," she told me proudly. She was sure she could have twelve animals on radio within a few short months. She was enthusiastic, brimming with ideas and utterly, catastrophically wrong.

The only local industry her work would support was the poachers and their craft. Her daily rounds to visit traps would be duly noted and the animals "liberated" long before she returned. Once the idea caught on, the traps would be liberated as well. Why suffer through a long and fruitless hunt when the animals could be harvested from a convenient cage? And live, no less; they'd bring a premium on the Chinese market.

Worse still, her detailed drawings would teach the poachers to construct their own live traps. The new technology would spread like a contagious disease and devastate any species that carried a price upon its head.

I could read her future in my own past. In the Peace Corps I had been just as enthusiastic and sure of my ideas. I had caused untold damage in a Filipino village with a misplaced rice cooperative, a well-meant school, and sorely needed drinking wells.

But the collars had already been purchased, the cages designed, and the project's future determined. Perhaps, I thought as I drifted off to sleep to the purring of contented kittens, she might yet manage to tag a few endangered animals. Then when the locals shot them, Tilo could track down the carcasses and maybe even catch himself a poacher or two.

The next morning the station echoed with the inquiring hoots and whistles of the forlorn gibbons. Everyone had gone to Hanoi: Tilo, Manuela, Emma . . . and Polonius. A short note explained that the eagle would be given to the Bureau of Forestry to do with as they wished. A postscript in Emma's distinctive scrawl demanded that I make no further attempts to interfere.

When I returned to America I would undoubtedly unfurl my hang glider and once again set sail upon the wind, to swoop and soar as only birds were meant to do. I had seen a half-grown eagle with broken tail and balding head in the Saigon market, a defiant spirit who had known no life beyond a tiny cage and prodding fingers. I had wanted to give him a chance at flight, to spread his wings and feel the wind beneath them. Buying him had been an impulsive and foolish move. But more than anything I regretted the lost opportunity to release him to one long day of freedom, regardless of the consequences. He would never have that chance again.

Cuc Phuong held nothing for me now. I packed my bags and left.

22

Dear Mom,
Jay and I were comparing Moms the other day.
 "My mom," he said, "fixes houses."
 "My mom builds them."
 "My mom has a garden with 143 rose bushes."
 "My mom," I said, "grows 2-kilo tomatoes."
 "My mom paints."
 "My mom makes beautiful pottery worth millions of dollars."
 "My mom," he snapped, "wallpapers."
 "How big a pack can she carry?" I asked.
 "Twice as big as she is."
 "Peanuts!" I said. "Can she drive a motorbike?"
 "No," he admitted.
 I wasn't about to tell him you couldn't either.
Can you learn before you get here?

Despair

Hanoi had completely transformed itself with the advent of warmer weather. Its population emerged, bleary-eyed, from its winterlong hibernation and went about its business in the more spacious environs of the street. On every corner, women dangled long black hair into rusty buckets, attended to their toenails, scrubbed children and the evening's vegetables with equal energy, and spat copiously into the gutter. Music seeped through open windows, filling the air with the pulsating themes from *Flashdance, Hawaii 5-0*, and James Bond movies. The mobile brush man appeared in a dozen incarnations, each accompanied by a cart overflowing with handy implements to simplify spring cleaning. Mangy kittens with pus-filled eyes and life spans slightly shorter than the average dragonfly tumbled headfirst onto the street.

I hurried across town, all but oblivious to the sights and sounds around me. The only thing I wanted to see was that squat gray building beside the lake—the post office. I knew that somewhere among the general mail would be the answer to that all-important question—whether Mom was coming to visit me.

There were four envelopes this time. I hurried back down the street, struggling against the impulse to slide my finger under a corner of the first flap and inch it open. There it was, my noodle shop, just setting up for evening business. The old man smiled when he saw me and wordlessly swabbed out the wok to prepare my favorite dish. I sat in a corner seat and tried to make out the postmarks in the fading light. I had long ago done the numbers—three weeks for my letter to find its way from Hanoi to Virginia, a likely four-day turnaround, eighteen long days before the reply found its way into the slot market *M* at the Hanoi post office.

There it was. Somehow I knew exactly which one it would be. I wondered whether I should read the others first, but my fingers were already busy, and before I knew it my eyes were racing across the page. *The Hmong sound fascinating . . . lovely embroideries . . . hiking hut to hut . . . I spoke with Dad about coming to see you . . . Oh no . . . he wouldn't hear of it . . . he is so afraid of losing me . . . Nothing I could say would calm his fears. I had to choose.*

The last line burned itself into my soul. *I guess I'll just have to be an armchair traveler from now on.*

Mom not travel? Mom, who could spend endless hours exploring pond water under a microscope? I couldn't name a travel book she hadn't read. She was the only person I'd ever met who knew where Ilo-Ilo was. Not travel anymore? It wasn't possible. She was the one who sent me out to see the world. . . .

I folded up the letter and put it aside. The others could wait. I leaned back against the wall, wanting only to be alone. But there was no getting away from the pulsing heartbeat of the city, its sounds and smells.

I closed my eyes. In the distance I could hear the steady tap of wood on wood. Somewhere out there a young boy was cruising the streets, advertising soup for another stall. I had seen him before, trotting back and forth until the wee hours of the morning. Tonight he sounded tired.

When I opened my eyes a sticky sweetcake had appeared in front of me. The old man smiled and turned back to his wok. He must have seen my tears.

Other city sounds blended together into a background symphony. The bread seller hawked the last of her day's wares before resigning them to the rooftops. The ice cream man, still honking his two-tone horn to the pitter-patter of small feet. The tofu seller, who managed to stretch his one-word call into a seven-note, trilling melody. It had become strangely familiar—this exotic blend of Asian sounds.

I sat there until midnight, wishing that I could share it with her.

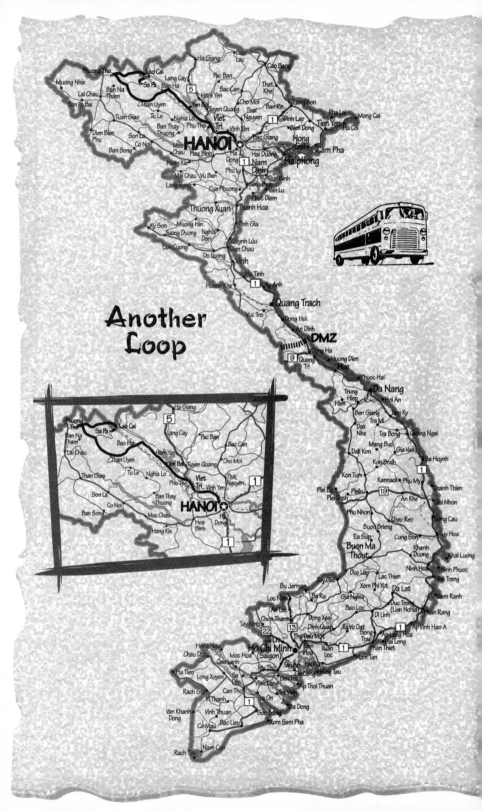

23

Dear Mom,
Halfway through the evening a one-legged man
hobbled into our mud hut and pulled a bloody
enormous ruby out of his pocket. It was, quite
literally, large enough to use as a doorstop.

The Burdensome Beast

I planned an extended loop through Sapa and across the Tonkinese Alps, past Dien Bien Phu, and back through the paddy delta to Hanoi, a rugged and mountainous 500 miles that would take at least three months. I tacked a note on a cafe message board, inquiring if there might be a motorbike for sale. A week went by with no response. Finally a time and date appeared at the bottom of my note, and an address in the old city. I hurried over—and found Jay. He had the perfect bike, he told me, reliable and roomy and guaranteed to crest the highest summit without breaking a sweat.

"The beast," I said, with less than overwhelming enthusiasm.

"The beast," he agreed, but magically transformed by the gurus of 73 Fu Dong Street. They had replaced the shorting spark-plug wires, welded the broken kick starter and the tottering stand, renewed the chain and cables, charged the battery, fixed the blinkers, taken the cylinders apart . . . in short, engineered a brand new bike with only a superficial resemblance to the unreliable beast. "And," he finished with a flourish, "it even comes with a driver—me."

I wasn't convinced. Jay was about as reliable as his bike and had thus far shown little interest in village life. Moreover, getting him to take the video camera out of its bag was like prying an oyster off a rock. Why, I asked, the sudden change of heart?

"Well," he said, "I figured I might as well get something out of the time I spent here. Besides, I've been thinking about it. A career in adventure documentaries could be just the thing for me."

"What would it take," I asked, "to make you reliable?"

He leaned back in his chair. "I'd want a copy of all the footage you took in Vietnam."

"What would you do with it?" I asked, suddenly suspicious.

"Maybe put together a short piece to show my friends. Nothing professional. But you'd have to give me credit if you got anything on the air."

"Sure," I said.

"And a piece of the back end."

"Hell no."

He shrugged again. "All right. When do we leave?"

I sat back and gave it some thought. It was hard to forget the many times I'd looked up during a critical moment only to discover that filming had once again taken a back seat to smoking, sitting, or simply a fit of pique. Hadn't I learned my lesson on Highway 14, and again in Sapa and Nha Trang?

But as usual there was no one else, and very little chance of finding someone for such a long and arduous trek. The more I thought about it, the more I realized that Jay and the documentary had become inextricably linked. I both loved and hated the camera—loved it in those moments when I caught a magic image on tape and knew it would be there forever. Hated it when it intruded upon new friendships and interfered with conversations and events.

Without Jay the crucial footage would be missing, and I would have the perfect excuse to put the camera aside, relax, and enjoy my travels. With him I would have the possibility of one day sharing the journey with others.

The documentary was costing far more than I had bargained for. Was it worth the price?

℮   ℮   ℮

Jay and I were thirty kilometers out of Yen Bai when the chain broke with a sickening crack. I let the bike free-wheel to a small cluster of houses and pulled over. The local mechanic took the beast willingly enough but soon pointed out that the chain had lost a link and was therefore irreparable. I marshaled together the usual crowd of thirty curious children and—on the theory that they were closer to the ground and happy to get dirty—organized a scavenger hunt with two dollars as the prize. After a half-hour's dedicated search I knew the missing link had gone the way of single socks and wallets left on crowded trains. The mechanic, sensing his moment, offered to have his cousin drive one of us into the township of Yen Bai to pick up his famous fix-it brother and a new chain. We flipped a coin, and I sat down to sip a cup of tea.

Darkness fell and still no sign of Jay. A nagging cold had blossomed into yet another flu, and I was swaying blearily. The mechanic's wife took pity on me and led me to a nearby wooden plank to sleep. I was afraid that our presence might cause trouble with the local authorities and mumbled something about police and passports. The mechanic only laughed and pointed at the wall. The hanging decorations gradually swam into view: a pair of handcuffs, a machine gun, and a shelf with several clips of ammunition. He was the local police chief, moonlighting as mechanic. He also, he told me proudly, served as matchmaker, doctor, and grocer and could mend a shoe in a pinch. A man of many talents.

The next I knew his wife was tugging at my sleeve for dinner. The main house, hidden behind the mechanic's shed, was spacious and well built. The floor was tiled, and a shiny new

Honda sat next to a complicated built-in stereo. I wondered which of his many professions had led to such material success.

My host, his fix-it brother, and Jay were already well along the road to that masculine form of bonding that comes from too much whiskey and endless repetition of the word "friends." I ate a little and excused myself again to sleep, but soon the insistent tugging dragged me back from swirling fever dreams. The happy, hearty drinking club had now expanded to seven, added "America" and "Vietnam" to their collective vocabulary, and would soon, apparently, be moving on to "love." But no, they'd reached an impasse, and my services as translator were urgently required. I sat down wearily, then came instantly awake as an unwashed man pulled a two-pound ruby out of his pocket and handed it to me. "Five hundred dollars," he said casually and scratched the stump of his missing leg.

I had never before seen a ruby that could double as a doorstop. It was larger than my fist.

More stones appeared from various hideaways, wrapped in bits of shopping lists or still damp with earth. One man spat out a bloodred polished gem that he had kept safely tucked under his tongue through several beers.

I knew little about rubies except that they had many imitators and so my interest was halfhearted at best. They agreed among themselves that America had huge amounts of money and fixed their asking prices. We agreed to disagree and settled back to admire the pretty stones. We were, they explained, sitting on an enormous ruby mine with outcroppings in farmers' fields throughout the province. The one-legged man was the local dealer. When he had sufficient stones, he made his way to Hanoi where he sold them by the pound, like pork.

When at last I stumbled back to bed, I dreamed of laughing pigs with ruby eyes and handcuffs made of mangled motorcycle chains.

The next morning our discreet gift of cash was summarily rejected and a much more elaborate bill drawn up. The sleeping plank, the chain, the whiskey, and the friendship came at an aggressive price. We paid and Jay made his final farewell affirmation of "friends" with considerably less enthusiasm than he had the night before.

The cold, damp night and the toxic clouds of raw tobacco smoke had prostrated me completely. We drove back to Yen Bai in search of softer beds and perhaps even the luxury of a lukewarm shower.

We had been this way before. I remembered a dusty town that boasted little more than a happy drunk who had offered Jay fifty cents to make me his wife for an hour. The monsoon season had since transformed it into an oozing, glutinous wallow that quickly coated our packs, our bike, and ourselves with an inch of splattered mud. My sinuses pressed up against my brain like overfull balloons, my joints had long since petrified, and my tongue tasted like a rusty spring. One thought penetrated the misery in my skull. A shower. A hot and steaming, infinitely relieving, soak in fresh, clean water. The hotel was almost in sight.

With a now-familiar crack and shudder, the chain broke again.

We wheeled the bike off to one side and discussed our afternoon plans. I opted for the repair shop just down the road since we now had plenty of spare links from the old chain. Jay wouldn't hear of it. The last vestiges of midnight camaraderie had faded with that mangled snap, and he was out for blood. Without another word he set off down the street in search of the famous fix-it brother. The man would redo his work for free or there would be hell to pay.

Three hours later they woke me from a fitful slumber, half draped across the bike. My services as translator were urgently required. The mechanic brother had agreed to do the work, but only at twice the price of the original repair. The second break was not his fault, he said. We had obviously been driving too fast and shifting without the clutch.

We wheeled the bike to the nearby repair shop, and I found the ancient owner. He heard me out in silence, then pointed at Jay's fix-it friend and sealed our fates with just two words. "My son."

We paid him what he asked.

It was almost dark, and raining, when at last we wheeled the beast out and climbed on board. The mechanic puttered along beside us, insisting that we follow him to a guest house of his choice. We suspected it would be owned by more in-laws who would relieve us of whatever money his side of the family had not yet managed to secure, and waved him off. "Good riddance," Jay said, and slowed to let him go. He let out the clutch, and with a cheerful crack, the chain broke yet again.

24

*A cave! With glittering stalactites and stalagmites
. . . Oh Mum, you can't imagine. I think we are the
first ever to be inside. . . .*

Medieval Medicine

It would never have occurred to me to spend a single night
at the dirty little outpost town of Phuong Tho. The bus
driver had other plans for us. He parked the bus in front of the
village flophouse, muttered "tomorrow, 5:00 A.M.," and left.

We wearily hoisted packs and followed. The beast had long
since found a comfortable retirement home in distant Yen Bai,
and we were learning to negotiate the vagaries of the Vietnamese public transportation system. Perhaps this driver had
a mistress here or an aging aunt. Or possibly the tea leaves
planted on a nearby patch of dirt were so succulent that he
couldn't help but stop and buy a pound or two. The only guar-
antee was that, with sufficient time and stoic patience, we
would eventually see him clamber back into the driver's seat to
take us on our way.

In the meantime I wasn't particularly impressed with our
new digs. The flophouse was little more than a filthy warehouse
with broken doors that opened periodically to empty brimming
bedpans onto the street. I picked my way through creeping yellow streams and dropped my pack in an unkempt room with a
dirt floor and several porthole-size ruptures in the walls.

The outdoor toilet was grimmer still. Two narrow planks
spanned an open pit with a wall built to belly-button height

around it. The pit itself seethed with a living carpet of maggots speedily digesting the remains of the last occupant's efforts. I watched in fascination as a piece of inedible toilet paper drifted off to one side over the backs of the rippling larvae.

I could hear my neighbors spitting, shouting, coughing, and urinating against the wall beside my bed. The market-place, I suddenly decided, seemed a much more palatable place to spend the remainder of the day.

There wasn't much happening this late in the afternoon. The best sugarcane sticks had long ago disappeared in the hands of eagle-eyed children with stumpy brown teeth. Bread was on the verge of going stale and in another hour would drop to half price. The resident pig had spent the morning dragging his fifty-kilo belly from stall to stall in search of scraps and now snored monotonously in one corner. It was too early to spectate the slow-motion slugging matches that occasionally erupted from the nearby drinking dens once the sun went down.

I was busy negotiating for a small bag of roasted peanuts when a stout Hmong woman walked by in full embroidered splendor. I followed her, bewitched.

I had done cross-stitched samplers in my time—long hours perched at my mother's kitchen table counting threads and trying not to pull too tight. This woman had taken micro-stitchery to an entirely different level. Her armbands were a miracle of complex, woven patterns all done in perfect crosses no larger than a pinhead.

She laughed at my amazement and passed me around to all her friends, who jostled each other in their eagerness to offer up their embroidery for my inspection. One young girl was crestfallen to have left her newly completed masterpiece back at her hut and quickly solved the problem by inviting me home for tea.

We set off through fields of roundly manicured tea bushes planted in endless marching lines. Soon we were clambering up the forbidding limestone mountain slopes along a path the width of a water buffalo hoof. All around us people were forsaking their sharply terraced fields for the long trek home. An occasional market-bound stallion with its double load of kindling wood trotted down the path against the flow of traffic, causing endless, good-natured entanglements. Wood seemed to be the principal export and women the most efficient beasts of burden. I passed three Hmong girls plodding barefoot down the track, their heads thrust forward into forehead straps to counterbalance a hundred pounds of kindling in the baskets on their backs. They were closely followed by a fine-looking young man, as straight as a young sapling and with a spring in his step, his muscular arms cradling a ten-pound infant.

The shadows lengthened and finally I could see nothing more than the flashing feet of my indefatigable guide on a trail so steep that her ankles were level with my nose. By the time we reached her village I was both enchanted and exhausted, and quite ready to forgo the maggots and the hawking, grunting guest-house patrons for a more wholesome evening on the mountaintop.

The huts were made of wood and thatch and glowed dimly from a single candle set in each kitchen window. Everything was made of wood—the troughs, the plows and scoops, the buckets, the pigpens and the tiny chairs. The cows clonked softly with their wooden bells, and even the seasoned rafters were secured with wooden pegs, not nails. The floors were made of hard-packed mud and cob-webbed corn hung from the ceiling beams.

Within minutes I was surrounded by women thrusting their embroidered jackets into my hands. Although I was their first Westerner, my visit had obviously been preceded by the tireless Sapa secondhand traders. The village was eager to cash in on foreign prices and loaded pocketbooks.

The armbands were, quite simply, works of art. I threw morals to the winds and began to bargain.

Most Westerners believe the key to successful bargaining is to get as close as possible to the true market value of the product before closing the deal. This philosophy, though superficially rational, has little bearing on reality. The real purpose of the extended negotiations is to convince each party that they have wrung from their opponent the best deal they can possibly get. This allows them to walk away secure in the knowledge that not only have they not been cheated, but if possible have made a killing into the bargain. Assume, for example, a typical American faced with a magnificent embroidery. She offers the Vietnamese equivalent of ten dollars. The locals respond with a demand for fifteen. The Westerner, foolishly assuming that time is money, immediately offers to split the difference—twelve-fifty—and assumes the deal is as good as struck. The locals withdraw suspiciously. If she is so willing to raise her bid, they reason, then their initial asking price is obviously too low. They return with a new price of twenty dollars. She is piqued at their irrational behavior and briefly considers backing down to her original offer of ten dollars. But no, she made the offer in good faith and must stand by her word. They haggle for a while, apparently getting no closer to an agreement. The locals are just coming to the conclusion that she will go no higher than twelve-fifty and that they would do well to accept this price. She is getting bored with the lack of progress—time is money—and makes a suicidal move. They originally wanted fifteen dollars, she recalls. So be it. She will pay that much.

But that was then and this is now, and clearly they misconstrued her upper limits. The price jumps to twenty-five.

The two long hours it took to purchase one grubby armband left me limp and wilted, and ready to go back to town.

The guest house was in full swing by the time I had made the hike back down the mountain. My initial resentment at having to share the single lightbulb dangling from the rafters with four teams of rowdy truckers evaporated completely when I realized that it had long ago burned out and we were all on equal terms in the dark. I had no trouble locating the toilet through its unique odor but, try as I might, I couldn't track down the showers. The proprietor waived my inquiries away with an impatient "no!" and showed up half an hour later with a leaking bucket half full of rusty water. I was to shower in the middle of the floor, she said, and reminded me to return the bucket promptly.

The bus left early the next day—without us. We were already trekking high into the hills, peeking over mountain saddles in search of hidden villages and terraced fields. It was a crisp spring morning and the Hmong were out in force, plowing, planting, weeding, and fertilizing the crumbling gray soil. The setting was idyllic: birds hopping from stone to stone in search of seeds and grubs, the clonking bells of browsing buffalo, the whooping call of Hmong to Hmong.

Jay and I continued along the mountainside until we turned a corner and came upon an old Hmong woman walking slowly toward us along the path. She took one look at Jay's six-foot frame, hitched up her skirts, and jumped with remarkable agility over the lip of the nearest terrace. By the time we reached the edge she was nowhere to be seen. Not wishing to scatter the elderly population like chickens, we left the trail and continued our climb straight up the mountain slope.

Lunchtime found us in a field above the highest village. The early start, the hike, and the caressing sun all took their toll. I unslung my camera, made a nest of my pack and jacket, and drifted off to sleep.

I jerked awake a few moments later when I heard Jay shout. I leaped to my feet and tumbled down the hill in time to see a small black head and fleet bare feet disappear into the almost impenetrable undergrowth below us. The youngster had apparently crept close enough to grab my camera bag and was slipping away with it when Jay woke up. The shock of discovery made the boy drop it before darting down the mountainside. I sat and cradled the bag with a pounding heart. My camera, money, airplane ticket, and passport were all inside.

The valley spread out before me: rolling, terraced fields, a gemlike pond or two. In the valley below, a small cluster of thatched huts nestled among stands of fluffy bamboo and buffalo wallows. What was wrong with this picture? The pint-size thief couldn't have been more than eight years old. His mother, like the women I had bargained with the night before, wouldn't have recognized the Vietnamese equivalent of a five-dollar bill. What would the little boy have done with five thousand dollars' worth of cameras and cash?

We crept back down the mountain, glaring suspiciously at the friendly farmers who waved at us as they worked their wooden plows. We were following a weed-choked trail when it opened abruptly onto a blackened field. At its base a flurry of snow-white butterflies hovered above a patch of yellow mustard plants. I wandered down to make grateful use of my camera and stumbled upon a hole in the ground no larger than a half-size door. A bubbling, crystal stream poured out of it and disappeared into a cairn of rocks. I wormed my way inside.

It opened into a low-slung cavern filled with bulbous stalactites and ankle-deep in frigid mountain water. I borrowed Jay's cheap lighter and worked my way upstream, foot by foot, until the flame died . . . and still there was no end in sight. I pulled out my camera and used the flash, imprinting an instant memory on my brain and feeling my way blindly forward. When the camera gave up I crawled back out, determined to return with chalk and flashlights.

We took the shortest path home, our aversion to the scattered villages forgotten, arguing all the way. Jay had not the slightest desire to explore the mysterious cave. We would have to hike back up the mountain, he pointed out, our Vietnamese flashlights were unreliable at best, and what if the damn cave ended five feet beyond what I had seen? And by the way, how was he going to light his cigarette now that I had broken his Bic?

I listened, smiled, and dreamed of crystalline caverns, towering cathedrals, and glittering waterfalls of stalactites.

The next morning we reached the cave before noon, armed with four flashlights, a dozen bulbs, batteries, and candles. I forged ahead and was brought up short by a smooth, blank wall some ten feet further than I had gone the day before. I heard a sour laugh behind me. Bitterly disappointed, I waved the flashlight off to the left where the stalactites grew down to the shallow, rocky stream. There was a six-inch gap trailing backward into blackness. I dropped my cameras and squirmed lizardlike upstream, leaving bits of shirt and skin on the low-hanging stalactites. Ten feet, fifteen, and the ceiling abruptly sloped up and away. I slithered along a narrow channel, over a rock, and there it was—my crystal cavern. A tumbling water-fall of glittering rock, sinuous sheets of smoky stone, a hun-dred hundred stalactites. I stood in awe.

I eventually crawled back to collect my cameras and coax Jay through. We lit candles and explored the chamber. Another small opening followed the water yet further upstream. I appropriated a flashlight, dropped low into the water, and wormed my way forward. I crawled through corridors, over dome-shaped stalagmites, up narrow chimneys, and down sta-lactite stairs. At every bend I promised myself I'd turn around, but always there was one more stretch and I needed to see where it led. At last I heard the thunderous roar of rushing water and stumbled into a mist-filled cavern. A solid jet shot out of the wall above me and tumbled down over two stories of jagged rocks, to plunge into a thigh-deep pool. Not a hint of light crept through that black, forbidding wall. I turned back.

The journey out seemed far longer than the exciting adven-ture in. What if I should slip and drop my tinsel flashlight into the watery void? What if the Vietnamese bulb should live up to its reputation and last no longer than soap bubbles on a windy day? What if that wall caved in behind me? I crawled through the final gauntlet of grasping stalactites and staggered into the candlelit chamber beside Jay.

We emerged, shivering and filthy, into the impossibly bright afternoon sunlight. I had kicked up a lot of silt in my upstream trek, and it had found its way into our pockets, sneakers, seams, and socks. We spread our outer layer of clothing out to dry and grimly contemplated the long hike home. Waterlogged jeans permeated with abrasive grit and squishy sneakers—not a pleasant thought.

When the clothes were half dry we squirmed back into them and straggled up the blackened hill. I struggled with my myriad straps to minimize the chafing over my collarbones. Up ahead of me Jay had reached the runoff ditch that ringed the field. As he tried to jump it, his sneaker lost its purchase and he slid two feet down the slick clay wall.

"Are you all right?" I asked. He seemed to be having trouble climbing back out.

"No," he said, way back in his throat. I jumped down behind him and caught a glimpse of his leg impaled on a bamboo stake. He hung suspended halfway down the wall, like an insect struggling on a pin. I gave him a push from below and he scrambled upward, his leg finally sliding free.

The wound was two inches wide and twice as deep, angled into the muscle right below his knee. It was barely bleeding, but Jay's face was bone-white and he was panting with pain. We were several miles' hike from Phuong Tho, eight hours by bus to Lao Cai, and a twelve-hour train trip to Hanoi—and from there by plane to Bangkok. It didn't look good.

"I guess I'd better hike," Jay said heavily and levered himself to his feet.

We took the shortest route down. At the first village I spotted a horse and hammered on a nearby door to negotiate its rental. The farmer came out, noticed the blood that had begun to soak the lower cuff of Jay's pants, and demanded an absurdly high price. When I agreed he immediately doubled it. In the meantime two women who had been watching the proceeding disappeared into their huts and reemerged with half-finished tunics. "Buy embroidery!" one shouted and tugged on my arm. I agreed to the farmer's second price and asked him to saddle the horse immediately. "Buy embroidery!"

both women demanded, increasing their volume and hauling away on my sleeves. A saddle, the farmer informed me smugly, would run me as much again as the horse. "Embroidery! Embroidery!" the women screeched and thrust their handiwork under my nose in case I hadn't gotten the point. Jay called me over and told me, his voice ragged with pain, that he'd rather walk. The wound would bump against the horse's side, and the negotiating process was sure to take at least an hour. If I could just cut him a staff . . .

He hobbled away while the women hurled imprecations at us and the farmer gradually lowered his price until we were out of earshot.

Jay lowered himself onto the filthy flophouse cot and I plied him with painkillers, then hit the apothecary at a dead run. They had neither curved sewing needles nor catgut, but were well stocked with anesthetic and eventually pulled out an ancient Chinese glass syringe. The village doctor, they told me, could provide whatever else I needed.

"Where is he?" I asked.

They pointed down the road.

A half mile and a dozen breathless inquires later I was directed to a narrow courtyard where an old woman slowly swept up unhusked rice.

"A tourist man is badly hurt," I said in Vietnamese. "There is much blood. I need the doctor—please."

"Where is your man?" she demanded. I indicated the flophouse. She thought it over. "Is he your husband?" she asked, then "Where did you learn Vietnamese? How long have you been in North Vietnam? Do you have children?"

I reworded my request, emphasizing that Jay was on death's door.

"How old are you?" she replied, and invited me in to tea. I had just assigned her to the ranks of elder child when a young man shuffled out of the house. She immediately explained to him with perfect clarity who I was and what I wanted.

"Where did your friend get hurt?" the young fellow wanted to know. He demanded all the details, down to the size and shape of the wound. Finally, his curiosity fully satisfied, he pointed me in the direction of the doctor, yet further down the road.

"Is it near enough to walk?" I asked.

He nodded yes, while glancing over my shoulder at the TV. The excitement over, he was anxious to return to the show.

"Then you may show me the way," I said.

The young man contemplated this undesirable turn of events. "The doctor," he said after careful thought, "is in Dien Bien Phu." Two days' drive away. We haggled back and forth until the TV show abruptly ended and resolved the issue in my favor. My reluctant guide spent several long, rebellious moments rooting about for his flip-flops before slouching into the sunlight.

To my surprise he led me back toward the flophouse rather than down the road he had initially indicated. On the way he stopped to buy a stick of sugarcane, then paused to chat with two young girls on bicycles. A woman called to him when we were opposite the flophouse, and he waited while she searched at great length through all the pockets of her jacket for the money to repay a debt of twenty cents. She counted out the money three times in one-cent notes. We walked another quarter-mile before his sense of purpose began to falter and he cast about for a convenient place to rest.

I implored him once again for the whereabouts of the elusive doctor. He thought it over while gnawing, ratlike, on his sugarcane. "Where is your man friend?" he asked eventually.

I pointed at the flophouse. He immediately hoisted himself to his feet and set off to investigate the spectacle of an injured Westerner. By this time a nearby road crew had gathered around to find out what had happened. I asked them hopelessly for a doctor. They discussed it among themselves.

"He lives in Dien Bien Phu."

"He'll be back tomorrow."

"He won't return until next week."

"There is no doctor."

By this time I was already halfway to the apothecary, calculating antibiotics, dental floss, and whether I could bend a sewing needle if I held it to a flame.

The pharmacist mysteriously insisted I visit the next-door tailor shop before he agreed to serve me. Three seamstresses invited me inside and listened with little squeaks of excitement while I retold my story. They waved their hands at a nearby couch and bade me sit for tea. The doctor, I reminded them curtly.

"Yes yes," they said, "he's here, now drink your tea."

"Where is here?" I asked.

"Your Vietnamese is wonderful," they said enthusiastically. "Does your friend speak as well? You must bring him here to talk to us."

"Where is the doctor?"

They pointed down a long hall. I could see nothing but a man in grimy overalls dismantling a voltage meter on the floor. I went back to see him.

"Yes yes," he said, and waved a pair of pliers at an empty bed. "The doctor is here."

I had just decided to return to the apothecary and squeeze the necessary items bodily from the man behind the counter when I noticed an ancient stethoscope lying amid a rusty box of nails, a can half-filled with oil, and a glass of dirty yellow water with an old syringe and a dead fly floating in it. Some forceps, too, peeping out behind some balled-up wire. This really was the doctor's office. I squatted and described the accident.

The doctor pointed at the plywood bed. "Bring him here."

I reemphasized that Jay could no longer walk. This was apparently beside the point. We argued until he tired of the voltmeter and excused himself to wash his hands and comb his hair. He found his sports coat and checked himself carefully in the mirror before waving me to the door. "Let's go."

"You've forgotten your medical kit," I pointed out.

"No matter," he replied. How could he know what he might need before he'd examined the patient?

We walked into Jay's room to find it overflowing with a noisy crowd of casual spectators. They wandered in and out, ogled Jay in his underwear, and played with our flashlights, my expensive cameras, and film and accessories that lay strewn upon the bed. The circus had come to town and admission was free.

The doctor looked, clucked, asked a dozen unrelated questions, and strolled home to collect his stitching kit. He returned with two vials of Novocain and the syringe still bobbing in its dirty yellow water. I insisted he boil the needle before using it. He informed me stiffly that he had worked five years at the Ho Chi Minh City hospital and two years in Hanoi, and clinched his credentials with a worn card that said "Orthopedic and Traumatology Symposium—America-Vietnam."

"Nevertheless," I said, "the needle must be sterilized." I whipped it out of his hand. The nearest source of boiling water was a soup shop down the street. I appropriated their flaking teakettle and dropped the syringe inside. When I returned Jay was pale as parchment and the doctor was using filthy forceps and a heavy hand to swab out the wound without anesthetic.

He snatched the syringe, filled it with difficulty, and poked around for an injection site.

"The bubbles!" I snapped. "Knock out the bubbles first!"

He ignored me to jam in the needle and vigorously depress the plunger. The Novocain squirted through the leaky connection between the needle and the glass bulb. "No matter," he said, and began to stitch. Jay groaned.

The room had darkened considerably. I looked up to see the doorway and the window completely blocked with faces. A dozen people sat on the other bed, watching two children eviscerate my backpack. The doctor ordered me to hold a flashlight to the wound and, playing to his attentive audience, became the star of his own soap opera. He scrubbed vigorously and insisted that I swab his hands dry with an old rag while he held them high out of harm's way. He picked up several bloody swabs with the tip of his forceps and flung them to the floor. He plunged in the sewing needle with a flourish, ignored Jay's low-pitched moan, and pulled the stitches so tight that his hands shook with the effort.

I protested, watching the skin pucker and turn white. I raised my voice when he snipped the threads a scant millimeter above the knots. We glared at each other over the top of Jay's quivering leg. I hated this man. By now he hated me.

He added two more ugly stitches, issued strict instructions to exercise the leg and eat nothing but three bowls of rice a day, and took his leave. I emptied the pockets of a score of uninvited guests and saw them to the door, forcibly ejected a child who was playing trampoline with my backpack, and shuttered the window over the objections of a dozen street hawkers who had abandoned their wares to watch the spectacle. Jay and I sat in darkness, miraculously alone.

"At least that's over," he muttered softly. He had been extraordinarily courageous. Even now his injured leg jerked and shivered with remembered pain. I filled him up with Valium and took stock of our scattered possessions as he drifted off to sleep.

I packed our bags for the early morning bus ride and toppled into bed. Sleep came instantly, then gradually gave way to an insistent hammering noise. Every exhausted muscle in my body fought against returning to reality. The knocking continued. I rose and stumbled groggily to the door. The proprietor thrust me aside and marched over to Jay's bed. He snatched back the covers to inspect the wound and demanded a detailed accounting of the accident.

"Shoo," I said in English. Eight adults, two children, and a dog had already followed them inside. Everyone ignored me.

"We're sleeping," I said. A little girl crouched down to unzip my pack. I picked her up like a cat and put her out the door, then pushed and shoved until the room was clear. And then, while Jay lay sleeping, I threw up into the rusty bucket in the corner.

25

Dear Mom,

I just returned from my 324th bowl of soup, the highlight of my day, and am looking forward to the 325th bowl for dinner. My underwear has several charred holes in it from trying to dry it with my hair dryer, and nothing short of a depth charge will unstop my sinuses. My bowels, on the other hand . . .

I shouldn't complain—the Hmong are all sleeping outside, wrapped in plastic with their bare feet sticking out one end. They use bricks for pillows and nestle together like spoons against the cold.

Letting Go

The bus clawed up the foggy mountain pass at a determined five miles per hour. We had built a protective cave of packs around Jay's outstretched leg and padded it with our much-needed jackets. The bus was crowded, and nearby passengers cast covetous glances at our spacious niche. My guilty explanations triggered an avalanche of excited questions and prodding fingers, and in the end I simply imposed myself between the new arrivals and their intended perch. One piqued passenger, less inclined to resignation than the rest, hefted the hindquarters of a full-grown pig into my lap. I let it stay.

The driver abruptly cut the engine and reversed direction, struggling to keep the bus centered on the narrow lane as we rolled backward down the hairpin turns. It took me a moment to realize that there was a fire burning between his knees. He kept going until he found a convenient place to pull over and then calmly subdued the blaze with the business end of his rubber thongs. He briefly inspected the molten wires, then released the brakes and continued his backward roll down the hill. The bus shuddered twice, reversed direction, and we were on our way again. The connection to the battery had clearly lost its life in the conflagration. Thereafter the driver simply ignored all stops that weren't positioned on a hill. Ingenious.

We rumbled into Lao Cai by early afternoon. Jay's leg had ballooned to the size of an embedded football, and the wound was red and hot to touch. We watched it carefully through three long days while I scrubbed laundry, ran down medicine and food, and ferried meals through the hotel lobby. The curious staff were soon following me up the stairs whenever I went by. Whole gaggles of them began visiting our room several times a day to check on Jay's condition and sit down to chat with me in Vietnamese. When Jay asked me to lock the door, they calmly let themselves in with the master key, insisting that he would not recover without company to keep him in good spirits. I wilted at the thought of adding full-time hostess to my duties and thereafter clambered over the balcony, tray in hand, whenever we needed food.

The wound swelled further, all three stitches popped open, and then it began to drain. A plastic, viscous fluid flowed day and night, soaking towels and T-shirts. Eventually, tired of scrubbing homemade bandages, I tracked down sanitary napkins in the marketplace and, over Jay's objections, strapped them to his leg.

Our soup shop diet of noodles, beef broth, and the occasional egg had grown increasingly tiresome. Late one afternoon I set out on a hope-filled hunt for a few ounces of the squishy, processed cheese I had once seen for sale in faraway Hanoi.

"Cheese?" the stall owners repeated in confusion and offered me a block of tofu soaked in fish sauce.

279

I carefully described it to a dry goods seller: soft and eggshell white, smooth, salty, slightly sour. Made from curdled milk. I suddenly wanted some more than anything in the world.

"Curdled milk?" he repeated, his nose wrinkling well up into his eyebrows with distaste. The liquid that came out of lactating animals, left to go sour?

He had a point. I bought the tofu.

        (((

The next morning I woke up with a curious feeling of anticipation, like a child on Christmas day. I had promised myself a special treat today—I was going to call home.

I spent the morning pacing restlessly around my guesthouse room. With a thirteen-hour time difference, Mom wouldn't be awake until at least 5:00 P.M. my time. The afternoon hours dragged by.

Five o'clock. My feet had already found their way to the local post office. I gave the woman behind the counter my parents' number in Virginia, then sat in one of the tiny, superheated booths while she dialed the Hanoi operator. Half an hour later no connection had been made, so I handed in a second number—a cherished friend in Boston who I hoped might come to visit me in Vietnam. Another hour passed. Finally, the main phone rang. "Boston," the woman called, "booth four."

It was Larry. "Hi," he said across the static. "Have you talked to your mom?"

Strange question. "Not yet—what's up?"

"She's had an accident."

My world went gray. It didn't spin around or get fuzzy. It just drained of all its color. "What kind of accident?" Please God, don't let it be a car.

"She fell down some stairs."

My knees turned watery with relief. She was strong and fit. The stairs at home were carpeted. A sprained ankle, some bruises, perhaps a broken leg—certainly nothing more.

"Those stone steps out in Williamsburg," Larry was saying. "It was pretty bad. She broke her collarbone and both wrists, I think, and cut her head and had some sort of seizures. I don't know if she's still in the hospital or not."

"How long's it been?"

"About three weeks."

Three weeks was forever to be in a hospital. Intensive care? She might have died and I would still be writing her letters. Three weeks. For the first time, I felt far away, inconceivably remote, a million miles from where I wanted to be. "Larry, call my folks, please. Tell them to call me here. I need to talk to them. I'll keep trying from this end."

"Will do," he said, and hung up.

The next two hours refused to pass. A month, a year, went by and still I was sitting there, waiting for the phone to ring. The post office was supposed to close at nine. At seven the woman behind the counter began to shut the doors; I was her only customer and she was bored. I begged her to stay open. I chatted with her endlessly in cheery Vietnamese. I looked at her photos of her children and told her how handsome her husband was—and all the while my mind was numb.

It just didn't make sense. I was the one trekking through the jungles, facing poachers and parasites. She was supposed to be safe at home, ready to welcome me back. It had never occurred to me that she might one day not be there. I felt utterly lost, directionless, like a kite without its string.

I had always wondered what it would be like to have a home. It was something I'd thought I'd missed out on with all the moving and family turmoil growing up. Now I knew how wrong I was. Mum was my home, my roots, the reason I could set out with confidence and explore the world. If only I could tell her. . . .

I should be home.

The phone rang. It *rang!* It was Mum, her voice strong and clear over the line.

281

"I'm fine," she said gaily. "Dad says I'm always charging up and down the stairs. From now on I'm to hold the rail."

She did indeed have two broken wrists and a fractured collarbone. She had lost 15 percent of her blood through the gash on her head and had been unconscious for hours. After several days in the hospital they had let her come home, and she was recuperating under my father's care. "I'm typing all your letters now," she said, "but it's rather slow. I can only use one finger."

And at last, I started to cry.

26

Dear Mom,
You have to tell me what gifts I can get for you. . . .
Vietnam has beautiful silk scarves, lovely musical
instruments, and stunning embroideries. If you
simply ignore this letter then I will buy you a
clouded leopard cub. Do you remember when I
threatened to bring you a baby water buffalo from
the Philippines? Well, I wasn't kidding then, either.

Collision

A week later I took Jay back to Hanoi by train. His wound
had finally stopped draining and was closing up. He
would regain full use of his leg, though there would always be
an ugly scar. I split the next two weeks between nursing him
and staying in touch with Mum. She was adamant that I not
come home. I wasn't sure whether to believe her—wasn't sure
whether I wanted to believe her. The days went by in a haze.

One morning Jay announced that he was sick of Vietnam
and would shortly be on his way to Thailand. He knew just
where he wanted to go—a little beach resort outside of
Bangkok—but before he could limp aboard a plane, he had to
recover the beast from its storage space in Yen Bai. He insisted
that I accompany him to pick it up. I agreed. For the moment,
I had no idea what else to do.

I rented a Honda large enough to tow Jay and his bike back
to Hanoi, if necessary. We arrived in Yen Bai to find the beast
still safely stabled where we had left it. We split the baggage

and swore a blood oath to stick together in case the beast should decide to regurgitate a piston or a spark plug.

All went well for the first few miles. Jay's bike coughed laboriously up the hills and gurgled wetly on the flats. On the downhills its dual engines easily outran my smaller, lighter bike. It wasn't until we had negotiated the steepest hills that disaster struck. I was on a long, winding descent. Jay had drifted out of sight ahead of me. The road, though narrow, was clear of traffic. There was no honking horn to let me know a vehicle was overtaking, no warning shout. Just a glancing blow to the left handlebar and, as the bike spun around out of control, a quick glimpse of a white van, its door open wide enough to frame a grinning face. After that I saw nothing but black earth as I tumbled down the mountainside.

The bike had turned sharply to the right, the front wheel locking as it fishtailed out of control. I went over the road's edge and slid sideways down the mountain, my leg caught between the bike's frame and the tilled earth. The wheels eventually dug in, and I came to a stop ten feet below the road, in a cornfield so steep that the stalks barely grew free of the ground. Several Hmong gathered as I extricated myself from the bike and checked it for damage. The crowd grew to twenty, then thirty, all staring silently at my shaking knees and dirt-smeared clothes. They offered not a word of sympathy and made no move to help as I dragged the heavy bike back up to the road. They were afraid to get involved, fearful of the consequences of interfering with even a lowland Vietnamese, let alone a foreigner. They had been taught their place. Had I lain bleeding on the slope, they would have let me die, despite the moral imperatives of their culture. Somewhere in the mighty collision between their ancient society, the stringent edicts of communism, and the thrill of capitalism, something had gone terribly wrong.

I kick-started the engine and wobbled off, hoping to find Jay waiting around the corner. He was nowhere to be seen. As the kilometers ticked by, my adrenaline gradually drained into a growing anger. I was still stunned enough to miss the first signs of a police roadblock and saw the flashing white baton when it was too late to turn and run. A soldier pulled me over. "Papers?" he demanded and thrust out a hand.

I glanced at my belongings and realized instantly that my camera bag—with passport, papers, and all but a trivial amount of money—had migrated to Jay's shoulder in the scramble to pack the bikes and was now speeding toward Hanoi.

The lieutenant was not amused. Nor was his mood lightened by my mention of a tall man on a large bike who had apparently blasted through the roadblock with enough speed to ratchet down the lieutenant's lips at the mere memory. Jay was, at any rate, nearly an hour ahead of me and unlikely to return. Time to bargain.

I arrived in Hanoi penniless and coaxing the Honda along on fumes. I found the beast parked out in front of the guest house and Jay sitting on the balcony, cheerfully swigging a beer. "Hey," he said, "what took you so long? I've been here for hours."

I packed my bags and left. I never saw him again.

Last
Loop

27

Dear Mom,

You may be getting a call from some friends who are thinking of coming to visit me. Could you encourage them to bring the following things?

1) A curved needle for suturing
2) M&M's
3) Tampax
4) Breathable shoes so that they don't get jungle rot
5) M&M's
6) Leather gloves for handling wild animals (the problem is rabies)
7) A miniature baby's bottle
8) M&M's

Thank you!

The Real Vietnam

I decided to make that last journey into the Tonkinese Alps, to finish what I had come to do. In the end I didn't stay because Mom told me to—we both knew she would be fine—I stayed because I wanted to.

Mom had always been an extraordinary influence on my life. She had taught me curiosity, passed on her restless spirit, and then sent me out into the world. I had come to Vietnam in part to fulfill her dream for me.

Her decision not to travel anymore had profoundly shaken my belief in many of the things I'd learned from her. If she no longer wanted to see the world, then what was I doing here? And then her accident, making me realize that I had a home— and that I could lose it.

But somewhere along the way I had taken over her dream and made it mine. I was ready to carry on, not in her name but in my own. I would still write letters to her daily, but in the end, I was no longer doing it for her. I was doing it for me.

Still, when I finished packing, her letters had somehow found their way into a pocket of my pack.

℮   ℮   ℮

Sapa had changed. In eight short weeks it had given birth to two hotels, three Western cafes, and a guest house that now accepted both traveler's checks and foreign currency. An itinerant government official with an all-important visa extension stamp arrived each week to set up shop in one corner of the post office. The original pair of Honda-for-hires that had once spent their day lounging on the street corner had multiplied into a good-size fleet and had acquired a grizzled old whiskey peddler who shuffled through their midst at intervals to service their needs. Foreigners were arriving in lemming-like hordes, and Fridays were conspicuous for the nose-to-tail buses that lined the market street. The backpackers clothed in grunge and sporting three-day shadows had begun to give way to impractical shoes and matching pocketbooks as the Sunday market became "A Primitive and Exotic Weekend Getaway" at the more avant-garde Hanoi hotels.

The introduction of haute-couture had not been lost on the ever-observant Hmong. Shoes were now *in* among the minorities, except for the most stubborn old men. Cracked and callused rhino feet were giving way to softer edges and less dramatic toes.

Skyrocketing demand, a dwindling supply: Capitalism had done well by the Hmong and Zao. The price for their embroidery had doubled, then doubled again. The wholesalers were mobbed, their ragged secondhands becoming even more ragged jackets. The traders responded to the influx of wealth with a deluge of trinkets that no self-respecting Hmong household should be without. Hard on the heels of the first truckload of Classic Coke to reach Sapa, the Hmong had introduced their own new brand of native wear. Gone were their intricate embroidery and appliqué collars, stitched with the finest thread. A monstrous impostor had taken over like a weed among roses. Yarn. No longer willing to spend long hours making tiny stitches by candlelight, the Hmong had substituted lumpy strands of store-bought acrylic for their delicate thread. And not just any yarn, but skeins of glowing neon reds and greens. With thicker stitches and fewer layers, the women could now produce an armband or collar in record time, and the tourists seemed to prefer the eye-stopping colors. The children, too, had developed a much more sophisticated attitude toward foreigners, cutting short their games to tag along and mime an empty stomach, a pen, a dollar bill.

But I didn't really understand what was coming until I heard a cassette deck making its way through the market, sawing out a scratchy Christmas tune. The crowd parted before the approaching ditty and I was treated to the utterly incongruous sight of a Hmong boy, his head completely shaved and his eyes obscured behind wraparound reflective sunglasses, swinging along with his ear to a boom box cranked to full volume.

It was time to move on.

As I journeyed deeper into the Tonkinese Alps, the traffic thinned and rides grew scarce. One morning I rose at three and ventured out into the predawn darkness to catch the thirty-year-old bus to Son La. It was already full, the only space left atop a mountain of sharp-edged mailbags. I kneaded a place for myself, curled up around my cameras, and tried to sleep.

The back end of the bus fishtailed along the washboard road, its vintage shocks chattering like teeth on a cold night. The mailbags, initially tossed into a towering stack, were settling like cereal during shipment. The ceiling was now several feet further away, my backpack half-engulfed in a quicksand of dirty canvas. Those passengers unfortunate enough to array themselves around the edges of the pile were being squeezed into a smaller and smaller space. A young man near the door was the first to go. He stood to stretch weary legs, and when he turned to sit again his tiny space had been taken up by three knees and a bucketful of eels. Without a word of protest he hoisted himself through the window of the careening bus and clung there for a moment. Several disembodied hands reached down to steady him, and he clambered onto the roof and out of sight.

The canvas glacier moved inexorably. Soon two more middle-aged men were expelled as several hard-edged bags threatened to tumble down upon their heads. Everyone else sat hip to hip, their legs drawn under them, their bare feet tucked out of harm's way. When I sent them sympathetic looks, they replied with smiles that held no trace of resentment over whatever indignities the next eight hours might bring. I felt guilty that my weight was helping to redistribute the pile, but there was no place else to go and I couldn't risk leaving my heavy pack unguarded if I climbed up on the roof.

It seemed such a simple task for all of us to stand and toss the mailbags back into a pile, buffer them with our luggage, and rearrange ourselves more comfortably in the newly opened space. I couldn't understand why no one seemed inclined to make the effort. I stewed over their apparent indifference for a while until I realized that I was the only one who seemed annoyed with the tight fit. The other passengers had probably never known any other form of transportation and were grateful to be moving faster than a walk. Perhaps they had scrimped and saved for this journey and were going to see loved ones or experience the city for the first time. They seemed quite content. I looked out the window and thought of plodding up the steep passes with my backpack, or standing for long afternoons at empty intersections waiting for a ride, and in five minutes I was blissfully asleep.

I awoke to a sharp, biting odor and recognized it with instant, stomach-curdling fear. The brakes. We had topped the pass and were heading down, moving at a good clip around steep turns that fell away into a sheer ravine. It came again—a chemical odor that grew stronger by the minute. Suddenly the driver began to shout. The conductor vaulted out of his sleeping niche and stumbled to the door, slapping bags and feet out of the way to get at a three-sided wooden block jammed somewhere under the baggage. He hauled it free, leaned out the door, and dropped it just ahead of the back wheel. With a jarring thud the bus rolled over it and kept going. Urged on by a continual stream of high-decibel inspiration from the driver, he jumped out of the bus, ran back for the block, caught up with us, and tossed it under the wheel again. We slammed over it. Undaunted, he retrieved the block. I watched him dash back and forth, falling progressively further behind as the bus picked up speed, and began to plan which exit to use before the upcoming crash. The windows yawned over the ravine, a dizzying drop but padded with steep plowed earth along the road's shoulder. The narrow door opened to the mountainside, but was certain to be plugged by other passengers and would turn into a death trap if the driver chose to try to stop the bus by dragging it along the rock wall. With a final thump we left the conductor behind and slew around a corner. An army truck, heavily burdened, was churning its way up the hill in a cloud of black exhaust. In the best of times two such monsters would have to maneuver, inch by inch, in order to clear each other on the narrow road. The bus driver aimed to pass, the truck held its ground, and both vehicles locked together with an agonized shriek of metal on metal. The bus stopped, the two drivers started to shout, and the passengers nonchalantly descended to squat in the shade and await further developments. Once the altercation had run its course, the conductor poured spring water on the burning brakes, releasing clouds of scalding steam, until they were once again in working order. Everyone climbed back in, and we were on our way.

(e   (e   (e

Son La was a gentle, backwater town that had somehow been promoted to the status of provincial capital. It called itself The City of Flowers, but the only blooms I saw were the dusty plastic plants wrapped around the handlebars of the school-girls' bikes. It was too small to have a street map. Son La's main road boasted three cavernous, government-sponsored hotels where one could sit at dusk and watch water buffalo snarl traffic as they rambled home, unattended. A stretch of road was being repaired with a watering can full of tar and a row of women in conical hats tossing gravel. Here and there bright splashes of color gradually resolved themselves into gloriously attired minorities with black hair wound tightly around bright silver headpieces.

It may not have had cheese, pineapples, or even Indonesian chocolate, but Son La did have a provincial extension office. My visa was in the last throes of expiration. It was time to pay the government a visit.

Mr. Phuong looked ready to pass out in his heavy wool suit and tie. He had just come from a wedding, he explained, where he had been asked to give a speech. He fingered the knot of his tie, obviously wishing he had taken it off before he let me in. He encouraged me to visit the local hot springs, assumed I was in Son La only as a stopover on my way to historic Dien Bien Phu, and in the end admitted that he was so unused to issuing extensions to foreigners that he had no idea what price to charge. We agreed on two dollars and an English lesson upon my return. I left him with my passport to complete all the necessary paperwork at his convenience.

The guest house was crumbling and completely empty. A stocky young man paused from his inspection of the weeds in the middle of the courtyard and introduced himself as Mr.

Phan. He quickly took charge of my pack and all its contents, locking them securely in his office and personally conducting me on a tour of the hotel's services. Two types of rooms were available: a tiny cubicle with several lumpy, grease-smeared mattresses and a thermos of hot water, or their luxury model, identical but for a toilet squatting in one corner and a jutting sink with rusty fixtures. As the communal latrine was several hundred feet away and clearly overflowing, I chose the room with a toilet. Since I was already wallowing in decadence, I agreed to Mr. Phan's services as guide for the morrow, starting at seven in the morning, to visit the hot springs and the local tribes. When I disagreed to his demand that I sign up for an exorbitant dinner at the hotel's nonexistent restaurant, he flounced off in a huff. I sank onto one of the rock-hard mattresses and, completely indifferent to the stains of a thousand other patrons, fell into an exhausted sleep.

Seven A.M. came and went without a hint of Mr. Phan. At nine I rented a bicycle from a young lawyer working at the corner sugarcane stand. Armed with my hotel brochure featuring a photo of the legendary hot springs barely visible behind two reclining, bikini-clad models, I set off to find them myself.

Son La was only as wide as the trio of hotels along its main street. A few yards further and the town ended with minority villages taking the place of suburbs. Civet and panther skins hung stiffly in the breeze, bits of drying flesh still clinging to their tufty hairs. Small groups of elegantly clad Thai women ambled by, their tight skirts and graceful walk belying the hoes and shovels slung over their shoulders. The hot springs, when I found them, were as ugly as the women were beautiful—two cement cubicles fed by a large pool, layered in green scum. I pedaled on.

A hanging bridge appeared, unexpected and stunning. The slender walkway was held up by nothing more than the arching curves of its supporting wires. In the river beneath it, several water buffalo bathed leisurely and a teenage boy fished for darting minnows. I parked the bike and sat for a while, my legs swinging over the edge, enjoying a scene so idyllic that I wondered if there could be anything in the world more satisfying than the dreamy joy of basking in the sunlight.

They materialized out of nowhere—a horde of them, a tidal wave, pounding across the bridge on their way home from school. When the children caught sight of me, they stopped dead with shouts of wonder. They gathered a short distance away and held a serious discussion at the top of their lungs, pushing and shoving to make themselves heard. One girl, older than the rest, slipped away and disappeared around the corner. I was sure she would return with the local police, or at least a sour-faced elder or two. She reappeared with a double handful of speckled red fruit the size of large grapes, and without a glance in the direction of her friends stepped forward to offer them to me. She stopped a little bit away and carefully leaned forward, as though feeding a wild animal that might not take her gesture for a friendly one. I smiled and patted the ground beside me. Behind her the dam broke as the howling mob virtually bowled her over to accept my invitation. They swirled around me, snatching at the fruit, touching my hair and clothes, showing me with snorts of laughter that the soft berries had first to be kneaded into pulpy blobs to remove the bitter aftertaste. I wanted to stay on the swaying bridge, but they saw nothing unusual in the peaceful scene below us and soon dragged me off to knock down more fruit with sticks and pick succulent clover shoots from the muddy paddy walls.

They were remarkable mimics, these children, parroting snippets of songs in several languages as we marched up the hill with homemade carts in tow to practice kamikaze courage on three-inch wooden wheels. We played pickup soccer with a rotting chunk of wood that rapidly disintegrated under the onslaught of three dozen dexterous bare feet and a pair of clumsy sneakered ones. We made our way along the river to a crippled, leaking waterwheel. The boys clambered over it like monkeys until one slipped and got stuck where the buckets full of water dumped continuously on his head, to the delighted shrieks of his suddenly unhelpful friends.

As the shadows lengthened I took my leave with some reluctance, for the children had been a joy in their friendly innocence. When one of the girls saw me pick up my bicycle, she pointed up the hill to a large hut on stilts and asked if I would come back and visit with her family. I agreed but insisted gently that I meet her parents to insure their blessing on their daughter's openhearted invitation.

Her mother was one of the most beautiful women I had ever seen, with masses of jet black hair pinned up in thick swirls around her head, high cheekbones, and lovely skin that crinkled naturally around her eyes from years of smiling. She nodded immediately to her daughter's breathless request, pointing to her own bed and promising a hearty dinner if they might be privileged to share their home with me. I agreed to return the following day and climbed aboard my bicycle to pedal back to the hotel.

Mr. Phan was nowhere to be found, but his office was inhabited by a sharp-faced man with a stubbly chin. I had come, I told him, to settle the bill. He consulted an enormous ledger. The total, when he presented it to me, came out at somewhat more than eight times the agreed-upon price of the room for one night. I questioned his arithmetic. He reconsulted his books.

"You requested but did not attend dinner last night," he noted. "Ten dollars."

I disagreed, pointing out that the dining hall where dinner had apparently been served was little more than a gutted warehouse, with neither tables nor lighting.

"You hired the services of Mr. Phan for the day and did not meet him at the agreed-upon time. In addition, there is a charge for the motorbike you wished to use."

Mr. Phan had been less than forthcoming at our 7:00 A.M.

meeting, I explained, and if he had hired himself a motorbike for the day, that was his problem, not mine.

"And there is the room charge," he continued, unperturbed, and indicated a number somewhat more than twice Mr. Phan's original quote. I explained that we had bargained for the room.

"Mr. Phan is not a regular employee of this hotel. He is not authorized to offer discounts," the manager informed me.

"But he was sitting in this office!"

"I was unavailable at the time. You should have waited upon my return."

"Mr. Phan," I said in a reasonable voice, "had a key to every room."

"That is not my problem."

We sat and stared at each other in silence across the desk. I eventually pulled out my money belt and he smiled.

"Mr. Phan quoted me a price on a room without a toilet," I said, counting out bills. "My room had neither a functioning toilet nor running water. I would be happy to pay the outdoor latrine price for my one-night stay."

His smile fell away. "This is a government facility," he told me. "I will be forced to pay the difference from my salary."

"That is not my problem."

"If your sink was not working, then you should have informed the management."

"I told Mr. Phan."

"He did not inform me of the problem."

"Perhaps," I said, laying the bills on the table and rising, "you should take that up with Mr. Phan."

By the time I had hiked into the village with my pack, it was late afternoon. Several children came running down to meet me, but none faster than Lu, the young girl who had first brought me the fruit. She grabbed both my hands and held them, and refused to let go until I had climbed the hill with her and was safely on her terrace, greeting her mother and siblings who came pouring out the door.

Dinner was a feast, a smorgasbord of meats and cabbage, rice and noodles, broth and field greens. Afterward I brushed Lu's long black hair, as beautiful and shiny as her mother's, and drank whiskey with her father and his five-year-old son. Family members wandered in and out, sat for a while or simply nodded greeting. Through the complicated introductions an extended village lineage gradually took shape. Although there were only four children in Lu's immediate family, her mother had nine siblings and her father eleven, all grown and raising families of their own. There must have been well over a hundred relatives living within a mile of the hut, with several branching lines extending outward from the grandparents. I wondered what it must be like to live in a place where the entire world might be greeted with the prefix "uncle" or "cousin," and decided that I would like it.

As I was drifting off to sleep, the silhouettes of strange animals appeared to dance along my tattered yellow mosquito net. Dogs with droopy ears and lolling tongues, plodding turtles with long necks. A giggle escaped the bed beside me, and a coxcombed rooster temporarily disintegrated into a tangle of fingers and palms. The girls continued their shadow-puppet show by the light of the rising moon until my dreams were filled with frolicking shapes that laughed like children in an undulating, moonlit landscape.

The next morning I explored the village, built along the steep hillside above the river. Several bridges spanned the waters below it, and silver-green paddy stretched to the horizon. I was captivated by the rhythm of the water buffalo dragging wooden plows in ever-tightening spirals around the fields and the creaking of the waterwheels, raising buckets of muddy river to run along bamboo aqueducts that fed the village. I returned to the hut in a peaceful daze and ran smack into five policemen sitting in the living room with Lu's father. He looked up and for the first time did not smile at me.

My passport was still at the extension office, along with all the other paperwork the grim-faced men in uniform were sure to ask for. I ducked out without a word and started back for town.

Mr. Phuong was still at his desk. He greeted me pleasantly and invited me to take a seat before pulling out his briefcase with my paperwork. I relaxed. Once I had my extension in hand, there was little real damage the police could do to me for another month.

He paused in the act of opening the case, reconsidered, and folded his hands across the top. "We have . . ."—he searched for the word—"information concerning your stay in Son La last night."

I wilted. I pleaded ignorance. I begged for clemency. The briefcase remained firmly shut. How on earth had he figured it out so fast? I had entered the hut at dusk and not left until morning.

"I received a call from Central Command telling me there was a foreigner staying in a village under my jurisdiction," he told me with obvious pride. Apparently the local police had seen me arrive with my pack last night and reported the matter to the Son La police station, which sent the information on to Hanoi, which got in touch with the Son La extension agency for confirmation of my identity.

"Perhaps," I suggested cautiously, "they were referring to someone else."

He opened his briefcase and took out a note. "White woman, American, long blond hair, tall, speaks Vietnamese," he read. Not bad for fourth-hand information. I complimented him on the efficiency of his police system and privately wished that the government would put a little more effort into its roads and a little less into its spying. Then, hopelessly, I began to bargain.

My punishment was far lighter than I had any right to hope for. My visa extension was reissued for the full thirty days. I was made to write out my day-to-day itinerary for the next month in painstaking detail, complete with the names and addresses of hotels where I intended to stay and the sights I planned to see. I left with my passport firmly in hand and the assurances of Mr. Phuong that my lovely host family would be in no way held accountable for my misdeeds.

I waited until dark, hiked back out to the village, and snuck up the stairs to the terrace. I was surprised at their joyous greetings. They wondered where I had been, insisted that I once again stay the night, and dismissed my questions about their morning's visitors with assurances of powerful family ties within the village. Tonight they had planned a real feast and both sets of venerable grandparents were invited. No one would dare interfere.

Relieved and childishly happy to be allowed another evening with my new family, I gathered up my clothes and set off for the river to bathe and make myself presentable to the elders. A dozen children followed me and immediately stripped, to splash and play in the milky brown water and watch with fascination as I shaved the stubble from my legs. It was half an hour before I made my way, dripping wet, back to the hut. I found Lu's mother in tears and Lu looking bewildered. "You can't stay," her mother told me. "The police came again while you were swimming." She begged me to at least share their meal before I left. Even her husband wept in shame at the right of hospitality that had been taken from him. The elders arrived and we had a sad supper, which gradually turned merry over promises of letters and toast after toast to the wonders of Vietnamese-American friendship. My unborn children's children were blessed with a dozen offspring apiece and I with a wedding that boasted six fat pigs and a hundred-kilo sack of rice.

They walked me to the edge of the village, and I continued

on alone to Son La. They waved frantic good-byes and I promised insincerely to return, for I could not risk the trouble they might face if they saw me again.

Perhaps it was their lovely smiles, or the way they offered me their home, but walking in the moonlight I suddenly felt as lonely and forlorn as the day I had left my own family to come to Vietnam.

28

Dear Mom,
I consulted a Buddhist monk about your future
and was told that if you do not hike across Borneo
with me next year, then you will most certainly fall
up an escalator and do disastrous damage to your
pantyhose.
   I'm not kidding.

The Ancestral Flame

The days were measured in potholed roads and friendly
rides, in farmers' craggy faces and filthy flophouse rooms.
A young bangle seller entreated me for some Western-people
pills that would give him the bushy beard he yearned for. He
changed his mind only when I warned him that such powerful
medicine would be sure to grow black hair on his chest and in
his armpits. I sat through a long and dusty afternoon at an
intersection beside three barbers' trees, and by the time day
turned to dark their endless background snipping had became
a part of my drowsy consciousness and for weeks crept
through my dream-wanderings.

I had thought my filming was over without Jay, but I was
wrong. The camera gradually became a part of my life, and I
learned to see the world through its lens. I discovered those
few precious moments at the end of the day, when the sun

turns the air to liquid gold and even the dullest colors seem to glow with an unearthly light. I learned how to follow action, and capture details, and sense that peculiar, restless moment in a crowd when something is about to happen. And I learned to recognize when the camera had no place in a conversation or an intimate event, and to put it away without regret. I had yet to see a single moment of the footage I had already shot, but as time went on I worried less and less about how it would all turn out. The very act of waiting for that perfect morning light or watching for a child's smile had already burned the image into my memory. And who was I kidding, anyway? I wasn't doing it for anyone else. I was doing it for me.

My journey took me in a great loop to the border of China and across northwestern Vietnam, always in search of a village where I could settle for a while. I passed the battlegrounds of Dien Bien Phu with nary a glance but spent hours walking in the moonlight amid the growing paddy fields of Lai Chau, watching the fireflies dance over the dense green shoots. I spent a day making roofing out of sharp-bladed grass and a night tossing and turning from the thousand red-raised cuts along my arms. I sat with an old woman who seemed to laugh without end while she made toothpicks, her enameled teeth flashing coal-black in the afternoon sun. I followed footprints as flat as a duck's webbed feet, with fallen arches and rough-ridged scars, and discovered a village whirring with hand-pedaled cotton gins and perfectly spun thread. I never knew quite where I was, and didn't really care. The road would take me onward. In the meantime, there was always hope that I might find a place to put down my pack, where there was rice to weed and harvest, fish to catch and meals to share.

℮   ℮   ℮

The bus climbed up and up, winding along drop-offs so steep that straggling vegetables barely clung to the hillsides. I caught brief glimpses of tiny hamlets nestled deep in the mountain folds, their checkered fields glinting in the morning sun like flashing strobes. Without thinking I got off the bus and hiked down a narrow dirt road. At its end I found the village of Mai Chau, an island of tidy huts and fruit trees in a rippling sea of the greenest green I had ever seen.

Walking down its main street I discovered Tau—or perhaps he discovered me. He was sixty-nine years old, lean and leathery with short gray hair that grew straight out of his head like porcupine quills. His wife had sad eyes and a friendly, hopeful smile that belied her proud back and capable hands. They sat together on the doorstep of their elevated house, and when I greeted them they immediately invited me up for tea. Their home was in the center of the village, overlooking the only dirt road wide enough to allow two buffalo carts to move side by side.

Times were changing, Tau told me while he rinsed and filled my cup. I thought he was referring to my arrival, but instead he pointed to the pigsty under the kitchen, filled to bursting with an enormous, brooding sow. In 1954 a leopard had come slinking down from the surrounding mountains in the dead of night and taken three of his precious piglets. He shook his head at the remembered loss, then became sadder still at the thought of what such a predator would bring in the medicinal markets of Hanoi at today's prices. It had been many years since leopards had been seen anywhere in the surrounding hills. Nowadays to find even a civet or a half-grown porcupine one had to travel nearly fifty miles and spend days setting traps and camping out in blinds. "Everything sold out," he murmured.

We talked and drank through the afternoon. He had worked the fields his entire life and raised six strapping children. Their support had eventually earned him an airy house, an intricately carved double bed, a hand-dug well, and a shallow cement fishpond filled with gasping fish and floating cigarette butts. He now spent the better part of his day sitting on the floor beside his living room window and watching the goings-on in the village below him. The fishpond was close enough to spit into. In the evenings a long procession of ducks marched down the lane and toppled into the cool water, to splash and flap and jostle happily while waiting for their daily dole of rice.

The village itself was as immaculate and well-cared for as Tau's house, with trash-free lanes and well-bred buffalo that scarcely twitched their tails when children climbed up on their heads. Elaborate scarecrows adorned every field, though they seemed more ornamental than useful: The village's homemade shotguns and a well-developed taste for meat, no matter what the source, had long since taken care of any birds.

When evening came Tau invited me for dinner, and afterward told me I could stay.

The fertile valley provided two crops a year, the rice harvested four months after initial preparation of the seedling beds. Both the planting and the harvest were times of hard labor, but the months in between were by no means fallow. The daily needs of the household required hours of tedious chores, not the least of which was gathering wood to feed the cooking fires. Every morning at six, Tau's daughter rose, slipped the bark strap of a homemade basket over her forehead, and padded barefoot toward the rolling, tree-lined hills. One morning I asked to go along, and after much debate over my soft white feet and apparently boundless need for drinking water, she agreed to let me come. Armed with the confidence of my broad shoulders and long legs, a pair of stout sneakers, and an oversize water jug, I swung into step behind her along the narrow path.

The flat paddy turned abruptly skyward as we approached the forest's edge. We were joined by several other women just as we began our climb, hand over foot along a washout gully punctuated by sharp limestone outcroppings. The summit seemed only a few hundred meters away, but when I crested the hill it was only to see another, steeper one, and the retreating backs and flashing feet of the women disappearing into the undergrowth. The morning was already hot and windless, pregnant with humidity and clearly lacking in the oxygen necessary to sustain life. I struggled on.

The women were tireless, laughing and chatting as their stringy calves ate up the miles, their only concession to the heat the occasional banana frond they cut to fan themselves as they walked. It was with infinite relief that I heard chopping in the distance, the echoing puk-puk of wood on wood somewhere in the dense tropical forest. The path opened out into a clearing lined with meter-long sticks that had already been cut and split for kindling. My companions set down their baskets, pulled out sharpened machetes with homemade handles, and set to work.

Once the yearling trees were felled and hacked into the proper length, the women fashioned wooden wedges and mallets. They curled their bare toes around the base of each log and set to splitting it with tools that had existed before the age of bronze. They worked methodically. Their calm, completely naive confidence in their own abilities made them seem larger than life. I, who had been called a tomboy growing up, athletic and unfeminine, sat watching these tiny, graceful women swing a mallet with the strength and precision that it would take me years to match. It was a revelation.

But more was yet to come. When the wood was cut, they fetched their baskets and began to fill them, carefully choosing each piece of kindling and placing it beside the others until every inch of space had been accounted for. They removed their head scarves, folded them into pads, squatted down to slide the bark forehead straps over their heads, then rolled smoothly onto their feet. One by one, like animals in a yoke, they passed me, plodding heavily under a load that exceeded their own body weight.

The climb down was now complicated by their heavy cargo, balanced only by the inclination of their necks. Their movements became a complicated and precisely choreographed ballet. They gathered at the tops of steeper sections and turned slowly to face the mountain before lowering themselves, stiff-backed, feeling for the handholds they dared not look down to see. Two young girls joined us on the lower slopes, one twelve years old and the other fourteen, each carrying a full load home to her family. Their apparent ease stiffened my resolve to try the yoke, but I was still coward enough to wait until the road had turned flat and smooth and we were a scant half-mile outside of Mai Chau. The women paused to rest, and I traded my water bottle for a basketful of wood. I squatted, amid great hilarity, to ease the strip of bark over my forehead. I rolled forward and struggled to shift the wood onto my back, and got no further than if I had been tethered to a fire hydrant. Several of the women, their baskets already in place, helped me to my feet. I stood, swaying dizzily, quite sure that someone had dropped a circus bear onto my head. The load dragged my body backward from a single point in the middle of my forehead. The effort to keep my neck stiff when I walked sent shock waves up and down my spine. I could almost feel my vertebra fusing with every step. I lasted barely two hundred meters before looking for a place to sit. When I collapsed the laughter redoubled. Everyone gathered around to pat my broad shoulders good-naturedly. The woman who took my basket back was barely five feet tall and lifted the hundred and ten pounds as though it was no heavier than a two-month-old child.

When I got home I dropped onto my mat and drifted into an exhausted sleep. It was a week before I could sit up without supporting my neck with one hand.

The days meandered by and almost without my knowing it, collected into weeks. It was the planting season. Every morning a vast, slow-moving migration took place as houses emptied and whole families wound their way along the foot-wide paddy dikes to work their fields. I joined them, stooping for hours over the flat, wet ground, my legs sunk into the silt up to my thighs as I separated the bundles of rice seedlings and poked each three-inch stalk into the silky mud. The women around me worked with machinelike speed, their nimble fingers tuned to the exact dimensions of a healthy plant, their eyes no longer needed to ensure its proper place in the mud. My initial, painstaking efforts and wobbly rows were greeted with muffled laughter, and improvements pointed out with delighted claps and cries of wonder. When my planted seedlings toppled into my huge footprints, they pretended not to notice until my back was turned. Then they dug them out and smoothed over the holes, and looked up and smiled as though nothing had happened.

When the sun dipped under the mountaintops, the women planted their last few seedlings, put their hands on their hips, and painfully straightened their backs. Everyone shouldered hoes and empty baskets and joined the growing flood of villagers returning home. They stopped at the deeper channels and rinsed off the mud, their lower legs emerging white and wrinkly from the daylong immersion in silt. It seemed a simple life, filled with the rhythm of the seasons and the daily growth of the all-important rice. The work was hard but unhurried, and their lives held few surprises. They could look into the future, at any given month or time of day, and tell you exactly what they would be doing. They knew where they had been born, and where they were going to die. They did their chores cooperatively and in relative harmony. As much as such a thing is possible, they seemed to have created a place where the individual worked toward the good of all.

℮   ℮   ℮

Somewhere between the paddy fields and the afternoons spent drinking tea with Tau, I found the Vietnam I had been looking for. In this tiny village not yet touched by the modern world, I discovered an ancient and universal celebration

307

of community and family. I knew at last why I had come halfway around the world in search of this—because it had been lacking in me. Although it seemed much easier to create community in a place like Mai Chau, I knew that there was nothing here I couldn't find in America, if I just took the time to make it so.

I would return with many memories—of an old man patiently shifting rocks to build a new field for corn; of the peace offering of a conductor for whom the past had become nothing more than a reason to share bread; of the women climbing hand over foot down a mountainside, balancing their loads with strong backs and serene courage; of a Zao patriarch who could look around and know that what he built would shelter his children and his children's children long after he had gone on to join the ancestors.

But most of all, I would take back a sense of place, an understanding of what I had left behind, and why it meant so much to me.

It was time to go home.

Nuts and Bolts

I was twenty-nine when I left for Vietnam. The entire trip, including airfare and visas but excluding equipment, cost about $6,000. The following is a list of what I brought with me:

Cameras and accessories:
One-chip Hi-8 camera
Nikon 8008s with 35-135 zoom lens
SB25 flash
5 filters for the Nikon, 3 for the Hi-8
An amazingly heavy Bogen tripod with a fluid head
60 hours of Hi-8 tape
27 pounds of customized batteries that didn't work
Hi-8 camera battery recharger
130 rolls of slide film
50 AA batteries (every piece of equipment operated on AAs, including the flashlight)
Microcassette and 42 two-hour tapes
Lens cleaning solution
70 resealable plastic bags
Pelican case

Other:
3 pairs of socks and underwear
Polartec light jacket and 3 shirts
2 pairs of pants
1 pair of shorts
Reebok shoes and sandals

A large assortment of medication, both prescription
and nonprescription
Toiletries: shampoo, toothbrush, soap (detergent),
toothpaste, hair-ties, deodorant
Sunglasses
Hat
Not enough Tampax
Flashlight
Compass
Pocketknife
Basic motorcycle repair tools
Duct tape
Sewing kit
Toilet paper
Pens, paper, notebooks
Water bottle
Iodine tablets
Vitamins (eventually)
Too many books
Origami
Juggling balls (fillable)
Life magazine (for locals)
Laminated photos from home
Dictionary and grammar book
Passport and visa (and photocopies of them)

Things I wish I had brought:
More Tampax
Mom
Frisbee
Vitamin C
Sunscreen
A real cameraperson
My SB25 user's manual

Anatomy of an Adventure

7 months
6,400 miles
4,000 dollars (excluding airfare and visas)
63-pound backpack
Vietnamese vocabulary: 1,800 words
Transportation: bicycle, motorbike, train, bus, hitchhiking, truck, water buffalo, horse, fastboat, plane, outrigger canoe, hiking
113 hours on the train
42 hours waiting for rides
52 motorbike breakdowns
Small companions: mosquitoes, bedbugs, spiders, ants, bees, mites, fleas, centipedes
Large companions: 1 rugged Alaskan, 1 handsome German, 1 unfriendly eagle, 4 leopard kittens, 1 infant endangered gibbon
14 arrests (2 in Cambodia)
1 expulsion (from Vietnam)
4 haircuts
134 lodging houses
52 hours of Hi-8 video footage
4,644 slides (129 rolls)
Consumed: 429 bowls of soup
            8 pounds of weeds
            endless green tea
Stolen: 1 glove, 1 bottle of shampoo, 1 liter of gasoline
Purchased: 23 uncut rubies
Injuries and illnesses: 1 punji stake impalement, 5 colds, anemia, giardia, scurvy, assorted motorcycle burns, split ends

311

About the Author

Karin Muller was born in Switzerland and raised in the United States, the Caribbean, and Australia. After earning her degree in economics at Williams College, she spent two years in the Peace Corps in the Philippines. She speaks five languages. Several years as a management consultant and small business owner convinced her that she was more suited to backpacks than pantyhose. She now writes about, films, and creates websites for her travel adventures. In her spare time she is a competitive hang glider pilot and judo/jiujitsu instructor.

Her previously published works include the short fiction "Dreams" and "Global Warming," both published in the 1994 *Sideshow* anthology, and "Castles in the Tide," a nonfiction excerpt from the manuscript by the same name, published in the *1994 Deep South Writer's Conference Chapbook*. An excerpt from *Hitchhiking Vietnam* will appear in *Travelers' Tales: Women in the Wild* (O'Reilly & Associates, 1998).

Karin is planning five more trips along major, historical highways, all of which will become documentaries. The next trip, down the Inca Trail, is scheduled for fall 1998 and will be linked, via the Internet, to schools nationwide.